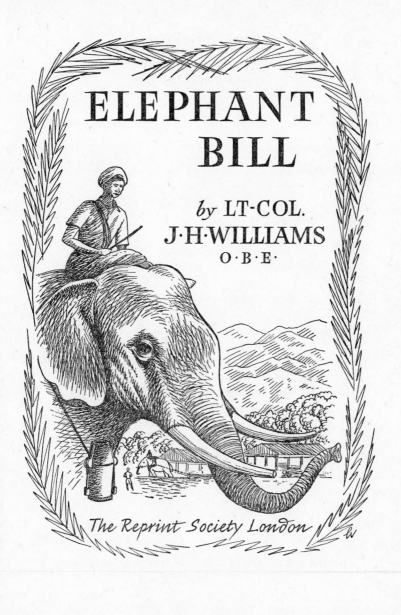

ELEPHANT BILL

by LT·COL.
J·H·WILLIAMS
O · B · E·

The Reprint Society London

FIRST PUBLISHED 1950
THIS EDITION PUBLISHED BY THE REPRINT SOCIETY LTD.
BY ARRANGEMENT WITH RUPERT HART-DAVIS, 1951

Second Impression October 1953

PRINTED IN GREAT BRITAIN BY RICHARD CLAY AND COMPANY, LTD.,
BUNGAY, SUFFOLK

FOREWORD

by

FIELD-MARSHAL SIR WILLIAM SLIM

G.B.E., K.C.B., D.S.O., M.C.

In the XIVth Army our soldiers varied in colour from white, through every shade of yellow and brown, to coal black. The animals we used reflected a similar variety. Pigeons, dogs, ponies, mules, horses, bullocks, buffaloes and elephants, they served well and faithfully. There were true bonds of affection between men and all these beasts, but the elephant held a special place in our esteem. It was not, I think, a matter of size and strength. It was the elephant's dignity and intelligence that gained our real respect. To watch an elephant building a bridge, to see the skill with which the great beast lifted the huge logs and the accuracy with which they were coaxed into position, was to realise that the trained elephant was no mere transport animal, but indeed a skilled sapper.

I could never judge myself how much of this uncanny skill was the elephant's own and how much his rider's. Obviously it was the combination of the two which produced the result, and without the brave, cheerful, patient, loyal Burmese oozie our elephant companies could not have existed. And we should have had no oozies had it not been for men like " Elephant Bill " and his assistants. It was their jungle craft, elephant sense, dogged courage, and above all the example they set, which held the Elephant Companies together under every stress that war, terrain and climate could inflict on them.

They built hundreds of bridges for us, they helped to build and launch more ships for us than Helen ever did for Greece. Without them our retreat from Burma would have been even more arduous and our advance to its liberation slower and more difficult. We of the XIVth Army were—and are— proud of our Elephant Companies whose story " Elephant Bill " tell so modestly but so vividly.

A Good-bye to
the Elephants
and their Riders,
and to the Up-country Staff
of Timber Assistants
in Burma.
Also as an appreciation
of two Sappers,
Bill Hasted and Tich Steedman
of the
XIVth Army,
who did everything possible
to help the
Elephants in War

ILLUSTRATIONS

PHOTOGRAPHS
(*see over*)

Apart from a few of my own, the photographs in this book were taken by Muir Wright, Fish Herring, John Booth, and the late Peter Bankes, to whom I am most grateful. J. H. W.

DRAWINGS

made by John Bruce from sketches by the author

MAPS

drawn by K. C. Jordan

A young male calf, about two and a half years old, and his mother. He is eating a leaf and challenging an intruder. The mother's turned-over ears show that she is at least forty-five years old

Homeward bound after the day's work

Inseparable. This young oozie is almost part of his animal.
They are both about the same age, twenty-one. He is a Shan,
with pale copper skin, and the elephant has pink edges to
its ears and trunk contrasting with its blue-black hide

Two pushing and one pulling

A determined tusker rolling a very heavy log

Taking the strain

Pulling his weight

A young tusker of eighteen years, saddled with a Siamese pack

The author about to operate on a dangerous tusker in a "crush." The Burman in attendance is U Nwa, whose tragic death is recorded on page 215

The tusker in the "crush" before an operation on his injured forefoot

Elephants being scrubbed with dohnwai creeper, which lathers like soap, and much enjoying it

Bath time

Forest Assistant watching his elephant transport cross a river

Travelling elephants of sixteen and seventeen years of age about to cross the Yu River. One is belly deep in mud which he would not have entered unless he could feel the firm bottom. The leading animal has Burmese panniers

Three elephants in tandem, dragging heavy logs

The first elephant bridge for the XIVth Army over the Lokechao Creek

Two female calves stealing salt, which they love

Easing logs out of sand

An elephant inspection

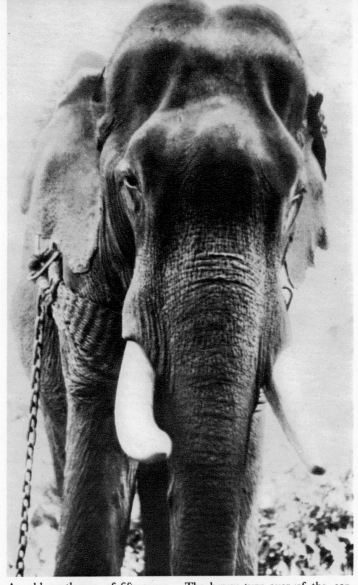

An old gentleman of fifty-seven. The heavy turn-over of the ear, sunken cheeks and head reveal his age

PART ONE

Chapter One

I HAVE always got on well with animals. I like them and, with one or two notable exceptions, they always seem to have liked me. When I was a boy in Cornwall my first animal friend was a donkey. He had free range over the moors, but I always knew where to find him. Then, during the World War of 1914–18, I was in the Camel Corps, and then, later on, Transport Officer in charge of a lot of mules. These experiences taught me much about animals, for both camels and mules are temperamental beasts, and mules have also a remarkable sense of humour, so that in dealing with them one gets plenty of exercise for one's own. That was valuable. My life has been spent east of Suez in places where if you lose your sense of humour you had much better take the first boat home.

And in one respect camels were a preparation for elephants, since the male camel, like the male elephant, is subject to coming into " season," or going on musth. In all other animals it is only the female that comes into season.

Like millions of other fellows, when the war was over I began to think about finding myself a job. A friend told me that he knew a man who knew someone else who knew a chap who did something or other with elephants in Burma. This sounded to me as though it would be just what I wanted, particularly as when I was in the Camel Corps I had read a small book called *The Diseases of the Camel and the Elephant*, by Hawkes. I took for granted that such a job would mean living in the jungle, shooting, riding ponies and putting up with a good deal of loneliness, though no doubt I should meet a fine crowd when I went on leave.

We looked up Burma in an atlas, and that night both of us wrote letters. My friend wrote to the fellow he knew, introducing me as a suitable candidate for elephant management, and I wrote direct to the head of the Bombay Burma Trading Corporation—the company concerned.

It was 1920 before I got back to England, but my letter led to an interview, and before the year was out I was in Burma.

My first vivid memories of Burma are not of the pagodas and rice-fields and all I had read about, but of my first *jungle salt*, Willie, the man under whom I was to begin my training. It is said that '' you can take a man out of the jungle, but if he is born to it you cannot take the jungle out of a man.'' No man I ever met was a better example of the truth of this saying, or believed it more than he did.

I met him at his camp on the banks of the Upper Chindwin River, Upper Burma. He was, in his own words, down with fever, but he was sitting at a table, about midday, outside his tent, drinking a whisky-and-soda and smoking a Burma cheroot with as much loving care as if it had been a very fine Havana.

His welcome—if welcome it could be called—was icy, and I immediately guessed that he jealously resented anyone sharing his jungle life. I hoped that I should be able to break down that attitude and that then all would be well. It was, however, to take me some time to do so.

Although it is nearly thirty years ago, the following incidents seem to have happened yesterday. About four o'clock in the afternoon I asked for a cup of tea—and was laughed at for not drinking whisky-and-soda. I vowed, privately, that I would see him under the table later on. About five o'clock seven elephants arrived in camp, and were paraded in line as though for inspection. Willie did not speak one word to me as he got up from his camp chair and walked off to inspect them. However, I followed him, uninvited. Judging by appearances, there was one worn-out animal which looked as though it might be the mother of the other six. Each animal was closely inspected in turn, and Willie entered some remark about each one of them in a book. This took up about half an hour, during which he did not address a single word to me. I was careful not to ask any questions as I saw that I should only be called a damned fool for my pains. However, when the inspection was over, Willie turned on me, saying: " Those four on the right are yours, and God help you if you can't look after them."

For all I knew, I was supposed to take them to bed with me. However, I saw no more of them till the next evening, when Willie told me to inspect my own four myself and to see that their gear was on their backs comfortably—as though I could tell! However, I followed a lifelong rule when in doubt: I trusted to luck.

After the inspection that first night, as my tent had been pitched near his, I joined Willie at his camp table. On it were two bottles of Black Label—one of his and one of mine.

After half an hour or so Willie thawed sufficiently to ask me: " Are you safe with a shotgun? "—not " Do you shoot? " as is more usual.

Silence reigned after my answer. Willie emptied and refilled his glass several times. At last he suddenly opened up, and, passing his bottle to me, remarked: " I drink a bottle a night, and it does me no harm. If I never teach you anything else, I can tell you this: there are two vices in this country. Woman is one and the other the bottle. Choose which you like, but you must not mix them. Anything to do with the jungle, elephants and your work you can only learn by experience. No one but a Burman can teach you, and you'll draw your pay for ten years before you earn it. To-morrow I'll give you some maps, and the day after you must push off for three months on your own. You can do what you damned well like—including suicide if you're lonely—but I won't have you back here until you can speak some Burmese."

After this speech he walked off to his bed without even saying " Good night." Unfortunately the following day he heard me address a few words of Urdu, that I had picked up in India, to my Burmese cook. Willie just sacked him on the spot as being a hindrance to my learning Burmese.

At dinner that night he gave me some chili sherry of his own brew. The bottle had a sprinkler top, and I gave it two shakes, as though it were ordinary tabasco sauce. When I had swallowed a few mouthfuls of my soup he asked me if I were homesick. His chili sherry burned a hole in the roof of my mouth, but I finished the soup, and then, wiping the tears out of my eyes, replied: " No. But I'd like to start off on my jungle trip to-morrow."

That remark got inside his guard. For the time being his hostility collapsed, and he kept me another two days in camp.

Going to bed that night he was staggery; and when he got up from table he corked his empty whisky bottle and turned it upside down, saying:

" By dawn it will have drained its last pau peg into the neck. It'll do to lace my early morning cup of tea."

He ignored my " Good night " as he staggered off. The new recruit was not to be allowed to forget that he had disturbed the peace of jungle life.

I greeted him with " Good morning " at six a.m. next day.

He looked at me and replied: " Good Lord! you still here? "

He had become just like the jungle—as hard and as unyielding and unfriendly as a tree seems when one is lonely. But a few years later he had become a great friend of mine. He accepted me slowly, as the trees and forests did.

After four and a half years' service in the Army I believed that I was past the age of adventures; but leaving on my first jungle trip certainly gave me a thrill. With four elephants carrying my kit, a cook, two bearers and two messengers, I was on my own again. After going nine miles it dawned on me that my life in charge of elephants had begun.

.   .   .   .   .

I started that trip in November, when every day was like a perfect English summer's day. Every evening a log fire beside my tent gave me the companionship of its warmth and the homeliness of its glowing embers. I moved camp for the first four days, so as to put sufficient distance between myself and Willie for me to feel reasonably sure that he would not pay me an unexpected visit—then I stayed in camp for a day to sort out my possessions.

I had been well equipped in England before leaving, with a new shotgun and a new 450/400 high-velocity rifle, and the Bombay Burma Corporation had issued me with excellent camp equipment. Among the treasures and curios it contained was a teak office box filled with books, circulars and papers for my information. The most interesting of them was a small textbook on elephant management by Hepburn, a young veterinary surgeon who had spent a few years as an Assistant with the firm, but who unfortunately had died of enteric. The book did not contain either a photograph or a diagram of an elephant, being concerned only with a brief account of the treatment of various accidents and diseases to which elephants are liable. My first impression was that they were likely to get every possible complaint to which man, woman and child are subject, except whooping-cough.

The book was, however, a gold mine, and all too soon I had to put it into use. For before I arrived at my destination the ancient female elephant known as Ma Oh (Old Lady) was discovered dead an hour before I was due to move camp. Willie had, I now know, somewhat unscrupulously palmed her off on me—and his terrible words, " God help you if you can't look after them," now rang in my ears. Seeing her enormous carcase lying in the jungle—just as she had died in her sleep—was a terrible sight, and it was awful that she had died within a few days of my being made responsible for her. How on earth, I wondered, should I get out of this mess? This was the nadir of my misfortunes. Willie's reception of me, the dead elephant, and his threat ringing in my ears, combined to fill my cup with bitterness. " At the worst," I thought, " I can only lose

my job. I'm damned if I'll buy them a new one!'' It
was a bad business, but as I had no one to help me out,
I had to help myself, and I decided that the best thing
I could do was to hold a *post-mortem* and see what I could
find inside to account for her death.

Tragedy soon turned into farce. The "Old Lady"
was scarcely cold before I was literally inside her, with
her arching ribs sheltering me from the sun. I learned
a good deal about elephant construction from her.
Spare parts galore had been hauled out and arranged
neatly in a row before tea-time. Her carcase proved to
be a cave full of strange treasures, such as the heart,
the gizzard and the lungs. The only snag was that, do
what I would, I could not find any kidneys, and I was
almost tempted to conclude that she must have died for
lack of them. However, when I came to write out a
report that evening I decided that " no kidneys " might
not be an acceptable cause of death—so, in desperation,
I left it at " found dead," and did not even mention my
Jonah's journey. Later on I found out that many
strange explanations of the deaths of elephants were
made by Assistants, and that most of them were taken
with a grain of salt. The unwritten law of the Bombay
Burma Corporation was that some cause of death had to
be given if the deceased animal was under fifty-five
years of age. Over that age the explanation of " old
age and general debility " was accepted. If one is lucky
one may get away with the explanation, " struck by
lightning," once in one's career of twenty years—but
one cannot try it twice. The Assistant who described an
elephant as dying of " broken heart " did not get away
with it, though he may have thought he had good
reason if he examined the heart and found it looked as
though it had been split in two, with two apexes instead of one, as in man and the lesser mammals. This
formation of the heart is a peculiarity not only of the
elephant, but of some of the other large mammals as
well.

The loss of one transport elephant seemed to make no
difference with the type of pack being used. Ma Oh's

load was easily divided among the remaining three animals, and on I went. My instructions were to march to a certain village in the Myittha Valley, where I was to meet a head Burman named U Tha Yauk. I shall never forget his welcome. I was on foot with my messengers and the two bearers, and we had outdistanced the elephants by several miles by taking a short cut up the bed of the creek. U Tha Yauk had come some way out of the village to meet me, and was squatting on a rock beside the creek up which we were travelling. I think that he formed his first impressions of me before I had ever seen him. He heard me laugh with the Burmans before he saw me, and he watched me eagerly bounding from rock to rock before I had seen him. Then he saw my quick reaction on seeing him, and noticed the tone of friendly authority in my greeting. I think these little things may have counted in my favour.

I greeted him with my three words of Burmese and laughed because I could say no more, and he laughed back; then we marched on in single file until we came into a big open clearing around which there were about ten bamboo huts, all standing on bamboo stilts and thatched with grass. A Burmese girl dressed in her best, with a pretty little white coat, and a flower in her hair, came forward with a cane basket-work stool for me to sit on. Three men came up with green coconuts and, cutting them open at one end, poured the juice into a cup of hand-beaten copper and gave it to me with the reverent gestures of priests administering the sacrament. I drank off at least six cups of the cooling drink before I realised that a dozen people had gathered round to stare and gaze at me.

Unfortunately, I attracted quite as much attention from all the biting bugs and flies as from the Burmans. But at once a small boy came forward, and offered me a fan to keep them off. In order to interest him and make some return, I first showed him a handkerchief on which there was a design of a fox, with hounds and a huntsman, and then tied it round his head. The watching crowd laughed with delight. I was relieved

B

when U Tha Yauk and his son-in-law, who could speak a few words of English, reappeared and explained that the elephants would soon arrive, but that, as it was already late in the afternoon, it would be better if I were to sleep in the hut reserved for my occupation during the monsoon rains.

Directly the elephants turned up, the crowd moved off to help unload them, and my cook was at once installed in his hut. In a few minutes a chicken had been killed and plucked, a fire lit and cauldrons filled with water. My kit was soon piled up in one corner of the big room twenty-four feet by sixteen, which was divided into my bedroom on one side and my living-room on the other, by a bamboo matting wall.

In a quarter of an hour the room was furnished— with a ground-sheet covered with bright blue cotton dhurries on the floor, my camp bed, camp tables and camp chair; my bedding roll was undone and the mosquito net put in position. Meanwhile other Burmans were filling my tub in a bathroom at the back of the hut with tins of water from the brook. After dismissing the other helpers, my personal servant unlocked my basket packs and took out photographs to arrange on my dressing-table, and my revolver, which he put carefully under my pillow. Then, when all was ready, he asked me to come in. As soon as I had looked round and sat down, he took off my puttees and boots, and then disappeared. When I had undressed and gone to the bathroom, I found a Burmese boy, who poured two buckets of hot water into my tub and swirled it around, giving me a smile, as though to say: " Bath ready, sir."

I bathed, and by the time I went back into my hut I found the table was laid with a spotless white cloth, and that flannel trousers, socks and white shirt were spread out on my bed, but that my perfect valet had once more vanished.

My dinner was ready, and as I finished each course hands of unseen attendants passed up the meat and vegetables, the sweet and savoury to my valet, who stood silently behind my chair as I ate. While I drank my coffee, he drew down the mosquito net and tucked it in, and then gave a graceful bow saying, though I could not understand him:

" By your leave I will now go."

Left alone, I was overcome by a great homesickness. The overpowering kindness of the Burmans was too much for me, and I asked myself what I had done to deserve it. Surely life in the jungle would not continue on such a pattern? It never dawned on me that the Burmans wanted to show their sympathy with me in my loneliness and my ignorance of their language and all the difficulties that lay ahead.

Chapter Two

Next morning a new life began—my life as a pupil of U Tha Yauk. Fortunately, he was as eager to teach me and to show me everything as I was enthusiastic to learn. Every waking moment I had to study jungle lore, to observe every detail and, in particular, to observe elephants and all their ways.

That morning I woke to the sound of elephant bells of varying notes, and the camp was astir before I had dressed, shaved and had my breakfast. While I was drinking my tea I could see that the camp was already full of elephants standing about unattended, and that three or four groups of Burmans were squatting round having their early morning meal of boiled rice. Each man had a heap of it, steaming hot, served on a wild banana leaf instead of a plate. Not a word was spoken while they ate, and as each man finished he rinsed his mouth and washed his hands from a coconut-shell cup of water. Then he walked off to his harnessed elephant, mounted in silence, and in silence the elephant and its rider vanished into the jungle to begin their day's work. But before they had all gone U Tha Yauk was waiting for me.

With the aid of a good map of the Indaung Forest Reserve, he made me understand I was to go on a tour with him from the valley, crossing the creeks and climbing over the watersheds, and so on, up and down, crossing in all five parallel creeks flowing from east to west into the Myittha River. On the sides of each of the watersheds he had a camp of elephants, ten camps altogether, each with an average of seven elephants, or seventy working animals all told.

Judging from the map, the distance between the camps was six to seven miles, with hills three to four thousand feet high between each. No tracks were marked, the whole area of about four hundred square miles was divided into numbered and demarcated areas, though the boundaries were irregular, as they followed the natural features of creeks and ridges.

At the first camp we reached I found about twenty Burmans, including a carpenter of sorts, erecting a set of jungle buildings. It was explained to me that this camp was to be my headquarters during the coming monsoon months. I soon realised that the elephant was the backbone of the Burmese teak industry.

The history of the Bombay Burma Corporation went back to the time of King Theebaw, when a senior member of the firm, who visited Burma, appreciated the great possibilities of the teak trade and was able to obtain a lease of certain forest areas on agreeing to pay a fixed royalty per ton of teak extracted.

As a result, sawmills were established at the ports, and forests previously regarded as inaccessible were opened up, a system of rafting teak-logs down the creeks and rivers was organised and elephants were bought on a large scale. Teak is one of the world's best hard-woods, partly because of the silica it contains. In the mixed deciduous forests of Burma, teak grows best at heights between two thousand and three thousand feet in steep, precipitous country, though it is also found in the rich valleys. The trees often stand ten or twelve to the acre, but usually only one tree—the largest—is selected, and the remaining trees, which are immature or under the girth limit, are left for the next cycle of felling, which is probably twenty-five or thirty years later. Under this system the teak forests would never be exhausted. The tree chosen is killed by ringing the bark at the base, and the dead tree is left standing for three years before it is felled, by which time the timber is seasoned and has become light enough to float; for green teak will not float. As teak grows best in country which is inaccessible to tractors and machinery, elephant power is essential for hauling and pushing the logs from the stump to the nearest stream that will be capable of floating them during the flood-waters of the monsoon months.

When the logs reach the main waterways they are built up into rafts, which are floated down the rivers to Rangoon or Mandalay. There they are milled and the squared timber shipped to the world markets.

Not only do the streams, creeks and rivers vary very much in size, but the degree of flooding during the monsoon spates varies with each, and depends on the size and situation of the catchment area feeding it. A great deal of experience is required to judge how high the flood will reach—or, in other words, below what level the logs must be hauled. There are all sorts of natural indications to enable one to judge this, that one learns in time. Debris from last year's floods caught up in bushes is a good guide, but often does not last from one year to the next. Less obvious indications are that jungle weaver-birds, which build near the creeks, never let their pendulous nests hang low enough to touch flood-water, and that lower down, near the rivers, turtles lay their eggs only above the level of the highest flood.

All such pointers are invaluable, for much work will be wasted if the logs are hauled far below flood level. On the other hand, an error of judgment in leaving them too high may make all the difference between the logs taking eight years instead of one to reach Rangoon, a thousand miles away.

The value of the logs depends greatly on their being cut up at the stump to the best advantage. There are specialised demands for different types of logs. The " English Square " for shipment to Europe and South Africa requires the greatest length possible without defects, while for " White Star "—the old ship-building term—logs yielding large flitches are required, and so on. A lot of clearance work is necessary in the jungle. Gorges have to be blasted clear of the huge boulders in their beds, which if left would trap the logs in jams when they were coming down on a spate. Dragging-paths have to be cut through the jungle for elephant haulage, and these have to circumvent natural obstacles such as cliffs, ravines and waterfalls. The Bombay Burma Corporation had to build up herds of elephants. Some were bought, mostly from Siam, but a few also from India. The majority were, however, obtained by capturing wild elephants in Burma and breaking them in. This process is known as " kheddaring," and Burmans, Karens and Shans employ rather different methods in carrying it out.

When, however, the Bombay Burma Corporation had built up considerable herds of elephants, it realised the importance of the elephant calves born in captivity. These could be broken in and trained much more easily than captured wild elephants. Finally, when the Corporation's herds had nearly reached a strength of two thousand animals, it was found that births balanced the deaths, and that new supplies of elephants were required only on rare occasions. The kheddaring of wild elephants, on any extensive scale, thus came to an end, as it was unnecessary.

The health, management and handling of the elephants in this enormous organisation impressed me as the factor on which everything else depended. I well remember wondering how many people who had waltzed on the teak deck of a luxury liner had ever realised that the boards of which it was built had been hauled as logs from the stump by an elephant in the Burma jungles.

The routine work of elephant management in camp consisted in checking up gear-making, getting to know the oozies, or elephant-riders, inspecting elephants and dressing any galls caused by gear rubbing or wounds caused by bamboo splinters in the feet, and other common injuries.

For my early training in all these tasks I am indebted to U Tha Yauk. After our first trip we spent several days in camp. During these early days there often seemed no hurry to teach me anything, but I mixed freely all day with everyone, forever asking questions and being given answers packed with information that I had to remember. I went back to my hut for a curry lunch and for a cup of tea, and it was on such an occasion, I remember, that I first watched a most fascinating sight. About a hundred yards below my hut was a large pool in the brook.

Two elephants, each with her rider sitting behind

her head, entered the pool, and then, without any word
of command that I could hear, they both lay down in the
water. The riders tucked up their lungyi skirts so that
they were transformed into loincloths, slipped off their
mounts into the water, and began to scrub their respective
elephants from head to tail with a soap which lathered
freely. Then they washed it off the elephants, splashing
water over them with their hands. The soap they were
using turned out to be the soapy bark of a tree. Soon I
was standing on the bank of the pool, and from there I
watched five elephants being washed in the same way.
Two of them were cows with young calves, which rolled
over and over and played in the water like young children.
There were also two large males, with gleaming white
tusks, which were scrubbed with handfuls of silver sand.

After they had all been washed and dried off, the
elephants were paraded for inspection—all drawn up in
line abreast—with each of the riders dressed in his best.

U Tha Tauk advanced with military precision and,
after bowing instead of saluting, handed me the books,
all ragged and torn, but on the covers of which each
elephant's name was written.

I looked at one book and called out the name of the
elephant; and the rider, hearing me, rode it up to me
at a fast, bold stride. Rider and elephant both had a
sort of natural magnificence. Then the oozie halted
the animal just before me. He was a splendid beast,
with his head up, his skin newly scrubbed but already
dry in the sun, a black skin with a faint tinge of blue
showing through it, which seemed to make it so alive.
The white tusks, freshly polished, gleamed in the evening
sunlight. The rider was motionless, with one leg bent,
on which he appeared to be sitting, and the other dangling
behind the elephant's ear. On his face was an expression
of intense pride—pride in his magnificent beast.

Suddenly he gave a sharp order and the elephant
swung swiftly round to present his hindquarters, on
which there was a brand, made with phosphorous paint
when the animal was six years old.

I opened the book and read a number of entries,

each with the date when he had been inspected during the last ten years. On the front page was the history of the animal with his registered number and all sorts of details—such as that he had been born in Siam, bought when he was twenty years old, badly gored by a wild tusker, but had fully recovered after being off work for a year.

Thus I inspected each of the animals in turn and read their histories. As each inspection was finished the rider and elephant left the clearing and disappeared into the jungle.

When they had all gone I was taken round the harness-racks—just a row of horizontal branches of trees on each of which hung one of the animals' gear. All the harness except the heavy dragging-chains was hand-made by the riders. There were great cane basket panniers, woven breast-straps of fibre, wooden breeching-blocks, padding from the bark of the banbrwe-tree, ropes of every kind twisted from the bark of the shaw-tree.

One evening, as I passed the camp huts on the way back to my own, I noticed a Burmese girl unlike any Burmese girl I had seen. Her skin was a different colour and she looked ill. She was rocking a bamboo Moses basket hung in the shade of one of the huts.

She gave me a pleasant smile, so, plucking up all my courage, I went up to her, gave the cradle a swing and peeped inside at a new-born baby which was fast asleep.

Now that I was close to the girl, I saw that her peculiar yellow colour, so unlike the natural pale bronze of the Burmese, was due to something smeared over her skin— a saffron lotion used by Burmese women after childbirth.

In those first three months on my own I did most of the things worth doing in Burma. Tha Yauk helped me to achieve my ambition of shooting a wild bull elephant. My main reason for shooting him was not to secure the tusks, much as I coveted them, but to carry out a *post-mortem* so as to see what the organs of a really healthy elephant looked like and make another attempt to find the kidneys. This second *post-mortem* taught me a good deal about what had been wrong

with Ma Oh. In fact it showed me half a dozen sufficient
reasons why she must have died.

After three months, which passed all too soon, I
returned to Willie, having learned a great deal since I
had left him. Naturally, when I arrived I got the
greeting I expected: sarcastic remarks about my having
let one of my elephants die in the first two days—no doubt
by having overloaded her with all my blasted new kit.

I replied that I was surprised that she had lived as
long as she had. Her liver was riddled with flukes, and
her heart was as big as a rugger ball.

" How do *you* know how big an elephant's heart
ought to be? " snorted Willie.

" I shot a wild tusker that Tha Yauk told me was
forty years old, and I did a *post-mortem* on him in order
to see how the organs of a healthy elephant compared
with hers. His heart was only the size of a coconut."

Willie's whole attitude to me changed after I said
this. What pleased him was that I had shot an elephant,
not for its tusks, but in order to learn more about elephants. For Willie, like most men who live long in the
jungle, hated big game to be shot. He felt far more
sympathy with any creature which was part of his jungle
than with any new arrival, armed with all his new kit.

That evening I became a companion with whom he
could enjoy rational conversation, instead of an inter-
loper who had to be bullied and kept in his place. What
I told him about shooting helped, for he was a magnificent
jungle-fowl shot. I showed him my diary, and the bags
of jungle-fowl I had made in the evenings, using my
elephant-riders as beaters, surprised him. I had found
a very good ground for jungle-fowl in an area where he
had not shot, and he saw we had something to talk about.
What this really led to was gin before our whisky and then
double rations of that. We had jungle-fowl that I had
brought back with me for dinner, and we sat up drinking
for a long time afterwards. I did not see him under the
table, as I had once promised myself, because he gave up
the contest by falling asleep in his chair.

I did not dare wake him, and went slowly to bed.

At last I saw him get up and move over towards the fire, as though to shift a log. Next moment he had overbalanced into it. I raced from my tent to save him. He had rolled out of the fire, and I pulled him to his feet. He stood up perfectly to attention and said very sternly:

"What the hell are you doing? Do you insinuate that I am drunk?"

To this I replied: "No. But you've burned your arm badly."

He then ordered me to my tent and told me to mind my own business. This was more than I would stand and I turned on him, saying:

"Well, if you fall in again, I shall let you sizzle."

He appeared absolutely sober at once. The shock of being spoken to in such a way by a young subordinate had been greater than that of the red-hot embers.

Next morning we were back where we had started, but I could see that he was feeling sorry for himself. It was two days before he was forced to swallow his pride and ask me to dress his arm for him. The ground lost over the bottle was regained by tactful bandaging, and I think it was from that time that our friendship really began.

But the way in which I had pleased him was by my interest in elephants. His great ambition had been to get someone who would take up the subject of elephant management seriously, and it seemed to him that I might be the man he wanted.

Before I left him, two or three days later, he had advised me to take up elephants and to make them my chief concern and my life's work. I thus owe a great debt of gratitude to Willie.

The job of extracting teak and delivering it a thousand miles away has many branches, and European Assistants took up different aspects of the work. Up till that time nobody had specialised in trying to improve the management of elephants. Most of the details concerning it had been left to the Burman.

The average European Assistant joining any of the

large teak firms in Burma was put in charge of a forest area bigger than an English county. In it were scattered a total of a hundred elephants, in groups of seven. By continually touring during all the seasons of the year, he might be able to visit every camp about once every six weeks. In such conditions it would be a long time before he learnt to know his elephants even by name, still less by sight; and it would be a very long time indeed before he knew their individual temperaments and capacities for work.

I was more fortunate, as I was made responsible for seventy elephants, all working in a fairly small area. I was thus often able to visit my camps twice a month and to spend longer in each of them.

What follows is largely the result of my having the luck to start in conditions that enabled me to get to know my elephants really well.

Chapter Three

THERE are three distinct species of elephant, one Asiatic and two African.

The Asiatic elephant is the one most frequently seen in zoos and circuses, as it is easily tamed. African elephants are rarely seen in captivity and are very rarely broken in for work, but the large African elephant is well known by sight from photographs and films of African safaris.

Four races of the Asiatic elephant are recognised: the Indian or Burman, the Ceylonese, the Malayan, and the Sumatran. All these are very similar, and differ from the African elephant in having much smaller ears and a smooth, tapering trunk; the female Asiatic elephant has no tusks.

In the Ceylonese race tusks are absent in both male and female. This has been attributed to the fodder available on the island. The Ceylonese elephants do not work in harness, but will drag a rope gripped in the mouth and teeth.

The African elephant is a taller and more lanky animal than the Asiastic. It is easily recognised by the large ears and the segmented trunk. One exhibited by Barnum and Bailey was ten foot nine inches high at the shoulder.

There are four races: the Central, Sudanese, Eastern and Southern varieties.

It is often stated that the African elephant is not capable of being domesticated. This is not entirely true, but specimens kept in captivity have usually had more uncertain tempers than the average Indian elephant. The reason why African elephants are so seldom domesticated is partly because the negro races have not the temperament to attempt the task and have no tradition of working with elephants. The elephant, moreover, is far more useful for dragging or pushing heavy weights than as a beast of burden. The African elephant is not so well proportioned for dragging heavy weights as the Asiatic animal. It lacks the short hind leg, and the hindquarters do not fall away to the same extent. The tusks of the African elephant are far more massive. A pair on exhibition in New York weigh two hundred and ninety-three pounds, being eleven feet five and a half inches and eleven feet in length, respectively, and eighteen inches in circumference at the base.

At the time of writing a movement is on foot for importing Burman or Karen elephant-men into Tanganyika in order to capture and train African elephants. If this is undertaken as a last attempt to effect jungle clearing for the British Government Groundnuts Scheme, I shudder to think what the eventual cost will be to the British taxpayer.

It is true the Portuguese East African elephant has been used in harness, and I have seen photographs and read an account of this successful experiment. But the work done was never heavy, and did not go beyond dragging small cultivators and ploughs, and it required little expenditure of energy by the animal.

The African pigmy elephant is a distinct species, limited to the equatorial and Congo region. The largest males are said never to exceed seven feet in height. Specimens of the pigmy elephants have been kept in captivity, and I have seen all three species in America. The ears of the pigmy are similar in shape to those of the ordinary African elephant—like enormous cabbage leaves. The ears of the Indian elephant are triangular, like the map of India, and when cocked never protrude above the head, like those of the African.

The African elephant is confidently stated to have been the species domesticated by the Carthaginians who employed it in their wars against Rome.

In 218 B.C. Hannibal began his invasion of Italy with an army of ninety thousand foot, twelve thousand horse and thirty-seven elephants. He is believed to have crossed the Alps by the Little St Bernard Pass. If this is correct, he at first made his way over the Mont du Chat through the Chevelu Pass and up the valley of the Isère before climbing the Little St Bernard. He descended by the valley of the Doria to Aosta. Part of his route was through a narrow defile, and there he was threatened by the mountain tribes who appeared on the heights. At the white rock, still known as " La Roche Blanche," he halted his infantry and sent his cavalry and beasts of burden ahead to the top of the pass. The next day, the ninth, he stood with his army on the highest point and addressed cheering words to his half-frozen Africans and Spaniards.

The descent was difficult and dangerous. The Italian side is steeper than the French, and the slopes were covered with freshly fallen snow. Three days were spent in constructing a road for the elephants and horses. Three days later the army reached the valley of Aosta. But his army had shrunk to twenty thousand infantry and six thousand cavalry. The casualties among the elephants are not recorded.

Hannibal's feat of taking the elephants over mountain passes and along narrow mountain tracks is of immense interest to me, as I have faced and overcome a similar problem myself. Since Hannibal crossed the Alps during the autumn, and early snow had only just fallen on the Italian side, there must have been fairly plentiful fodder for the elephants for the greater part of the time. Thus they did not have to rely entirely upon a grain ration.

It is not clear what his object was in taking the elephants with him. They cannot have been for pack purposes, unless for some special load such as bullion, since their total load could not, at a maximum, have exceeded forty thousand pounds.

The chief use of elephants in Indian wars was in battering open fortified defences during the final assault on beleaguered towns, and in particular in knocking down gates. The gates of Indian cities and fortified places were frequently covered with enormous iron spikes three to five feet long, so as to prevent elephants from battering them with their heads. It is possible Hannibal wanted the elephants for sieges. But it is more probable that they were taken as a form of psychological warfare. Among the ancients, rumours and news became even more exaggerated than they do to-day, and the appearance of unknown gigantic beasts trained to warfare would have been terrible in the extreme.

The most puzzling thing, and the only part I find difficult to believe, is that the elephants were African. It was physically quite possible for the Carthaginians to import young domesticated elephants by sea from India to Iraq, and then to march them overland, either to Tyre for reshipment to Carthage, or overland through Egypt and Cyrenaica. The Carthaginians were a maritime race of traders, and not Africans. One would expect them to buy elephants and mahouts and to ship them. One would not expect them to explore Africa, and discover the secret of capturing wild elephants and of breaking them in. If elephants were being captured, broken in and trained for warfare in Africa it is extraordinary that the Egyptians did not continue the practice. But no tradition of elephant-training has survived in Africa, and there is no record of elephants being used by any indigenous African people, whereas Indian history is full of accounts of the use of elephants in war. In India the elephant has been domesticated from time immemorial. There were elephants in the armies which sought to repel Alexander the Great. But, however formidable looking, they could not withstand the dash of his well-armed and disciplined troops.

If an elephant's trunk is injured the animal becomes unmanageable, and wounded beasts probably did more damage to their own side than to the enemy. Sometimes elephants carried great wooden towers capable of holding, it is said, thirty-two soldiers. These were archers.

From A.D. 1024 onwards elephants are mentioned in trains of thousands in the Wars of the Princes; and those who are familiar with the subject find no reason to question such figures. After the battle of Delhi, Prince Timour is stated to have captured three thousand elephants from Prince Mohammed. It is said that they all had snuff put into their eyes so as to make them appear to weep tears of grief at having been defeated.

Indian elephants were on the strength of the Royal Engineers up till 1895, when Daisy, the last and oldest pensioner, died.

In India itself elephants have gradually disappeared. Only a few are kept by the princes for ceremonial purposes and shikar. The elephant is, however, an animal in which every Indian is interested, and it is invested in a haze of myth and legend which delights children and is a source of pride to the descendants of India's ancient warriors.

It is impossible to understand much about tame elephants unless one knows a great deal about the habits of wild ones. The study of wild elephants usually entails shooting a few of them at some period, either deliberately for sport or ivory, or in self-defence. Most men who have shot elephants come afterwards to regret having done so—but " to hunt is to learn."

The only attempted census of wild elephants in Burma is contained in *Big Game in Burma* by E. A. Peacock, who puts their number at three thousand. If I were to hazard a guess, I should double that figure, but all one can really say is that they are plentiful.

Wild elephants normally live in herds of thirty to fifty, and during the year cover great distances, chiefly in search of fodder. During the monsoon months—from June to October—they graze on bamboo in the hilly forest country, sometimes remaining on one watershed for a week or ten days, after which they suddenly move ten miles for another week's stay on another slope. After the monsoons are over they move into the lower foothills and the swamp valleys, feeding more on grass and less on bamboo.

It is at this time that the full-grown male tuskers join the herd, though they seldom actually enter it, preferring to remain on its outskirts, within half a mile or a mile of it. At this season they do their courting and mating, in the course of which the older bulls often have to fight some youngster who is pursuing the same female.

C

The herds know their yearly cycle of grazing grounds, and in their annual passage wear well-defined tracks along the ridges of the hills. In places where they have to descend from a precipitous ridge down the side of a watershed they will move in Indian file, and by long use will wear the track into a succession of well-defined steps.

Wild elephants hate being disturbed on their feeding-grounds, but they do not usually stampede suddenly, like many other herds of big game. With an uncanny intelligence, they close up round one animal as though they were drilled, and their leader then decides on the best line of retreat. He leads, and they follow irresistibly, smashing through everything, like so many steam-rollers.

If they cannot exactly locate the danger which threatens them, they invariably retreat along the track from which they have come while grazing, with their trunks on each other's backs, but in a formation of three or four abreast.

I once had the unpleasant, but exciting, experience of being a member of such a stampeding party, when I was mounted on one of my own elephants. The wild elephants were fortunately quite oblivious of the fact that Elephant Bill and tusker Po Sein (Mr Firefly) were among them. Fortunately my rider was able to extricate us from the party before they reached a muddy nullah with banks eight feet high. The leading elephants plunged their forefeet into the edge of the bank, broke it away, and, sitting on their haunches, made a toboggan slide for the herd following them.

Most wild elephant calves are born between March and May. I believe that, if she is disturbed, the mother elephant will carry her calf, during its first month, holding it wrapped in her trunk. I have seen a mother pick up her calf in this way. On two occasions I have found the tracks of a newly born baby calf in a herd. Later on, after I had disturbed them, there were no tracks of the calf to be found among those of the stampeding animals, nor could the calves have kept up with a stampeding herd. But there was no possibility of the calf being hidden or abandoned.

The birth of a calf is quite a family event in a herd

of wild elephants, and I have on several occasions camped close to what I may call the maternity ward. For many years I could not understand the bellowing and trumpeting of wild elephants at night during the hot weather, when most calves are born. The fuss is, without any doubt, made by the herd in order to protect the mother and calf from intruders—in particular from tigers. The noise is terrifying. The herd will remain in the neighbourhood of the maternity ward for some weeks, until the new arrival can keep up with the pace of a grazing herd. The ward may cover an area of a square mile, and during the day the herd will graze all over it, surrounding the mother and her newly born calf, and closing their ranks round her at night. The places chosen, which I have examined after the herd has moved on, have been on low ground where a river has suddenly changed its course and taken a hair-pin bend. These spots were thus bounded on three sides by banks and river. The kind of jungle found in such places is always the same. They are flooded during the rains, but during the hot weather— the normal calving period—they are fairly dry, with areas of dense kaing, or elephant grass, eight to twelve feet high, with an occasional wild cotton-tree giving shade. They are eerie spots, and to explore them is an adventure. Wild pig breed in the same type of jungle, and harbour their sounders of sucking pigs under huge heaps of leaves and grass which in size and appearance resemble ant-heaps four feet high.

It is common practice for a Burman oozie, or elephant-rider, to ride his elephant silently up to such a " pig's nest " of leaves and grass and then, silently controlling the elephant by movements of his foot and leg, to instruct him to put one forefoot gently on the mound.

Squeals and snorts usually follow from the old sow, and three or four sucking pigs join her in a stampede.

Once while an elephant did this I had the good luck to bag a right and left of sucking pig for the camp pot from an elephant's back. It was ridden by an oozie called Kya Sine, who knew every trick of the jungle and became my gun-boy until his death.

It is a peculiar thing that the elephant, which becomes so accustomed to man, and has such confidence in him once it has been trained, should be so afraid of him in its wild state. Owing to this fear of man, they do surprisingly little damage to village crops, considering the vast numbers of wild elephant. They much prefer their own deep jungles, and seldom leave them. The damage that they do has been greatly and most unfairly exaggerated, and the extermination of wild elephants in Upper Burma was actually started on unreliable advice. Solitary animals may, however, do great damage and become bold enough to drive off any human intruder who shows himself. They will do this almost as though they thought it was a joke. Such animals, however, are always eventually declared rogues and are killed—or at least shot at, or caught, or injured in traps.

Before the Japanese came into the war in 1941 we made it difficult for the Burmese cultivators to obtain arms. It was not that we distrusted the villagers themselves, but if one of them was known to own a firearm, the local robbers or dacoits were likely to steal it. Many robberies were carried out with one firearm in order to obtain a second. Rightly or wrongly, when a villager was allowed to possess a gun, it was usually a twelve-bore shotgun, which is scarcely an ideal weapon with which to kill a wild elephant. The Burmese villagers did their best with what they had, and a common practice was to remove the shot from a twelve-bore cartridge and then plug it with a pointed roasted cane about three inches long. It protruded about two inches from the cartridge-case, and was firmly fixed in with molten wax to make all as gas-tight as possible. Such a cane dart carries fairly accurately for about thirty yards, and if an elephant is wounded in the foot by one, the dart usually becomes deeply embedded and sets up such severe inflammation that the animal goes dead lame. In such a case it abandons cultivated crops and takes shelter in the jungle. I have sometimes had my own elephants wounded by these darts, and, indeed, have had to employ the same unpleasant method to capture savage animals that had gone wild after being loose for a long time. The operation of removing one of these darts from the foot is extremely difficult to perform and, like all operations on the foot, is exceptionally painful to the animal.

Ordinary fences round crops are no good as a protection against elephants. The Burma Posts and Telegraphs know only too well that an elephant has merely to lean against a telegraph post in order to push it over, and has only to grip it with its trunk and give a heave to pull it up with ease. And no ordinary fences have posts stronger than telegraph poles. The only effective fence against elephants is what is called the punge. This is often used as a trap, and it was a godsend to the XIVth Army, which often employed it instead of barbed wire. The punge fence, or trap, is made of a series of sharpened and lightly roasted, or smoked, bamboo stakes of varying lengths. One end of each is stuck into the ground at an angle of thirty degrees, with the point upwards and facing outwards. On the outside of the fence, concealed in the undergrowth, are very short stakes, protruding only three or four inches out of the ground, and behind these are stakes gradually increasing in length, the longest sticking out four or five feet. The depth of the fence may be as much as eight or ten yards. I have seen wild boar stampeded down a track across which a punge fence had previously been erected. They were killed outright, skewered through the chest and out between the shoulder-blades.

If an elephant charges a punge fence, a stake may easily pierce right through the foreleg before snapping off. On one occasion I had to extract such a stake, gripping the point with a pair of blacksmith's tongs and pulling it right through the leg. For, like a barbed fish-hook, a piece of bamboo cannot be withdrawn by the way it has entered.

Pit-traps which occur so frequently in books about elephant-hunting are very uncommon in Burma. I think the Burmese elephant is too intelligent to fall into them. An effective and heinous trap which killed one of my own elephants was a spear, about the size of a ship's spar or a light telegraph pole, heavily weighted and suspended in a tree over a game track. The release was by means of a trip-wire rope, and the spear came down with such force as to transfix the elephant, smashing his ribs and piercing his intestines. It must have taken at least a dozen men to erect this trap. I never traced the culprits. When I tackled them on the subject, all the villagers within a hundred miles round would only say that the tree must have grown like that.

Wire ropes of all sizes have become common in the jungle, and the simple wire noose can be very dangerous, and terrifies elephants, as the trunk is often caught; and if an elephant's trunk is seriously injured it will die of starvation, since everything it eats has to be torn down or pulled up and handled by the trunk.

The noose-trap is set with a very stiff but flexible sapling bent over as a spring. When anything is caught in the snare the sapling springs up and pulls it tight.

I was once confronted by a full-grown Himalayan black bear hanging by the neck, with his hind legs dangling three feet off the ground. The spring of the sapling jerking the wire noose must have broken his neck, as there were no signs of a struggle. I was glad it was the bear and not me, for I might easily have put my foot through the noose.

Herds of wild elephants are not always suspicious of danger. I have on many occasions ridden on one of my own tuskers into a herd of sometimes as many as fifty animals. Sitting on my own elephant, I have passed so close to a wild one that I could have struck a match on his back. Without being detected, I have watched and photographed wild calves of different ages playing in a mud wallow, like children playing at mud pies.

The mating of wild elephants is very private. The bull remains, as usual, outside the herd, and his lady love comes out where she knows she will find him. She gives the herd the slip in the evening, and is back with them at dawn. Sometimes a rival tusker intervenes, and a duel ensues. This is why elephant-fights are always between two bulls. There is never a general dog-fight within the herd.

Elephant bulls fight head to head and seldom fight to the death, without one trying to break away. The one that breaks away frequently receives a wound which proves mortal. Directly one of the contestants tries to break off and turn, he exposes the most vulnerable part of the body. The deadly blow is a thrust of one tusk between the hind legs into the loins and intestines where the testicles are carried inside the body. It is a common wound to have to treat after a wild tusker has attacked a domesticated one.

Some males never grow tusks, but these tuskless males are at no disadvantage in a fight, although to outward appearances they are the eunuchs of the herd. This impression is quite wrong. From the age of three all that the animal gains by not having to grow tusks goes into additional bodily strength, particularly in the girth and weight of the trunk. As a result, the trunk becomes so strong that it will smash off an opponent's tusk as though, instead of being solid ivory, it were the dry branch of a tree.

From the time that a male calf is three years old there is always interest among the oozies as to whether it is going to be a tusker with two tusks, or a tai (with one tusk, either right or left), or a han (a tuskless male, but with two small tushes such as females carry), or, lastly, a hine, which has neither tusks nor tushes.

One of the most delightful myths about wild elephants is that the old tuskers and females drop out of the happy herd life when they realise they are no longer wanted, and that they finally retreat to die in a traditional grave-yard in some inaccessible forest. This belief has its origin in the fact that dead elephants, whether tuskers or females, are so seldom found. I wish I could include a description here of how I had discovered one of these graveyards. But since I cannot, I shall try to explain away the myth by describing what really happens. I will take the case of a fine old bull that has stopped following the herd at about the age of seventy-five and has taken to a solitary existence. He has given up covering great distances in a

seasonal cycle, and remains in the headwaters of a remote
creek. It has become enough for him to devote all his
time to grazing, resting and taking care of his health. His
cheeks are sunken, his teeth worn out. Gathering his
daily ration of six hundred pounds of green fodder has
become too great a tax on his energy, and he knows he
is losing weight. Old age and debility slowly overtake
him and his big, willing heart. During the monsoon
months he finds life easy. Fodder, chiefly bamboos, is
easily gathered, and he stays up in the hills. As the dry
season approaches, fodder becomes scarcer, and the effort
of finding food greater, and he moves slowly downhill to where he can browse on the tall grass. Then, as
the hot season comes on, and there are forest fires, he is
too tired and too old to go in search of the varied diet he
needs, and his digestion suffers. Fever sets in, as the
showers of April and May chill him, and he moves to
water—to where he knows he can always get a cool
drink. Here, by the large pool above the gorge, there
is always green fodder in abundance, for his daily picking.
He is perfectly happy, but the water slowly dries, until
there is only a trickle flowing from the large pool, and he
spends his time standing on a spit of sand, picking up the
cool sand and mud with his trunk, and spraying it over
his hot, fevered body.

One sweltering hot evening in late May, when there
was not a breath of air stirring in this secluded spot, to
which he had come again for a drink, he could hear that
a mighty storm was raging ten miles away in the hills,
and he knew the rains had broken. Soon the trickle
would become a raging torrent of broken brown water,
carrying trees and logs and debris in its onrush. Throwing his head back, with his trunk in his mouth as he took
his last drink, he grew giddy. He staggered and fell but
the groan he gave was drowned by peals of thunder.
He was down—never to rise again—and he died without
a struggle. The tired old heart just stopped ticking.

Two porcupines got the news that night, and, in spite
of the heavy rain, attacked one of his tusks, gnawing it as
beavers gnaw wood.

They love the big nerve-pulp inside near the lip. They had only half eaten through the second tusk when the roar of the first tearing spate of the rains drove them off.

A five-foot wall of water struck the carcase—debris piled up while the water furiously undermined and outflanked this obstruction—at last the whole mass of carcase, stones and branches moved, floated, and then, swirling and turning over, went into the gorge down a ten-foot waterfall and jammed among the boulders below. Hundreds of tons of water drove on to it, logs and boulders bruised and smashed up the body, shifting it further, and the savage water tore it apart. As the forest fires are God's spring-cleaning of the jungle, so the spates of the great rains provide burial for the dead. That elephant never had to suffer months of exhausting pilgrimage to reach a common graveyard.

By dawn the floods had subsided and the porcupines had to hunt for their second meal of tusk. Other jungle scavengers had their share of the scattered parts, taking their turns in the order of jungle precedence. But the spate came again the next night, and in a week all traces of the old tusker had disappeared.

In South Kensington Museum there are three petrified mammoth's teeth, one canine and two molars, which I found in a gorge in Burma. They are entirely different in kind from elephants' teeth, which are large, serrated dentals on either side of the jaw. These mammoth teeth are all that is left of an incident similar to the one I have described, which must have happened many centuries ago.

Existing species of elephants are all that remain of a rich and varied family. Fossil bones of fourteen species of the genus *elephas* are known, and there are a still larger number of the allied genus *mastodon*, which had tusks in both jaws and more numerous teeth. The most interesting of all the extinct forms is undoubtedly the mammoth. It co-existed with primitive man, whose drawings and engravings of it are well known, and it may have survived to a late period in Siberia. Its remains are frequently found throughout northern Europe, America and Asia, and are so abundant in Siberia that the tusks form an important article of trade. Mammoths have been found frozen in almost perfect preservation. The remains of elephants have been frequently found in England, and in Malta remains of two pigmy elephants have been discovered.

Chapter Four

As civilisation eats into the jungle with its roads and railways, the herds of elephants grow fewer. The number of elephants in India has shrunk enormously for this reason, and I fear the same thing will happen in Burma. Fortunately, there are vast forests in the north of Burma into which the herds will gradually withdraw, and where they will, for a long time to come, find that peace characteristic of the jungle of which they are a symbol.

Low-flying aircraft are a new danger. They disturb and terrify herds of elephants, and may seriously affect their breeding for some generations.

The elephants which piled the teak in the sawmills of Moulmein, Mandalay and Rangoon were hand fed, and so are the great majority of ceremonial elephants kept in India. Such animals are kept in stalls, like horses, just as they are in the London Zoo. Sawmill elephants were at one time quite a show piece in the mills where they were used, and those invited to see them were usually asked to come by twelve-thirty p.m.; for at one o'clock, when the siren blew for the midday break, the elephants, like the men, just downed tools. They flatly refused to place the piece of timber they were holding between tusks and trunk on the stack, but just dropped it.

The fact that very few, if any, of these animals ever bred in captivity is sufficient proof of the unnatural conditions in which they lived. Very little could be learned from elephants kept in such conditions which was of any use in improving the general management of the thousands of up-country elephants. The conditions of these up-country elephants are completely different. They are far nearer to the wild state than any other domesticated animals. Indeed, one might

33

say that they are domesticated for only eight hours out
of the twenty-four. The great difference is that these
elephants feed on their natural fodder in the jungle,
and gather it for themselves. They are not hand fed.
As a result of the liberty which this involves, they breed
readily.

A conservative figure of the numbers of elephants
working in the mixed deciduous forest areas of Burma
before the Japanese invasion is six thousand. Seventy
per cent of them were born in captivity.

The purchase of newly captured kheddared elephants
was more often than not left to a Burman who was reputed
to be a good judge of elephants. But the purchase of
kheddared elephants was never really successful. A kheddared elephant seldom works as well, or as reliably,
as one brought up from a calf to be familiar with man and
with work, and it can be immediately recognised by the
terrific training scars on its legs. It was soon realised
that it was increasingly desirable to keep up the numbers
by taking greater care of mothers and newly born calves,
of which the death rate was very high. I arrived in
Burma just as a determined effort had been started to
improve the management of these elephants and their
calves. In order to do this, it was first necessary to improve the conditions of the oozie, who must be considered as part and parcel of the Burmese timber-working
elephant which he rides. These men are born with a
knowledge of elephants. Their homes are in camps in
the most remote parts of the jungle. They can sit an
elephant from the age of six, and they grow up learning
all the traditional knowledge, the myth and legend, the
blended fact and fiction, which is attached to this lovable
animal. At the age of fourteen the average boy in an
elephant camp is earning a wage. He starts life as a
paijaik—that is, the man who hooks the chains to the
logs—a ground assistant of the oozie who rides on the
elephant's neck.

It is a proud day in that boy's life when he is promoted
to oozie and has an elephant in his own charge. There
is no more lovely sight than to see a fourteen-year-old

boy riding a newly trained calf elephant of six. The understanding between them is only equalled by that of a child with a puppy, but the Burmese boy is not so cruel to his elephant as most children are with puppies. The Burman oozie is cruel to his elephant only if he loses his temper, but usually he has the patience of Job. He has a pretty hard life. In the first place, he has to catch his elephant every morning and bring it to camp. The camp is often a hundred miles from his village, and may consist of a few jungle huts, or even no more than a couple of tarpaulins making a shelter on the bank of some creek in the densest jungle. Catching his elephant involves tracking the animal a distance of about eight miles, starting at dawn through jungles infested with all types of big game. That in itself is a lonely job, and to do it successfully the oozie has to become one of the jungle beasts himself—as alert and as wary as they are.

He knows the shape, size and peculiarities of his own elephant's footprints with such certainty that he can recognise them at once and distinguish them from all other elephant footprints. Once he has picked them up, he sets off, following the trail. While he is doing so he notices many things: he finds the spot where the animal rested in the night, he observes its droppings, and, after giving one heap of dung a kick, can tell that his elephant has been eating too much bamboo and, for that reason, will probably have headed for a patch of kaing grass that grows on the banks of the creek over the watershed.

When he has gained the ridge he will halt and listen, perhaps for ten minutes, for the sound of the bell his particular animal wears round its neck. He can hear a bell perhaps two miles away but he decides it is not the note of the bell that he made himself, hollowing it from the teak with such intricate care. So he goes on again, descending to the creek, and when he is half a mile from the kaing grass he listens again and this time he recognises the sound of his own kalouk. Elephant bells are made with two clappers, one on each side, hanging outside the bell, which is made from a hollowed-out lump of teak. No two bells ever have the same note, and the sound of fifteen or more can only be compared to the music of a babbling brook.

As the oozie approaches his beast he begins to sing, so as to let her know that he is coming. He has taught her, or she has taught him, that it is dangerous for them to startle each other in the jungle. So, instead of bursting through the kaing grass that stands nine feet high, he sits down on a boulder beside the creek and fills his home-made pipe and lights it. Between the puffs he keeps calling: "Lah! lah! lah!" (Come on! come on! come on!) But no sound comes from where his elephant is grazing, so he changes his words to: "Digo lah! Digo lah!" (Come here! Come here!) And he will sit and smoke and call for fifteen minutes without showing impatience. He gives her time to accept the grim fact that another day of hard work has begun for her. If he hurried her, she might rebel.

Presently the elephant emerges from the kaing grass, and, chatting away to her, he says: "Do you think I've nothing else to do but wait for you? You've been eating since noon yesterday, and I haven't had a bite of breakfast."

Then his voice rings out with a firm order: "Hmit!"

Dropping first on her haunches, then reposing with all four legs extended, she allows him to approach her.

"Tah!" (Stand up!), he orders, and she does so, keeping her front legs close together. He then bends down and unfastens her fetter-chain and throws it over her withers. These hobbles are either chain or cane, and are put on fairly tight and with little play between the legs. When the animal is hobbled it can either shuffle slowly on easy ground or progress by a series of hops. But in spite of this it can go fast: for short distances it can go as fast as a man can run.

After unfastening the hobbles the oozie orders her to sit down, then he climbs on to her head, and away they go, back to camp, by the route she has been feeding along ever since the previous day.

When they reach camp the oozie has his first meal of

the day, washes his elephant in the creek, and then harnesses her for work. Their job for the day is to climb a ridge two thousand feet above the camp and to drag a log from the stump to the creek.

When the oozie reaches the log with his elephant and his paijaik, he will trim it, cutting off knots where there were branches with his axe, so as to make it easier for dragging. He also cuts a hole in the thinner end of the log, through which the dragging-chains are passed. This hole, called a nepah, is so useful in handling the log when rafting, as well as in dragging, that though it is wasteful of good timber it is preferred to fastening the chains round the log in a clove hitch, or to any other form of attachment.

Then he will make sure the chains are securely fastened. After that there begins the wearisome task of dragging a log twenty-nine feet long and six or seven feet in girth— that is to say, over a hundred cubic feet of timber, or four tons dead weight. For a mile the path follows the top of the ridge. " Patience! patience! patience! Yoo! yoo! yoo! " (Pull! pull! pull!), calls the oozie. As the elephant takes the strain, she feels what power she must exert besides that of her enormous weight. Tremendous energy is necessary. The ground is ankle-deep in mud, and there are dozens of small obstructions which must be levelled out by the log's nose—sapling stumps, bamboos, stones, even rocks. So the elephant puts out her first effort and, bellowing like hell, pulls the log three times her own length and then stops. She rests then to take breath, and her trunk goes out sideways to snatch at a bamboo. It is her chewing-gum as she works, but it earns her a sarcastic comment from the oozie: " My mother, but you are forever eating! " However, his patience is quite undisturbed. The elephant takes her time. " Yoo! yoo! yoo! " calls the oozie, but there is no response. " Yooo! yooo! yooo! " Then the elephant pulls again, but this time, as it is slightly downhill, she pulls the log six times her length before she halts. So it goes on, until they reach the edge of a precipice—a four-hundred-foot drop. The elephant knows the margin of safety to a foot, and when the log is ten feet from the edge she refuses to haul it any closer. The chains are unfastened, and the elephant is moved round behind the log. The oozie gives his orders by kicks and scratches with his bare feet behind the elephant's ears. So he coaxes her to bend down her massive head in order to get a leverage under the log with her trunk. Working like that, she moves it first four feet at one end, then rolls it from the middle, then pushes the other end, until she has got it almost trembling on the balance on to the very edge of the cliff. She will then torment her oozie by refusing to touch it again for ten minutes. Finally, when the oozie's patience is almost at an end, and the elephant can foresee that she will get a cursing and a vigorous toe-nail scratching behind her ears if she refuses any longer, she puts one forefoot out as calmly as if she were tapping a football; and the log is away—gone. There is a crash in the jungle below, and then a prolonged series of crashes echoing through the jungle, as the log tears down bamboos, until it comes to rest four hundred feet lower down, leaving the elephant standing on the edge of the precipice above, with a supercilious expression on her face, as though she were saying: "Damned easy."

Half an hour later elephant and oozie have reached the log again, having gone round by a circuitous game-track to the foot of the precipice. Once down there, she has again to drag the log with the chains along a ledge, which has been roughly blasted out of the hillside around a precipitous waterfall.

Such blasting is often done by a more primitive method than using dynamite. The rock is heated with a fierce brushwood fire and then cracked by pouring water over it. After that the fractured rocks are again broken with crowbars, and the big pieces disposed of by elephants.

Dragging a log weighing four tons while negotiating a not very wide ledge is a risky business, for the log might roll. But the elephant can judge what is safe to the inch —not to the foot—and she works with patience, patience, patience. Both oozie and elephant know that should the log start to roll or slide over the edge, all the gear and harness can be got rid of in the twinkling of an eye. The elephant has only to whip round in her tracks, step inside her chain, and bend down her head for all the harness to peel off over her head as easily as a girl will strip a silk slip off over her shoulders. For this reason it is very rare indeed for an elephant to be dragged over a precipice by a log suddenly taking charge.

After negotiating the ledge there is an easy downhill drag for half a mile to the floating point on the side of the creek. By that time it is about three o'clock in the afternoon. The oozie unharnesses his elephant, puts on her fetters, slaps her on her backside, and tells her that she must go off in search of food. For neither of them is their day's work really over. The elephant still has to find her fodder; not only to chew it, but to break off, pull down, or pull up, every branch, tree, creeper or tuft of grass that she eats. The oozie has to repair his gear, trim logs or weave a new laibut, or breast-strap of bark. This bit of harness takes the full strain of the elephant's strength when dragging, and has to be made accordingly. It gets a tremendous lot of wear.

Such is the oozie's day's work—and with it all he is a very happy man.

His chief relaxation is gambling. He does often literally lose the shirt off his back. I have seen one particular shirt worn by six different owners in a year. But they don't wear their shirts at work, but only dress up in the evening and when showing their elephants for inspection.

The hardest work, described above, lasts from June until March. Then for three months the oozie gets a rest from logging, but has still to look after his elephant every day.

He is, as I know Burma, all that is left of the real Burman—the cheerful Irishman of the East. I have watched him fraternise with all who played a part in the evacuation of Burma in 1942 and with those who recaptured it in 1945—the British soldier, the Gurkha, the Sikh, the Punjabi, the West African and the East African. He even fraternised with the Jap, because he would not abandon his elephant, and for a time both had to work for a new master.

One gets to know one's riders at the same time, and in the same way, as one gets to know the elephants. They are so much part of one another.

Living under such primitive conditions, not only the oozie but also his wife and family need frequent medical attention, and they have no one to look to but the European Assistant who lives nearest. Apart from all the diseases, accidents are constantly occurring in the jungle, and the Assistant has to be a bit of a doctor, and ready to take decisions which would make an ordinary medical man's hair stand on end. One may come into a new camp and find six people down with beri-beri—two women with their breasts split like ripe tomatoes from the swelling characteristic of that disease—and one has to decide at once what one is going to do about it. One has to be ready to tackle a girl with a bad afterbirth hæmorrhage, or a man scalped by a bear, with his long hair tangled deeply into the wounds and one eye out of its socket. Malaria is more common than are colds in the head in England, and is often followed by pneumonia. Dysentery, and even cholera and smallpox epidemics are all liable to break out in the jungle. I am convinced that life in such conditions would be impossible if it were not for the elephants, which exert a fascination over the Burmese, a fascination which Europeans soon begin to feel as well.

Like the elephant, the jungle Burman makes a marvellous patient. Both, when they are ill, have an implicit trust even in the most amateur of doctors, whose equipment is all too often only a first-aid box the size of a biscuit tin. Luckily, faith helps to make up for its deficiencies.

Chapter Five

THE fact that men and elephants live about as long as one another and come to maturity at much the same ages means that they can live together all their lives. They can thus acquire a lifelong mutual knowledge of each other's characters. With no other domestic animal is this possible. A baby boy may be born in an elephant camp, and at the same moment an elephant calf may be being born a mile or two away in the jungle; and that child and that calf may grow up together, play together, work together all their working lives, and they may still be familiar friends when sixty years have passed.

Elephants are not bred in captivity. The captive animals breed naturally in their natural surroundings. During the war I was talking about elephants to two war correspondents, one American and the other an Australian. The latter asked me: " Is it true that elephants are very shy about their actual love affair? " Before I could answer, the American chipped in with: " Of course they are: aren't you? " The mating of elephants is a private affair, and even the oozies of the tusker and the female concerned may not know that it has taken place. Often they know, but regard it as none of their business, and do not talk about it.

The most fantastic tales are told, and even believed, about the mating habits of elephants by Europeans. The tallest story that has come my way was told by a young Sapper officer to a very attractive nurse whom he took to the Rangoon Zoo, after the recapture of Rangoon in May 1945. Among the few animals left behind in it by the Japs were two young elephants, a male and a female, which led very boring existences hobbled and tethered by the hind legs to two posts in the elephant-shed. While watching this melancholy

pair, the young Sapper described how the female elephant
turns to thoughts of love in the spring time, and pre-
pares for her honeymoon by digging a deep pit, round
which she stacks a month's supply of fruit and fodder for
herself and her young bridegroom. When she has completed these preparations, she lies down in the nuptial
pit and trumpets a love-call to her mate. After his
arrival they live in one unending embrace for the whole
month, and do not separate until they have shared their
last pineapple or banana! No doubt the Sapper hoped
that his attractive listener would take the hint and act
likewise. The pretty girl to whom this story had been
told afterwards applied to me for confirmation of the
story. I felt sorry to have to disillusion her, though the
love-making of elephants as I have seen it seems to me
more simple and more lovely than any myth. It is
beautiful because it is quite without the brutishness and
the cruelty which one sees in the mating of so many
animals.

Without there being any appearance of season, two
animals become attracted by each other. In other
words they fall in love, and days, and even weeks, of
courtship may take place, the male mounting the female
with ease and grace and remaining in that position for
three or four minutes. Eventually the mating is con-
summated, and the act lasts five or ten minutes, and may
be repeated three or four times during the twenty-four
hours. The pair will keep together as they graze for
months, and their honeymoon will last all that time.
When they have knocked off from the day's work they
will call each other and go off together into the jungle.
My own belief is that it lasts until the female has been
pregnant for ten months—that is, until she has become
aware that she is pregnant. The act of mating can be
performed as easily by an elephant wearing hobbles as
without them, as the position of the male's forelegs lying
along the barrel of the back of the female is not interfered
with by the hobbles. In the final mating position the
male is standing almost vertically upright, with the
forefeet resting gently on the female's hindquarters.

The average female first mates between the ages of seventeen and twenty. She shows no sign of any particular season, but apparently feels some natural urge. It has recently been noticed that female circus elephants become moody in periods of approximately twenty-two months. Gestation lasts twenty-two months, and she does not appear to realise that she is pregnant until the end of the first ten months. After that the period of mating comes to an end, and the companionship of the male is replaced by that of a female friend or " auntie." From that time onwards the expectant mother and her girl friend, or " auntie," are never apart. They graze together always, and it becomes difficult to separate them. It is, indeed, cruel to do so. Their association is founded on mutual aid among animals, the instinctive knowledge that it takes two mothers to protect a calf elephant against tigers, which, in spite of all precautions, still kill twenty-five per cent of all calves born.

After the calf has been born, the mother and the " auntie " always keep it between them as they graze—all through the night—and, while it is very young, during daylight hours as well.

To kill the calf the tiger has to drive off both the mother and " auntie " by stampeding them. To do this he will first attack the mother, springing on her back and stampeding her; then he returns to attack " auntie," who defends the calf, knowing that in a few moments the mother will return. On many occasions I have had to dress the lacerated wounds of tiger-claws on the backs of both a mother elephant and her friend.

A mother elephant in captivity has no suspicions that man will injure her calf. I have only once been attacked by one of the many mothers whom I have congratulated by a pat on the trunk, often within an hour of the actual birth. That was an accident. I was patting a calf so young that it could not focus me with its little piggy eyes, and it bumped hard against my bare knees and yelled out the cry for danger. As I jumped back, the lash of the mother's trunk missed me by inches. She then chased me, but only for twenty yards, as she had to return to her squealing babe. On the other hand, I have handled a newly born dwarf elephant under the mother's belly, lifting it up so that it stood on a small platform, so as to reach its mother's nipples, and the mother seemed to consider this as much of a joke as I did.

A baby calf follows its mother at heel for three or four years. It is suckled by the mother for that period, from the breasts between her forelegs.

This position, between the forelegs, affords the calf perfect protection. At birth the calf's trunk is a useless object, or membrane, growing rather to one side, so as to allow the calf to suck more easily through the mouth. It does not become flexible and useful for three to four months. When the sacred white elephant of Mandalay Palace was a calf its mother died, and it was suckled by twenty young Burmese women daily as wet nurses, and so reared.

At the age of five or, at most, six years, the calf has learned to gather its own fodder, and gradually gives up sucking its mother. Female elephants have an average of four calves in their life-time. Twins are not uncommon, and two calves of different ages following their mother at heel is quite a usual sight. Larger families are not uncommon.

" Accidents " happen in the elephant world, and elderly females occasionally spring a surprise. Thus Main Hpo (a Shan name) gave birth to her eighth calf just after the Japanese War, in the Gangaw Valley, when she was sixty-one years old. All her previous calves had lived and had been trained—in fact her eldest son, a tuskless male named Hine Pau Zone (Mr Laziest), was the only elephant recorded as having killed a Japanese soldier. This incident took place at a Chin village in 1945, during the Japanese withdrawal.

After weaning, young elephants go through an awkward stage, becoming a bit truculent owing to the desire for independence—much like human boys and girls.

At fifteen or sixteen they become very much like human flappers and young stalwarts. They have reached the same adolescent stage of not knowing quite what they want. Some soon find out, others do not; for their temperaments vary.

Young male elephants do a lot of flirting with the females from the ages of sixteen to twenty, sometimes being most enterprising. But the average animal does not show any signs of musth until the age of twenty. A male elephant will mate when he is not on musth, in fact he usually does. But when he is on musth all the savage lust and combative instincts of his huge body come out.

From the age of twenty to thirty-five musth is shown by a slight discharge of a strongly smelling fluid from the musth-glands near the eye, directly above the line of the mouth. In a perfectly fit male it occurs annually during the hot months, which are the mating season. It may last about two weeks, during which time he is very temperamental.

From the age of thirty-five to forty-five the discharge increases and runs freely, eventually dribbling into his mouth, and the taste of it exasperates him and makes him much more ferocious. He is physically in his prime at that age, and unless he is securely chained to a large tree while on musth, he is a danger to his oozie and to other elephants. His brain goes wild, as though nothing would satisfy him, and nothing will.

From forty-five to fifty musth gradually subsides, and finally disappears. Tuskers that have killed as many as nine men between the ages of thirty-five and forty-five will become docile during musth in the later years of their lives. But no elephant on musth can be trusted unless he is over sixty years old.

Poo Ban, a magnificent tusker, was normally a friendly animal, and would allow me to walk under his head and tusks, but he went on musth in the Taungdwin Forest area, killed his oozie and another man, then killed two female elephants, and attacked on sight any man who came near him. Finally he entered villages, tore rice granaries open, and became the terror of the valley. I offered a reward of three hundred rupees for his capture, and decided to destroy him if he could not be captured.

He was marked down in a dense patch of bamboo jungle in Saiyawah (the Valley of Ten Villages), four marches away. With Kya Sine, my gun-boy, I set out, lightly loaded with two travelling elephants as pack. The evening before I was to tackle Poo Ban I was testing my rifle with a half charge, *i.e.*, with half the cordite removed, and with a soft-nosed bullet in the left barrel, keeping a normal hard-nosed cartridge in the right. I wanted to wound Poo Ban in one of his forefeet with the half charge, and then recapture him, break his spirit and heal his wound. At a hundred yards my practice-shooting was so accurate that I felt hopeful of success. Kya Sine, however, begged and implored me to let him go ahead and attempt to recapture him without shooting, so that he could earn the three hundred rupees. He intended to tackle him boldly, face to face, relying on his own authority and the animal's habits of obedience. Unfortunately, I gave in, and before dawn he had gone on ahead. I arrived at three p.m. next day to be met by men who said: "Kya Sine is dead." Poo Ban had killed him during his attempt at recapture.

That night I bivouacked in an open place which had at one time been paddy-fields. It was a brilliant moonlight night, and before I went to sleep I made my plans to recapture Poo Ban. I had no desire to avenge the death of Kya Sine—to whom I was devoted, and who had the greatest knowledge of jungle lore of any man I have ever known. The idea of revenge on an elephant would have been very distasteful to him.

I was asleep, lying in the open, when I was woken by a clank! clank! clank! Luckily for me, a piece of chain had been left on Poo Ban's off forefoot. I came suddenly to my senses out of a dream, and, jumping up, saw the finest sight of my life. Two hundred yards away, in the open, a magnificent tusker was standing, with his head erect in challenge, defiant of the whole world. He was a perfect silhouette. I did not dare move an eyelid. He was a bigger man than I was, and while I held my breath he moved on with a clank, clank, clank, which at last faded away like the far sound of the pipes over the hills.

At dawn I tried to put my plans into action. When he had been located, I took up my position, while twenty Burmans, with four shotguns between them, tried to drive him past me.

Poo Ban faced the lot, defying them four times. Shots rang out, but at last he changed his mind and, turning, came towards me. I was perched on a broken-down, dilapidated brick pagoda, a heap of rubble about six feet high, behind which was the hundred-feet-high bank of the Patolone River. Directly in front of me was a clearing of disused paddy-fields, and my hopes were that Poo Ban would cross it. I still meant to wound him in the foot, recapture him, break his spirit and then heal the wound.

Poo Ban came out of the jungle with his head held high. He halted, and then made a bee-line across my front, travelling fast over the open ground.

Kneeling, I took the shot at his foot on which my plans depended. The bullet kicked up a puff of dust in front of his near forefoot as he put it down in his stride. I had missed!

Poo Ban halted and swung round to face me, or the bark of my rifle which he had heard. Then he took up the never-to-be-forgotten attitude of an elephant about to charge, with the trunk well tucked away in his mouth, like a wound-up watch-spring or the proboscis of a butterfly. As he charged it flashed through my mind that I had no time to reload. I depended on the hard-nosed bullet in the right barrel. At twenty-five yards I took a chest shot. At twenty yards Poo Ban fell. His head dropped; his tusks drove nine inches into the ground. For a few seconds he balanced, and then toppled over, dead.

I dropped my rifle and was sick, vomiting with fear, excitement and regret. Poo Ban was dead, and I had failed to catch him alive. There was no court of inquiry. My report was accepted, and I was given the tusks as a souvenir, a souvenir of a double failure that I bitterly regretted, and of the death of the finest and bravest Burman hunter I have known.

Chapter Six

THERE is undoubted cruelty in breaking the spirit and training wild elephants after they have been captured by kheddaring. The ideal age at which to capture a wild elephant is usually considered to be from fifteen to twenty, as it is then only a few years before it is sufficiently mature to do heavy work and to earn its original cost. But the spirit of a youngster of that age, whether male or female, takes a lot of breaking. It often takes a matter of weeks, while it is tethered to a tree with chains; and its continual struggling and fighting to break free cause the most shocking galling of the ankles and neck. Food is thrown to the tethered animal, but insufficient and unsuitable food leads to great loss of condition, and the oozie, or attendant responsible for feeding and watering, often retaliates with a spear-stab in the cheek after the captive has lunged at him with its trunk. The wounds it receives are almost impossible to treat, and they naturally become fly-blown and ulcerated.

In the end the young animal becomes heartbroken and thin. Finally it realises that it is in captivity for the rest of its days, and after the last heartbreaking struggle will put up with a man sitting on its head. By then it is usually covered with sores and wounds.

But a calf born in captivity in the nearest possible surroundings to those of a wild elephant is far more easily trained. From the day it is born until it leaves its mother at five years old it is in contact with its mother's oozie. It flirts with him like a child, it pretends to chase him, then runs away again. But, though so playful, it seldom trusts him much beyond accepting a tid-bit of fruit or a handful of rice from his hands.

In November of its fifth year the calf is weaned, and from that moment becomes more independent. Five or six calves are trained at a time in one camp. A Burman specially picked as a trainer is in charge, assisted by two men per calf, with eight other men to do general work. A training camp should be in flat country near a stream. An area of a hundred yards square is cleared, except for a few trees to give shade, leaving only a carpet of earth. In the middle a " crush " or triangular-shaped pen is built of logs of about the height of the average five-year-old calf. The logs of which it is built are fastened with wooden pegs; no nails are used in its construction. The bark is stripped from the logs, which are rubbed smooth and smeared with grease—all precautions against galling the calf's hide while it is in the crush under training. In addition to the calves with their mothers in camp is an elephant known as the koonkie (schoolmaster). This animal is usually a tuskless male between forty-five and fifty years of age, chosen for his docility and patience.

There is a great deal of superstition connected with the whole business of training young elephants. Before any attempts at actual training have begun, offerings are made to the Nats or spirits of the jungle. A small shrine is built near the crush, and the actual day on which training is to be begun is chosen by the manner in which a series of candles burn out. All the ropes for training are made from raw buffalo hide, preferably woven, and kneaded in lard until they are soft and pliable. Stocks of fruit, such as bananas and tamarinds, are also laid in at the camp, so as to provide the calf with tid-bits while it is in the crush. These help to keep its mind occupied and soften the shock of its finding itself in a cage.

On the morning when the first calf is to be weaned, the mother and the calf are brought into the clearing and made familiar with the crush and its surroundings. Some calves are so unsuspicious that they will follow a man into the crush if he holds out a banana as a bait. Once the calf is inside, the attendant Burmans quickly slip two stout bars in behind its hindquarters. More often than not, however, the calf is suspicious, and has first to be caught by one foot when in the open. This is done by placing a number of raw-hide running nooses on the ground where the calf is likely to walk. Each man is responsible for one of these lassoos, and has to twitch the noose tight once the calf has stepped inside it. A short struggle and a good deal of yelling on the part of the calf follow, but provided its mother is near at hand, it soon quietens down. It is then gradually pushed and pulled into the crush. In obstinate cases the koonkie, or schoolmaster, has to be brought up, and, with no fuss at all, he puts his head against the calf's fat little rump and gently butts it forward. The mother is quite content to stand by watching these proceedings, and makes no attempt to charge the Burmans so long as she is loose. But she becomes terribly agitated if she is tied up, and will make every attempt to snap her chain to get free and go to its rescue.

Once the calf is inside the crush, the forefoot which is still in the noose is tethered to the apex of the triangle. Bribery is begun at once, but the calf is at first far too intent on getting out of the cage to take the tid-bits offered to it. It will usually struggle and kick for about two hours. Then it sulks, and finally it will take a banana from the oozie out of sheer boredom and disgust. The expression on its face is like that of a child who eventually has to accept just one sweet after it has sulked for half an hour because it cannot have the whole bag.

While the calf is being cajoled and persuaded that it will do better to make the best of what is offered it, instead of struggling and sulking, its future rider has been attached to a pulley a few feet over its head. Two men on the ground, on either side of the crush, control this pulley, and on a signal from the rider he is lowered slowly on to the calf's head.

" Damn you, get off! " screams the calf, bucking like a bronco. The would-be oozie has soon to be hauled up again, but no sooner has the calf quieted down and accepted another banana, than the rider is lowered once more—and so on, again and again and again, until the

poor little calf seems to say: " All right, damn you.
Sit there if you must."

When it has finished the bananas it will buck again;
but directly it starts eating, down comes the inevitable
oozie.

So far, so good. By that time it will be nearly midday. The poor calf is tired, but the Burmans, stripped
of all but their tucked-up lungyis, are thoroughly enjoying the game, though they are dripping with sweat,
which shows up their gleaming copper skins and rippling
muscles.

Suspended from another pulley above the centre of
the calf's back is a heavy block of padded wood. This
is also lowered on to its back and provokes more bucking
bronco antics, with sideways rollings and strugglings
against the greasy bars. A moment or two later the block
is lifted, but directly the calf stands still, down it comes
again. Once more there are determined struggles to get
free, and so it goes on, and all the while the calf is being
offered food and spoken to with kind and soothing words.
Finally, in utter disgust, the calf sits down with its front
feet straight out, hoping that it will get rid of the pests
riding on its back in that way.

A cheer goes up from the Burmans: a cheer which
soon becomes a chant of " Tah! " (Get up) " Hmit! "
(Sit down). As the weight is lifted, the calf gets up, and
all the Burmans chant, " Tah! " As the weight comes
down, and the calf sits, all of them chant, " Hmit! " in
chorus.

After a time the rider, still attached to the pulley,
remains comfortably seated on its head. By evening,
unless the calf is a really obstinate young devil, the
rider can turn and, putting his hand on its back instead
of the log of wood, order the calf to sit down by pressure
and by saying, " Hmit."

Once that is possible, the calf is considered as broken.
Often it takes less than twelve hours, with no cruelty
whatsoever. Sometimes, however, in dealing with obstinate and truculent young tuskers, the game has to be
kept up, by the light of bamboo torches, far into the night.

Occasionally it may last even till the morning of the next day. But however long it may take, the Burmans never give in and never give the calf any rest until their object is achieved. The great lesson is that man's will-power is stronger than its own, and that man will always get his own way, however long it takes him.

Before the calf is taken out of the crush on the following morning it is hobbled with well-greased buffalo-hide thongs, and it is then tied to a tree for twenty-four hours, being caressed and cajoled all the time by its future rider. He makes it sit down each time he approaches. He mounts on its head, remains there ten minutes, orders the calf to sit again, and dismounts, and sometimes keeps it in the sitting position for five or ten minutes. Extraordinary patience is needed throughout. Once the Burman starts, he goes on until he gains his point. He never lets the calf win a victory, however temporary. Meanwhile the calf's mother has been taken away. No doubt she misses it, as it is common for her to call her calf for a couple of nights after their separation. But the tie between them has grown slender at that age. She does not really want the calf with her, though she may feel some anxiety on its account. The calf is then taken for its first walk, attached to the koonkie by a buffalo-hide girdle. The koonkie has a surcingle over the withers and behind the forelegs, while the calf walks alongside. He thinks the whole thing a bore, but he stands no nonsense. If the calf jibs, sits down, or lags, he gives him one wrench that pulls him along. On occasion he will give him a real welt with his trunk, as though to say: "Come on, you wretched urchin."

It soon becomes a decorous walking-out, and at a later stage the koonkie can manage two calves—one on each side of him. By the time they are really well-behaved the koonkie puts on the airs of a stuffy old nurse taking a pair of well-behaved and terribly bored twins out in the Park. As they approach other calves, one can imagine him saying: "Don't you dare speak to those common children over there."

I once had a camp with nineteen calves in training

in it. They were a joy to watch. Each had a different
temperament, and their innate differences of character
were enshrined in a lovely lot of names. The trainer
really has the right to name calves, and long discussions
go on among the assembled riders and the trainer over
the camp-fires at night before the calves are finally
christened. Often some incident which occurs in the
initial stages of training will suggest the name. One
such instance I well remember. On the third night after
the calf had been taken out of the crush, and while it was
tethered to a tree, some little way off from the riders'
camp, it was attacked by a tiger, which sprang upon its
back.

The calf threw the tiger off, and managed to keep it
at bay for twenty minutes, until men from the camp
arrived with bamboo torches. That calf naturally became a hero, and the next day it was christened Kya
M'Nine (Chyarmanine), which means " The tiger could
not overcome him "—as lovely a name for an elephant as
Black Beauty for a horse.

Sometimes there is humour in the name, such as:
Ma Pin Wa (Miss Fat Bottom). One young elephant
of that name could scarcely have been called anything
else. How she wobbled as she walked!

The name given to a calf sticks to it for life, but it
never knows its name, as a dog does; for the oozies do
not usually call their elephants by name. The real
reason why they are christened is so that men can talk
about them to each other.

Some of the names are most attractive: Po Sein
(Firefly), always given to an animal with a bright fiery
eye; Ma Hla (Miss Pretty), always a good-looking
calf with a perfect figure; Ma Palai (Miss Pearl), an
animal with a pearl-coloured eye; Maung Kyaw Dan
(Mr. Straight-back); Bandoola (the name of a famous
Burmese General), rarely given except to an animal of
most outstanding temperament and build. In a herd of
two hundred animals in a forest area, it is rare that any
two have the same name.

On occasions the trainer will pay a European Assistant

the compliment of asking him to christen an animal.
In one forest I had a Hitlah and a Musso. In another I
had a solitary female calf named Susan Ma after my wife.
Twelve years later, by an extraordinary coincidence, I
spoke to the rider of a fine young elephant seventeen years
old—the first animal to be recovered from the Japs after
the evacuation of Burma.

" What's the name of your elephant? "

" Susan Ma," he replied, and smiled all over his face,
for he knew what the name meant.

Less than a year later Susan Ma was lost again when
we were overrun by the Japs—but seven months after
that, when the Japs retreated, Susan Ma became mine
once more, and her namesake still is.

From the age of breaking, young elephants are kept
under training until the finishing age of nineteen. For
about two years they remain in the camp nursery, merely
being caught daily and taught the simple words of command and the " aids " of the rider and by foot control,
behind their ears.

Perhaps this is the place in which to explain what
these " aids " are. Their nature will be familiar enough
to polo-players. They are simply movements of the
rider's body by which he translates his wishes, almost
instinctively, to his mount. Thus an intense stiffening
of his limbs and leaning back will be at once understood
as halt. A pressure on one side will be understood as
turn to the left, on the other as turn to the right. Leaning
forward and forcing downwards will mean stoop or
kneel. A dragging up on the right side will be correctly
interpreted as lift the right foot—on the other, as lift the
left.

At about eight years old, young elephants carry their
first pack and become " travellers," accompanying a
European Assistant when he tours the forest areas. They
thus become accustomed to going over the mountains
and down the streams, carrying light weights, such as
camp cooking-pots, or a light roll of bedding.

In camp the young traveller is learning something
new and useful all the time, even if it is only to pick up

D

the branch of a tree in his trunk and carry it into camp as firewood, or to disentangle his chain if it should get caught in some bamboos.

Such travelling, and all the odd jobs which accompany it, continue until the calf is nineteen years old, after which he joins a working camp and starts hauling timber.

During the early years the elephant never really earns its keep or does enough to pay the wages of its oozie, but is learning all the time. By the time it is nineteen its temperament is fully known, and it has developed physically sufficiently for its future value as a working animal to be gauged.

Up to the age of nineteen or twenty it will have cost about one thousand pounds, when the wages of the oozie, training costs and maintenance are added up. Any earning capacity it might have had during those years would be small, even if used for rice transport. Moreover, any attempt to increase its earnings during the early years is very bad policy, and likely to involve its being overloaded and its whole future usefulness put in jeopardy.

We may assume that the elephant has on the average a working life from its twentieth to its fifty-fifth year. In this period it may cost another one thousand five hundred pounds in the wages of its oozie and in maintenance.

Each working year consists of nine months' work and three months' rest, necessary both to keep it in condition, and on account of the seasonal changes. From June to the end of February are the working months; whilst during the hot weather season, from March to May, animals should not work, there being insufficient fodder and water for them in the teak-bearing and deciduous forest areas.

Each month consists of only eighteen working days and twelve rest days, animals working three days in succession and then resting two. Thus, during the nine months of the working year there are only one hundred and sixty-two working days. Each day averages about eight hours. Thus an elephant works one thousand three hundred hours a year. During this time an average animal delivers one hundred tons of timber from stump to a floating-point in a creek. This is only one of the steps in the transport of the teak to the mill.

Chapter Seven

By the time it is twenty-five years old, a well-trained elephant ought to be able to understand twenty-four separate words of command, quite apart from the signals or " foot-aids " of the rider. He ought also to be able to pick up five different things from the ground when asked. That is to say, he should pick up and pass up to his rider with his trunk a jungle dah (knife), a koon (axe), his fetter or hobble-chain, his tying-chain (for tethering him to a tree) and a stick. I have seen an intelligent elephant pick up not only a pipe that his rider had dropped, but a large lighted cheroot.

He will tighten a chain attached to a log by giving it a sharp tug with his trunk, or he will loosen it with a shake and a waggle, giving it the same motion with his trunk as that given by a human hand.

An elephant does not work mechanically, like many animals. He never stops learning, because he is always thinking. Not even a really good sheep-dog can compare with an elephant in intelligence.

I don't believe that " an elephant never forgets," but I should scarcely be surprised if he tied a knot in his trunk to remember something, if he wanted to. His little actions are always revealing an intelligence which finds impromptu solutions for new difficulties. If he cannot reach with his trunk some part of his body that itches, he doesn't always rub it against a tree; he may pick up a long stick and give himself a good scratch with that, instead. If one stick isn't long enough, he will look for another which is.

If he pulls up some grass, and it comes up by the roots with a lump of earth, he will smack it against his foot until all the earth is shaken off, or, if water is handy, he will wash it clean, before putting it into his mouth. And he will extract a pill (the size of an aspirin tablet) from a tamarind fruit the size of a cricket ball in which one has planted it, with an air of saying: " You can't kid me."

Elephants can also detach a closely clinging creeper, like ivy, from a tree far more skilfully than can a man working with two hands. This is due to their greater delicacy of touch.

Many young elephants develop the naughty habit of plugging up the wooden bell they wear hung round their necks (kalouk) with good stodgy mud or clay, so that the clappers cannot ring, in order to steal silently into a grove of cultivated bananas at night. There they will have a whale of a time, quietly stuffing, eating not only the bunches of bananas, but the leaves and, indeed, the whole tree as well, and they will do this just beside the hut occupied by the owner of the grove, without waking him or any of his family.

Catching a young animal at this is just like catching a small boy among the gooseberry bushes. For some reason stolen fruit is always sweetest.

Oozies are not always as innocent as they pretend on such occasions. I once had to pay a fine to the Forest Department for damage done by my elephants to some experimental plantations of teak saplings. Naturally, I gave the oozies a reprimand for their slackness in allowing their animals to stray into these plantations. A month afterwards I happened to meet the Forest Officer who had fined me, near a large village, where we both camped for the night. He had four elephants with him, and I had eight. Next morning his annoyance can be imagined when the village headman arrived to ask for compensation for no less than a hundred banana-trees, destroyed by his four elephants. Strangely enough, not one of my eight elephants had been involved in the mischief, a fact which made it even more annoying for him. It was not until a week after we had parted company that I found out that though my elephants were innocent, my oozies were quite the reverse. They had taken the bells off the Forest Officer's four elephants and during the night had led them quietly into the banana groves—and had thus paid him out for fining me for the damage to the teak plantation.

I have personally witnessed many remarkable instances of the quick intelligence of elephants, though I cannot claim that they equal the famous yarns which delight all of us, whether we are children or grown-ups—such as that of the circus elephant who saw a man who had befriended him sitting in a sixpenny seat, and at once picked him up with his trunk and popped him into a three-and-sixpenny one!

But the following incidents seem to me to denote immediate brain reaction to a new situation, rather than anything founded on repetitive training.

An uncertain-tempered tusker was being loaded with kit while in the standing position. On his back was his oozie, with another Burman in the pannier, filling it with kit. Alongside, on the flank, standing on the ground, was the paijaik attendant, armed with a spear which consisted of a five-foot cane, a brightly polished spearhead at one end and a spiked ferrule at the other. Another Burman was handing gear up to the Burman in the pannier, but got into difficulties with one package and called out to the paijaik to help him. The latter thrust the ferrule of the spear into the ground so that it stood planted upright, with the spearhead in line with the elephant's eye. Then he lent a hand. The oozie, however, did not trust his beast, and said in a determined voice, " Pass me the spear." The tusker calmly put its trunk round the cane at the point of balance, and carefully passed it up to his rider. But, unthinkingly, he passed it head first and held it as though waiting for the rider to catch hold of it by the head.

The rider yelled at his beast in Burmese: " Don't be a bloody fool—pass it right way round! " With perfect calm and a rather dandified movement, the elephant revolved the spear in mid-air and, still holding it by the point of balance, passed it to his oozie, this time ferrule first.

The oozie did not say thank you, but gave him a curse with a touch of endearment—as though saying,

" You are a damned ill-mannered wild elephant, and I
want no more of it." Then, with a quick movement,
he moved the spearhead beside the elephant's eye, an
action which meant that he would suffer for it if he
tried any tricks with his tusks on those engaged in loading
him up. The loading was completed without incident.

Sometimes an elephant will show its intelligence by
divining what its oozie wishes.

A case I remember concerned an animal which would
not work with a rider on its head, but was obedient
to the words of command given by its oozie walking
alongside. I was watching this beast straightening logs
in a creek—that is to say, placing them in rows of eight
or twelve parallel to each other and pointing down the
bed of the stream, in readiness for the first floods to carry
them away. The oozie was sitting on the bank; work
was almost finished, but, because I was around, he knew
every log had to be straight in line with the others before
they broke off.

There was one noticeable and unshapely log, and the
elephant came to the last row in which it lay. He was a
big tusker, and was doing all the work with his tusks
and head, free of all chains. Without any word of command being given, he let the first log alone, and began
shifting the second, keeping one eye on his oozie, as
though saying: " Come on, wake up and tell me what
you want! "

The oozie soon told him, shouting: " You old son of a
bitch! What's wrong with that one? Leave it."

The elephant moved on to the next log, keeping his
eye cocked on his oozie, like an old man looking over a
pair of spectacles.

" No," shouted the oozie. " You know as well as I
do," and made a gesture of picking up a stone to throw
at his beast.

The elephant gave a squeal of pure delight at having
pulled his oozie's leg, and, without hesitation, disre-
garded the next five logs and, without pausing, bent
down and rolled the one irregularly placed log over
four times, leaving it exactly parallel with the others

and about a foot from them. Then he walked up to his master, as though to say: " Enough fooling, let's break off! " and the day's work was finished for man and beast.

But one of the most intelligent acts I ever witnessed an elephant perform did not concern its work, and might just as well have been the act of a wild animal.

One evening, when the Upper Taungdwin River was in a heavy spate, I was listening and hoping to hear the boom and roar of timber coming from upstream. Directly below my camp the banks of the river were steep and rocky and twelve to fifteen feet high. About fifty yards away on the other side, the bank was made up of ledges of shale strata. Although it was already nearly dusk, by watching these ledges being successively submerged, I was trying to judge how fast the water was rising.

I was suddenly alarmed by hearing an elephant roaring as though frightened, and, looking down, I saw three or four men rushing up and down on the opposite bank in a state of great excitement. I realised at once that something was wrong, and ran down to the edge of the near bank and there saw Ma Shwe (Miss Gold) with her three-months-old calf, trapped in the fast-rising torrent. She herself was still in her depth, as the water was about six feet deep. But there was a life-and-death struggle going on. Her calf was screaming with terror and was afloat like a cork. Ma Shwe was as near to the far bank as she could get, holding her whole body against the raging and increasing torrent, and keeping the calf pressed against her massive body. Every now and then the swirling water would sweep the calf away; then, with terrific strength, she would encircle it with her trunk and pull it upstream to rest against her body again.

There was a sudden rise in the water, as if a two-foot bore had come down, and the calf was washed clean over the mother's hindquarters and was gone. She turned to chase it, like an otter after a fish, but she had travelled about fifty yards downstream and, plunging and sometimes afloat, had crossed to my side of the river, before she had caught up with it and got it back. For what seemed minutes, she pinned the calf with her head and trunk against the rocky bank. Then, with a really gigantic effort, she picked it up in her trunk and reared up until she was half standing on her hind legs, so as to be able to place it on a narrow shelf of rock, five feet above the flood level.

Having accomplished this, she fell back into the raging torrent, and she herself went away like a cork. She well knew that she would now have a fight to save her own life, as, less than three hundred yards below where she had stowed her calf in safety, there was a gorge. If she were carried down, it would be certain death. I knew, as well as she did, that there was one spot between her and the gorge where she could get up the bank, but it was on the other side from where she had put her calf. By that time, my chief interest was in the calf. It stood, tucked up, shivering and terrified

on a ledge just wide enough to hold its feet. Its little, fat, protruding belly was tightly pressed against the bank.

While I was peering over at it from about eight feet above, wondering what I could do next, I heard the grandest sounds of a mother's love I can remember. Ma Shwe had crossed the river and got up the bank, and was making her way back as fast as she could, calling the whole time—a defiant roar, but to her calf it was music. The two little ears, like little maps of India, were cocked forward, listening to the only sound that mattered, the call of her mother.

Any wild schemes which had raced through my head of recovering the calf by ropes disappeared as fast as I had formed them, when I saw Ma Shwe emerge from the jungle and appear on the opposite bank. When she saw her calf, she stopped roaring and began rumbling, a never-to-be-forgotten sound, not unlike that made by a very high-powered car when accelerating. It is the sound of pleasure, like a cat's purring, and delighted she must have been to see her calf still in the same spot, where she had put her half an hour before.

As darkness fell, the muffled boom of floating logs hitting against each other came from upstream. A torrential rain was falling, and the river still separated the mother and her calf. I decided that I could do nothing but wait and see what happened. Twice before turning in for the night I went down to the bank and picked out the calf with my torch, but this seemed to disturb it, so I went away.

It was just as well I did, because at dawn Ma Shwe and her calf were together—both on the far bank. The spate had subsided to a mere foot of dirty-coloured water. No one in the camp had seen Ma Shwe recover her calf, but she must have lifted it down from the ledge in the same way as she had put it there.

Five years later, when the calf came to be named, the Burmans christened it Ma Yay Yee (Miss Laughing Water).

In 1930 it fell to my fortune to do field work with a brilliant veterinary surgeon named Pfaff. He was a research officer who had been appointed to stamp out anthrax among domesticated elephants in Burma. Having isolated the germ from an elephant's whole ear which had been sent him, he cultured it and prepared vaccines from both oxen and horses. Then came the experiments in inoculating elephants. The first of these was carried out under perfect conditions, with picked animals in a special camp with a " crush " to hold the elephants while being inoculated, and with ample time and all that one could wish for. The first experiments were disastrous, a large proportion of the elephants inoculated either were very seriously affected or died. It was some time before he could get the dosage right. But he was determined, and we went on. But when inoculation had proved its value, the work fell on European Forest Assistants working under very different conditions.

Baby-trained calves, savage and dangerous animals, nervous females were all in the day's work for the Assistant working hundreds of miles away from the nearest help. But one had to overcome all difficulties and treat them as child's play, just because one had enough self-confidence to ignore or to forget any risk attached to the work —and the animals knew it. One cut out all the fuss and just walked up boldly to the animal, gave it a good smack with the left hand and exclaimed : " Hullo, old chap ! " while with the right, one thrust the needle through the hide and squirted in the vaccine. Then one gave it another smack and turned away, exclaiming, " Come on ! " to the next elephant. With that technique one could inject fifty animals in the morning and have them back in their working camps during the afternoon.

An Assistant working under me at that time once sent me a frantic message that while he was struggling to inoculate a particularly restive elephant he had unfortunately broken off three needles, and had not been able to recover the broken pieces. He asked for immediate instructions as to whether he should operate and try to extract them.

I replied at once, pointing out that the age of the

animal was forty, and we might hope that, considering the size of the elephant and its circulatory system, it would take another fifty years before the needles reached its heart. By then the animal would be getting on for a hundred, so there was no reason for operating now. Moreover, three needles in the heart would result in a most interesting *post-mortem* on an elephant of ninety! He went on with his work of inoculation, and, so far as I know, he lost no more needles.

Another Assistant had to report that inoculation had been held up, as a truculent elephant broke away on feeling the injection, and carried off the hypodermic syringe and needle firmly planted in his hide. The elephant was not recaptured for a fortnight.

Such humorous incidents helped us to make light of our difficulties in the early experimental days. But only those who have known and experienced the effects of an epidemic of this terrible disease can appreciate what it meant to overcome it. Wholesale inoculation, carried out in this cheery way, brought with it immense relief— one of the nightmares was banished.

I lived through such a nightmare once when thirty-seven elephants, out of the seventy in my charge, died in three weeks.

At nine o'clock one morning I inspected a camp of seven elephants and entered all of them, in their inspection books, as " fit and fat." That evening, when I was camped ten miles away, I received an urgent message from the Burman in charge of the elephants I had inspected to say that one of them was down with anthrax. I went back immediately, and reached the elephant camp well after dark, to find that the sick animal was dead and that another one was down.

Veterinary treatment of the disease in those days was amateur indeed, and I was working in the dark in more senses than one, as I started operations on a prostrate elephant by the light of a bamboo fire kept stoked by three Burmans.

Running along under the belly of the elephant was a swelling the size of a bath-tub. I made an incision about two feet long in this with a large knife, and poured almost pure carbolic acid into the wound. At that time the accepted cure was to get carbolic to circulate with the blood. There must be a providence that looks after honest fools. Going to my tent that night, sweating and tired and very gory, I prayed earnestly for success. Strange to say, that animal did recover, but next morning anthrax was reported from another camp ten miles off. And so it went on for that week, until the map of my forest area was closely dotted with crosses in red ink, marking where my elephants had died.

One night, after vainly pondering on how the disease could spread from one camp to the next, ten miles away, and from animal to animal, although by that time I was keeping them isolated, each tethered to a tree a mile from its nearest neighbour, I fell asleep, sitting at my camp table, and dreamed that I myself was the dread carrier of the disease.

When I woke up I found the two table candle-lamps were almost burned out, and in their guttering light I decided to take no action when the next case was reported, no matter how near or how far away it might be. Then I went to bed. I did not move camp for a week, and I shall never know whether my unconscious intuition had been correct, and whether I, like many others, had been the carrier of the disease. For then the rains broke, and the epidemic, mercifully, died out.

I once returned a pony-saddle that I borrowed, but advised that it should be burned, as I had used it touring the anthrax area. The owner did not burn it, which caused great indignation on the station among all who owned polo-ponies. But nothing happened.

Just before the war, experiments in the use of local anæsthetics, and even of general anæsthetics, on elephants were carried out. No doubt these will be resumed one day. But up till the time of the reconquest of Burma, after the Japanese invasion, all elephant surgery was on old and somewhat primitive lines.

It needs confidence to walk under an elephant's jaw and tusks, armed with a bellied knife with a ten-inch blade four inches across in one's left hand, and a six-pound wooden club in the right hand, and then to tell him to hold up his head while you drive the knife up to the hilt into a huge abscess on his chest with one blow of the mallet.

One blow of the mallet is all you can get—if you try another, you must look out for squalls. The elephant does not like it. But if you do the job properly and make a quick and quiet get-away to his flank, he will let you go back ten minutes later to clean out the abscess with your hands and then syringe it with disinfectant. Abscesses on the back are dealt with in the same way, when the animal is sitting down in the " Hmit " position. Elephants will bear a great deal of pain patiently and appear to understand that it is being inflicted for their own good. But they will only put up with it when the operator is full of confidence in himself and feels he is making a good job of it. For an elephant can sense the absence of self-confidence quicker than any other animal in the world—and when one loses confidence it is high time to hand the knife and the club to someone else.

Wounds caused by tigers, most often received by mother elephants protecting their calves, are exceptionally difficult to heal and frequently do not respond to the most modern antiseptics.

The Burman has cures for all the ills that may befall an elephant. Some are herbal, some are mystic spells and incantations, and some of them have had to be vetoed as being definitely harmful. But I have so far found no treatment for tiger-wounds that comes up to the traditional Burmese method of plugging the wounds with sugar. The Burman also used maggots to clean up gangrened wounds for centuries before the method was rediscovered in modern surgery.

It has been quite truly said that once an elephant goes down, owing to exhaustion or severe colic, he has only a twenty-five per cent chance of getting on to his legs again unaided. Any method of keeping him on his legs improves a sick elephant's chances of survival. The Burman will do this by putting chili-juice in his eye—

a counter-irritant that must be agony. But it is effective, and about doubles the animal's chances of recovery. No matter how far modern research goes in the veterinary treatment of elephants, we shall always rely to a certain extent upon the Burman's knowledge.

I know, without question, that an elephant can be grateful for relief given to it from pain and sickness. For example, I remember Ma Kyaw (Miss Smooth, an expression often used to describe any Burmese girl with a strikingly good figure). She had fearful lacerations on the barrel of her back from tiger-claws, and I treated her for them every day for three weeks. In the early stages she suffered great pain, but although she made a lot of fuss—rather as an eight-year-old child might have done—she always gave way, because I was determined, and she let me go on. When she was sufficiently healed I sent her back to camp under a reliable Burman, with instructions that she was to be given light dressings of fly repellent on the wounds. I did not see her again for two months, when I was having a cup of tea in camp outside my tent, while seven elephants were being washed in the creek near by, preparatory to my inspecting them. The last animal to come out of the creek and to return to camp to dry off before inspection was Ma Kyaw. As she passed me, about fifty yards away, with her rider on foot, following at her heel and not on her head, I called out, more in order to greet him and show that I recognised him than because of any interest in the animal, which I was anyhow going to inspect in less than an hour's time, " How is Ma Kyaw's back? "

Her rider did not reply, as he had not caught what I said, but Ma Kyaw swung round, at right angles to the direction in which she was going, and came towards me.

She walked straight up to me where I was sitting. I patted her on the trunk and gave her a banana off my table, and then, without any word of command, she dropped into the sitting position and leant right over towards me, so as to show me her back. Having patted her I told her to " Tah " (get up), and away she went, leaving me with the agreeable conviction that she had

come to say " thank you." Then I began to suspect that
perhaps, on hearing my voice—with which she had
become familiar—she had done it merely from habit.

But later on, when I inspected her, I got a surprise.
She was the last in the row, and I went over her back
very carefully, kneading the wounds with my hands,
and I found one little hole which still suppurated. There
was great tenderness along a line nine inches long
where the wound had healed over. There was undoubtedly a sinus. Ma Kyaw let me open it up to its
full length there and then, although my doing so obviously
gave her great pain. But she was a good patient.

This made me think over the incident again. I can
never be quite sure that she came and showed me her
back in order to tell me that it was still painful. But I
am sure that she liked me, trusted me, and was grateful,
and that we were very good friends.

Besides the surgical side of looking after elephants,
there is the medical side. This is not so much administering drugs and medicines as keeping the animals healthy
so that they never need them. This means understanding
the particular needs of individual animals. The elephant
is not a ruminant, and has only one stomach. He has to
collect about six hundred pounds of green fodder to fill
that every day, and the most likely thing to go wrong is
his digestion. To keep well he needs variety, but one
has to see he doesn't pay too high a price for it. For
example, an animal may be working in a place where
there is nothing but bamboo fodder. To get the variety
of food he needs, he may have to travel eight miles, and
this he will do. But to do this every night after a hard
day's work and to come back in the morning will soon
pull him down. And in three weeks he may lose condition that will take him at least three months to recover.
It needs a really experienced man to spot any loss of
condition when inspecting an elephant. A good man
ought to be able to answer the very frequent question,
" Do you know every animal by name? " by replying,
" Yes, and by its digestion too."

To divide up a herd of elephants into bunches of

seven at random and allot each group to a different camp would soon be disastrous to the health of the herd. Animals have to be chosen so that the fodder available in the part of the forest in which they will work corresponds to their individual needs. The type of ground, rocky or otherwise, precipitous or undulating, has to be taken into account. Moreover, the work they are expected to do must be adapted to their strength. Some can handle large timber, others only small logs.

Elephants' feet vary as much in size and shape as do those of human beings, although practically all of them have five toe-nails on the front foot and only four on the hind. But, in selecting animals for certain areas, one has to take their feet into account. Only elephants with well-shaped feet with thick ankles should work in mud.

Lastly, the sex of the animal is of the greatest importance in allocating work. Tuskers are needed more than females in forest areas where the timber is large and the country is very precipitous. Special tuskers, known as htoking elephants, do the work of clearing the log away from the stump and getting it to the dragging-path. Sometimes a tree, when it is felled, will skid three or four hundred feet into a deep ravine. Powerful animals with tusks are then required to htoke it up to the dragging-path after it has been cut into logs.

Chapter Eight

In 1931 I had the good fortune to be selected as one
of a party which was to explore the forests of the North
Andaman Islands.* There were three other officers
in the party, and we were given forty-eight convicts from
the penal settlement as our labour. Part of my job was
to discover whether the native flora, grasses, etc., would
provide sufficient natural fodder to enable elephants to
be completely self-supporting, as in Burma. I decided,
before embarking on this adventure—for it really was an
adventure—to collect all the plants on which elephants
feed in Burma, for purposes of comparison. The one and
only way to do it seemed to me to live with an elephant,
continuously, for three days and three nights. I did this,
moving with the animal as she browsed, and collecting
specimens of every plant she ate. Altogether I gathered
forty-eight species of common plants: the few rare
plants I ignored. I had my collection classified for me
by the Botanist of the Forest Department School, and
the specimens were pressed into a two-volume herbarium,
which later fell into the hands of the Japs, together with
the rest of the contents of my bookcase, when I left Burma
in 1942. With them was my diary of the four months'
trip in the Andamans, which showed how valuable that
knowledge of fodder proved, as it enabled me to decide
that the North Andaman Islands provided sufficient
natural fodder to support elephants. Elephants are not
indigenous to the Andaman Islands, but the Forest
Department had, some years previously, imported eighty
into the South Islands, where it was erroneously believed
that natural fodder had to be supplemented by a ration of
paddy—that is, rice in the husk.

During a trek across the largest island of the Northern
group, I was amazed to discover the tracks and droppings

* See map on p. 143.

of an elephant which I could only suppose was a wild one. Judging from the impressions of the pads and the size of the droppings, I came to the conclusion that it was a young animal, about twenty years old. I got quite close to him on two occasions, but, owing to the dense jungle, was unable to see him before he winded me. Thus I was left guessing, until the end of our exploring trip.

My enquiries then revealed that a seven-year-old calf elephant, one of the South Andaman Forest Department's elephants, had been missing twelve years before. It had been " written off " in the Forest Department records as " believed drowned," having been seen attempting to swim from island to island. The age of this animal coincided pretty well with my estimate, and there can be no doubt it was the same. It was a remarkable swim, for it was over two hundred miles from where he was last seen to where I found him, and some of his swims from island to island must have been at least a mile in the open sea, which is seldom without a swell, and in a country where there are two monsoons a year. Of course, he had twelve years in which to do it, and no doubt he had a good sojourn on each island before moving to the next. An elephant thoroughly enjoys swimming, and will entirely submerge for brief periods when in deep water. He must have been a considerable surprise to any of the wild Jarawa tribesmen who saw him, and he must have seemed to them like a sea monster. These Jarawas are sea gypsies who live entirely on fish and shellfish. They are still wild, and in the past, if they were in large numbers, used to shoot their poisoned arrows at anyone they met. Now they are practically extinct, and there are less than a hundred of them left. They are of negro type, and are said to be the only link between the African negro and the Australian aborigine. I was lucky enough to meet a small party of five, consisting of three men and two young girls. They were all small in stature, but the men were muscular and healthy, and the girls had exceptionally good figures. The men were naked, and the girls wore nothing but a leaf, the shape of a

fig leaf, which was traditionally designed for that very
purpose. The amusing part was that the girls each had
two spare leaves, which they carried rolled up, above each
ear. Thus they were able to change their frocks twice a
day, once during the midday heat, and again in the
cool of the evening. The whole party attached themselves to our camp for a few days, during which time
the men were most useful in showing us the few
fresh-water springs that existed on the coasts of the
islands.

No doubt the young elephant was just as surprised,
on emerging from the sea after swimming from a distant
island, at being confronted by a modern Eve, as the
Jarawa Eve was to see a sea monster rise up out of the sea
and disappear into the jungle.

But the Jarawas are used to strange animals. They
helped me to catch a dugong, the warm-blooded mammal
which some suppose to have given rise to the myth of the
mermaid. This dugong was a female, and it certainly
had a more uncanny resemblance to a human being than
any monkey. It had a repulsive little nose, human-
looking teeth, well-formed breasts the size and shape of
inverted tea-cups, flippers like deformed arms and fat
fists like little hands.

While I was on this exploring trip I learned a great
deal about Burman dacoits, or robbers, which confirmed all that I had imagined them to be from my
experiences in Burma. We had working for us, during
the four months of our trip, forty-eight convicts with
life sentences.

Before I set off to the Andaman Islands I stuffed the
bladders of two Rugby footballs full of opium, as I
knew that half of the dacoities which are committed are
done in desperation by opium addicts, in order to obtain
money to buy it.

I picked up our convicts—most of them dacoits—
at Port Blair, and from there I took them to the North
Islands, where we were dumped for four months. The
leader of them was a Burman called Nga Moh, with a
grey moustache, like a mandarin's, hanging to below his

chin. During the first week I never saw a smile on his face. He had wonderful control over his companions, who were a bunch of the biggest cut-throats I had ever seen. The only precaution I took with regard to them was to immobilise our two motor-launches offshore every night. They included men of all sorts of trades: mechanics, fitters, elephant-riders, and even goldsmiths; and every one of them had that wild look in the eye which indicated he would take any risk in order to see his native land again. They were all either murderers or accessories to murder, but they had a sense of humour, and we often had the camp ringing with laughter after the day's work was done—and it was at that hour that I gave out the opium ration. I heard the most astounding tales from them about the crimes they had committed, which eventually earned each of them a life sentence in a penal settlement.

Nga Moh told me he was one of a gang of eight dacoits when he was twenty. They attacked a mule caravan on the Burma-Siam border, but had no intention of using the one firearm they possessed, except to fire a couple of shots in order to stampede the mules. Unfortunately for him, the attack did not go as planned, and the leader of the dacoits had to fire his gun at a muleteer, killing him outright, in order to avoid being struck down with a Gurkha kukri-knife.

Nga Moh was unlucky, as he got badly knifed in the leg and was captured. The only two spare rounds of ammunition that the dacoits possessed were found on him. He told us the story round the camp-fire on the sands of a lovely and uninhabited island, set in the middle of the Indian Ocean, where he was spending the twenty-fifth year of his exile, at the end of which he would have served his time and would regain his freedom. He did eventually follow me to the Upper Chindwin in Burma, but he soon felt a nostalgic longing for the sea and the islands of his exiled years, and he went back to them.

These four months were months of freedom for the convicts, and they enjoyed every minute of them like children. Many of them were, no doubt, still prisoners there when the islands were occupied by the Japanese after 1942, but they will all have got their freedom by now.

The penal settlement on the South Islands is to be abolished, and the forests I explored in the North Islands are to be exploited. It is a melancholy thought that the peace of those islands should be disturbed. The spotted deer we encountered, right in the depths of the untrodden jungle, came up to meet one without fear, to sniff at one's clothes with nervous inquisitiveness. They greeted the unheard-of stranger, whose bad reputation was unknown to them, with friendship, as I greeted them. I did not disillusion them, and then, stepping softly and gently through the jungle, they went their ways.

I had known many dacoits intimately before I went to the Andamans. Sometimes I knew what they were, but sometimes I was quite oblivious of the truth and employed them believing they were good fellows and trustworthy. But, on the whole, the average Burman dacoit has earned a good name for himself as a gentleman outlaw, like Robin Hood. He has a sporting instinct, and plans his crimes with roguish humour. And, if it is at all possible, he tries to avoid combining dacoity and murder.

Once I set out from Paungbyin in the Upper Chindwin for the Kanti forests, with ten pack-elephants carrying over one hundred thousand rupees in silver, packed in specie boxes, each of which weighed about three hundred pounds. The trip was planned to take me eighteen days. The daily loading of each of these boxes on to the elephants was a real feat of strength, and the day after I left Paungbyin my head Burman suggested that I should hire a man from the village where I had camped who had the reputation of being as "strong as an elephant." I agreed that such a man would be useful, and sent for Maung Ngapyaw (Mr Banana Tree), as he was called. He was a man of magnificent physique, and a really pleasant rogue with a most cheerful temperament—and he could handle those boxes of rupees as though they weighed only fifty pounds apiece. Thus loading up in the morning became easy work. He accepted an offer of sixty rupees for the trip, and soon gained everyone's confidence and became the wag of the camp. We felt we had made a good find.

After a particularly hard trip, as we had been caught by the first break of the rains, I reached Kanti, my jungle headquarters, where there was a safe. I made it my first job to roll the money into hundred-rupee packets and put it in the safe. Ngapyaw became one of my chief helpers, and proved most expert at the job. Just as I had finished, and felt quite happy that all the money had been checked and made secure in the safe, the first jungle messengers since my departure arrived with the ever welcome mails. It was six p.m., so having called for a tub, I decided to read my mail after bathing, by which time it was late evening and peg time. I opened the mail-bags alone on the bamboo veranda of my hut, sorted home mail and private letters into one pile and official in another. As was my habit, I ran through the official first, so as to get the worst things done with. Among them was an envelope marked *Urgent and important*. I wasn't in the Army, and knew that only something really urgent and important would be marked in this way by the Corporation, so I opened it at once. It was to inform me that the police had reason to believe that a renowned dacoit named Ngapyaw, alias San Shwe, alias San Oo, was following my camp, and that every precaution was necessary. In my private mail was a note from my Forest Manager, a man of few words, which merely read, " Forewarned is forearmed."

I was not at all perturbed by the news, though I was extremely grateful for the warning. After I had had a meal, I debated with myself whether I should give him the shock of arresting him that night, or wait till next morning when I paid him off. Eventually I decided on the second course.

My position in this lonely forest camp was a perfect setting for a real armed dacoity, and as the night wore on I was not too easy in my mind. However, I eventually dropped asleep, keeping one eye and one ear cocked, but I was not disturbed.

In the early hours of the morning, when I got up I decided to send for Ngapyaw, but when I asked for him, my head servant informed me that he had disappeared from the camp during the night, together with one of the messengers who had brought the mails. Thus all of us had been forearmed and forewarned! The police and Forest Manager had written to warn me by letter, and the spare messenger had come along to warn Ngapyaw! It then became my turn to send messages off, warning one of my neighbours in the jungle. Ngapyaw was not heard of again for another year, when he was shot by the police in the notorious Shwebo dacoit area. He had, however, passed on all the necessary information as to the lie of the land and the lay-out of the safe in Kanti jungle headquarters to some confederates, as my successor in this district had his safe robbed, two years later, of twenty-five thousand rupees in notes.

The dacoits who did it had a really enviable sense of humour, as before they departed with their booty they impaled a ten-rupee note on each post of the fence round jungle headquarters. There were one hundred and twenty posts altogether, so they returned one thousand two hundred rupees as a jest.

One of the most interesting of my experiences, or close approach to an experience, with dacoits, was when I was forearmed and forewarned of their proximity by the behaviour of a common brown rat.

I was moving camp, travelling in a large dug-out country boat up the Myittha River from Kalewa, sleeping on the bank at convenient staging bungalows. I was bound for Kalemyo, where I was to be joined by some travelling elephants.

As usual, I had a considerable quantity of specie with me, and was not at all comfortable about it, during that stage of the trip. It would be safe enough after I joined my elephants and riders, for I always had great confidence in them. I was camped for the night at the

Chaunggyi Rapids bungalow, a poor apology for a rest house, consisting of one small room and a veranda, raised about four feet above ground level. The walls, door and floor were all made of bamboo matting. While I was having an early meal about seven o'clock, my head servant reminded me that I was some distance from where my servants were sleeping, and the sound of the rapids would make it difficult for them to hear me call. Also I was to remember that there were no elephant men in camp, and that it would be as well if I kept a sharp watch on the boxes of rupees. He knew something was in the wind, and his vague warnings were, no doubt, intended to put himself right with me after the event, but I did not tumble to it at the time.

It had been raining heavily, and it was one of those nights when every kind and shape of bug with wings had seemed to decide to commit suicide against my one and only hurricane lamp. Their varying stings, bites, stinks and noises eventually drove me to seek shelter on my camp bed under my mosquito net. I left the lamp on a specie box beside the bed, intending to read for an hour before I went to sleep. I had got settled comfortably under the net with a book, lying propped on my left elbow with the only weapon I had in camp, a .45 revolver, lying beside my knee. Keeping it handy was as much habit as anything else, as the very last thing in my mind was the possibility of a dacoity, although it was a lonely and isolated spot.

Presently a slight movement in a corner of the twelve-feet-square room caught my eye, and a very pleasant, cheeky-looking rat appeared. I watched him without moving my head, and his movements fascinated me. He first of all sat up on his hind legs and washed his face with his forepaws, then he came out into the room and picked up a small piece of biscuit I had dropped. I was watching him thoroughly enjoying nibbling it, when he suddenly dropped it and scuttled off to a corner where I could not see him, so I decided to remain absolutely still, hoping he would come back. While I waited, I wondered whether it could have been the movement of my eye that had

scared him. Presently he came back, and again repeated his trick of picking up the biscuit. I fully expected he would finish it this time, but, more suddenly
than in his first scurry, he dashed off again, dropping
the biscuit half-way to his dark corner.

As he did so, a sense of fear gripped me. I knew that
the rat and I were not the only occupants of the little
hut and veranda. My heart pounded in my throat, and
for a fraction of a second my arms and legs felt paralysed,
as though I could not move them. But my adrenalin
glands pumped their stuff into my blood, and my voice
barked out in Burmese, "Who is it?" I then heard
distinct whispering outside the wicker-bamboo door and
a movement under the floor of the hut. Without further
hesitation, I fired two rapid shots through the roof. A
frightful confused stampede from the veranda and from
underneath the hut followed instantly.

My four camp servants heard the shots and joined
me by the time I had got on to the veranda myself, and
we soon tracked the would-be dacoits by torchlight to
the river bank, whence they hurriedly made off downstream in a dug-out canoe which they had waiting.
They were a party of six, and had undoubtedly followed
me with the intention of rushing my hut that night. I
was never able to find out whether they were armed or
not.

Before I went away next morning I left an open tin
of Kraft cheese for my little pal, the rat, not on the
floor, where some dacoit might get it, but hidden in the
roof. A month or so later, when I passed that camp
again, I found the empty tin. Not only had the cheese
gone, but there was an empty nest inside. Mrs Rat
had reared her babies in it.

I was very glad to join my elephant men at Kalemyo, and from there sent off word that a party of river
dacoits was at large.

These experiences, and all the various mysterious
stories which I discovered my elephant men believed
about dacoits, helped me when I came to handle my
crowd of forty-eight of them in the Andaman Islands.

My riders believed that dacoits had acquired immunity to gunshot wounds by secret tattoo marks known only to themselves, and that they could carry out their dacoities in absolute silence, as a result of drinking the warm blood of the slow loris.

Superstitions of this kind, when firmly believed in, change human behaviour, and they naturally influence the European Assistant living alone among people to whom what we call superstitions are established truths. One of the most puzzling cases concerned a Burman called San Shwe Oo. I think I liked him better than any Burman I knew. He was really a Kadu gypsy. With his very fair skin and long black hair, which hung down to his waist when he let it down, he always looked a bit out of place among the other elephant men. He rode one of the most dangerous of my animals, a tuskless male called Han Po. He was particularly friendly with me whenever I visited the camp where he worked, and took pains to bring himself to my notice. I often met him unexpectedly, alone by some creek near camp, and he was always eager to accompany me, if I went out in the evening with my rifle for a shot at something. He liked talking to me, and I found him very good company, for he had a lovely sense of humour.

The headman of that camp, U Po See, was a man of the deeply religious, old-fashioned type who was regarded with respect by all his men. He had always discouraged the presence of women in his camp except for his own family, who lived in one hut, while his ten other men lived in one long hut twenty-four feet by sixteen, the bamboo floor of which was raised six feet above the ground.

The incident occurred in September, and although, since the war, enthusiastic Chindits have stated that the Burmese jungle is not " a green hell," I thought it was, there, at that time of the year. During a nine-mile march I had to swim the Kanti seven times, and I got into camp shivering with malarial ague like an aspen leaf. I was my own doctor, taking thirty grains of quinine a day, as long as the fever lasted. There was no question of my going sick, I had to carry on with my job. It was just part of the normal life of every Forest Assistant, until he finally developed immunity to malaria.

I had just got into my camp bed, and was almost delirious with fever, when I felt powerful sinewy hands working up and down the vertebræ of my spine. No one who has not been down with malaria and given massage can imagine the relief it gave me. I opened my eyes, saw San Shwe Oo bending over me and smiling. I blessed him in silence. By midday next day I was up and about, and U Po See came to see me. After enquiring about my health and telling me his news, in a happy and contented way, he suddenly changed his position by sitting down and falling into a shiko posture, with his hands together on his knees. He then asked me to dismiss San Shwe Oo from his camp. I enquired, with a pained expression, what his reasons were, and for five minutes had to listen to a long rigmarole in high Pali Burmese, which he used on purpose to confuse me. I did, however, gather that the camp was in terror of supernatural vengeance on account of San Shwe Oo's complete disregard of every tenet of the Burmese faith, and that, unless he were removed, a tragedy would ensue, owing to the presence of a Nat tiger, or Spirit tiger, which the men said was prowling round the camp.

I pretended that I had understood every word he said, and told him not to worry—I owed San Shwe Oo a considerable sum in wages, and would go into it when settling up, before leaving camp.

San Shwe Oo came to see me again that evening with a present of three minute chicken's eggs in a little bamboo basket, which looked like a child's Easter-egg present. He had come to ask me if I would like another massage for my malaria, as he was recognised as the most skilful man in camp. I gladly accepted his offer, as the aches and pains of another bout of fever were upon me. He persuaded me to let him tread the small of my back with his bare feet. I was already in a new malarial rigor. San Shwe Oo's company and sympathy and understanding of the loneliness I felt in this outlandish jungle camp where the torrential rain was falling incessantly, strumming endlessly upon the large teak leaves, while I was in the grip of continuous bouts of malaria, made his dismissal the very last thing I would have agreed to. He had nothing to say about any unhappiness in camp, but, strangely enough, he did say that I should be quite fit again in a day or two, and then added, as a joke, " You might even have a shot at the Nat tiger." With those words he departed. Later that night I asked my personal servant Maung Aung Net—a dear, faithful, simple fellow, if ever there was one—when he came, about midnight, to change me from my clothes soaked in sweat into dry ones, what all the tommy rot was in camp about a Nat tiger. He told me that he had heard in camp that when it was San Shwe Oo's turn to do the cooking and washing up of the rice-bowls he treated it as a joke, and had even played boats in the brook with the rice-bowls and ladles, as a child might have done. And it was also said that he did not take any rice that was left over to the Nat Shrine, or present it to the fishes in the creek, but would actually scatter it in the mud. I thought this was probably a true account of San Shwe Oo's offences in U Po See's eyes, and the explanation of why he would like to banish such an atheist from his camp. The European Assistant has to respect all these jungle superstitions, even if he is not in some degree influenced by them. I had another three days in that camp, performing my ordinary duties, and on the last day, having got rid of my fever, settled up the men's wages. To my surprise, Maung San Shwe Oo asked that the balance of the money owing to him—sixty-eight rupees—should be retained by me. I granted his request and gave him a credit note, though it complicated my accounts. He gave me no reason for this request, and I asked for none, but it occurred to me that perhaps he intended leaving the camp after my departure. I did not at all want him to, as it would not have been easy to find his equal as a rider for Han Po. At the same time, I did not wish to get involved in any way with a breach of their superstitious beliefs.

I saw U Po See alone again late that evening, telling
him that I should leave at dawn and be back in six
weeks. I gave him orders and said, " Au revoir," and
there was no mention of either San Shwe Oo or the
Nat tiger. I went to bed feeling I had been very
successful in dodging a domestic complication in the
camp.

Dawn had not quite broken, when I was aroused by
an excited camp servant calling out to me, " Hurry,
Thakin, hurry. A tiger has just killed Maung San
Shwe Oo."

There was a faint glimmer of the green light of dawn,
breaking through the jungle saturated by rain. By the
time I had got on a few garments and a pair of gum boots,
I could hear an excited commotion going on in the camp,
three hundred yards away. The first person I met, as I
stumbled through the mud down the slope, was U Po See.
" Nat kyah, Thakin! " (A Nat tiger, sir) he exclaimed.
He appeared terror-stricken. When I got to the oozies'
hut I found an excited party of five men, all examining
the indisputable pug-marks and tracks of a tiger that had
sprung up into the hut and down again. There were
clear tracks of a dead body having been dragged through
the mud down the slope to the creek, which was half in
spate, but only a foot deep. On the near bank, fifty
yards away, was another group of Burmans examining
the marks and on the far bank a third group. All were
yelling to each other. The interior of the hut was a mass
of dishevelled blankets and clothes. A wailing friend of
San Shwe Oo's told me some sort of story, of how two
men had woken up, scared, and found him gone, but no
one had heard him scream or any sort of scuffle. Every
spear in camp had been got out, and U Po See was carrying his single-barrel shotgun. Even in the excitement of
the moment, I got hold of it and unloaded it, as I knew
that there would be no need for a supernatural explanation if an accident happened with that weapon. I then
plunged on, down through the mud, to the edge of the
brook, which was sandy. The tracks led into the water,
but when I crossed to the other side there were no

tracks of pug-marks or of a dragged body coming out. Apparently the tiger and San Shwe Oo's body had evaporated into thin air after going into the stream.

The men, who were all skilled trackers, were dispersing—small parties going upstream and downstream on both banks, which were sandy for a very long way. The air was filled with the cries of excited men, calling " Cheeyah m' twai boo! " (Can't find a track), and their excitement grew into hysteria. I fired two rifle-shots in the air, with a faint hope that the tiger might drop his kill and leave it where he was hiding. Every minute I expected one of the men to cry that he had found the track, but the minutes passed by . . . half an hour later it was broad daylight.

Someone made the suggestion that the tiger must have swum away with the body and travelled a long way. I set off barefoot, with five spearmen, downstream, while another party, under U Po See, went upstream. It was clear that the tiger could not have kept to the river below a place called Kyauk Shin, as at that point there are boulders, rapids and broken water. I felt sure we should find something when we got there. It was less than a mile from where the track had disappeared, but there was an unaccountable absence of tracks, and, when we got there, no trace at all. Judging from the river banks, there might not have been a wild animal in the jungle.

After that I went upstream, and again there was not a tiger pug, new or old, to be seen.

In camp there was still an uproar going on. U Po See sat with his gun beside him, perfectly satisfied that the tragedy was due to a supernatural cause. It made me angry to hear him speak so confidently of a Nat Kyah.

I cancelled orders for my departure and went to the hut to be alone—drank some hot tea, which I laced with whisky, and lay back in a long camp chair.

U Po See soon appeared. He was a pathetic sight, a dear old deeply religious Burman of the old school, stunned by the event, but quite disposed to accept it unquestioningly.

I sent him away, and told him to join the other men, who were still continuing the search.

I drank several more cups of tea and whisky, before I rejoined the camp. By evening all the men had returned to camp, and no trace of San Shwe Oo's body had been discovered. I was beyond attempting any further investigation myself, but I was angry and depressed at having to accept something, of which I knew there must be an explanation, which I had failed to discover. All San Shwe Oo's possessions were intact. I stayed three more days at the camp, in order to restore the morale of the men and convince them that the Nat Kyah would pay no further visits. Nor did it, and during the two years following which I spent in that forest area I never heard any explanation other than that San Shwe Oo had been taken by a Nat Kyah or Ghost tiger. My name was often mentioned by the Burmans in connection with the affair, as evidence of the truth of the story. I have heard the facts discussed by dozens of men and women and various explanations put forward. A jungle man whom I greatly respect summed up one view by saying:

" Billy, my boy, in spite of your knowledge of the jungle and the presence of your men, I believe that U Po See and some of his men murdered San Shwe Oo and provided perfect evidence to convince you that a tiger had taken him. Yet, who are you and I to decide what strange gods or supernatural forces are not masters of the jungle? "

I replied: " San Shwe Oo was never murdered, and you, and every other man who knows the jungles of Burma intimately, have often to accept things that you cannot understand."

He drained his glass and nodded his acceptance. There are thousands of unexplained and unsolved stories, but not all of them are gruesome or tragic.

I was once moving camp through jungle which had not been crossed for many, many years, if ever, by a

European. I camped one evening in a creek that my
Burmans called Yauk Thwa. The name puzzled me,
and I was told that it meant " Oyster." I was a young
Assistant then, and I was quite thrilled when, strolling
down to the creek, I found dozens and dozens of petrified
oyster-shells in its bed. In spite of being fifteen hundred
miles from the nearest point on the sea coast of Burma,
I sat up late pounding them open, hoping to find
a fossil pearl. When I went to bed at last, I was no
richer.

Next day I moved camp in a direction far away from
any traces of Burmese village life. I knew from my map
that I should have to follow a well-defined ridge for
one or two marches, before I dropped down into the
watershed for which I was heading. When I reached
it I found it was more of a razor edge than the map
indicated. The progress of my pack-elephants was
impeded by thick undergrowth, which was uncommon
on a ridge.

Towards the end of the second day's march I was
becoming anxious, because there seemed to be no way
down. It was already near sunset, I was ahead of my
elephants, when I suddenly came to an open glade,
where there was an obvious drinking-pool used by
game. It was only a few square yards in area, but it was
large enough to water my travelling elephants, and I
knew we could camp there. I waited an hour, and
rejoiced as the sound of the elephant bells grew nearer.
Well before dusk we were settled in, and my men were
pleased with me for having called a halt. I pitched no
tent, but bivouacked under a spread tarpaulin. I gave
orders that the elephants should be tethered after they
had been watered, as otherwise they might wander
down two thousand feet on either side of the ridge.
My last order was that we were to be moving before the
mists of dawn had risen.

My servants were camped within a hundred yards of
my bivouac. I was near enough to hear their chatter,
but they were silent, and insisted on giving me my
evening meal before my usual hour. When I had eaten

E

I soon turned in. But an air of uneasiness lay over the camp; there was a strange eerie silence. The drip of the night dew from the great leaves seemed to begin unusually early and was unusually heavy, so that it soon pattered steadily on to my stretched tarpaulin. I was comfortable and happy but for some reason I lay awake. The elephants must have been motionless, although tethered, for not a bell sounded. The last glow of the camp fire died down. At last I fell asleep, feeling perfectly confident of my safety, for all around me were men whom I trusted, elephants and the jungle that I had come to love.

I woke suddenly, feeling that I had only been to sleep for a short time, and found myself listening with fear, such as the European alone in the jungle often experiences. I sensed it was near dawn—but what had woken me? Was it one of my servants moving about to light a fire or put on a kettle?

I sat up in bed. The camp was still wrapped in sleep. Not a sound or movement came from my men. Then, as I sat listening, I heard a village cock crowing, and almost at once after it, I could distinguish the sounds of a baby crying. There was no question about it. I was wide awake. A village pungyi kyaung gong chimed clear as crystal, and the wailing of half a dozen pi dogs took up the echo of the chimes. Then I could hear someone begin chopping a log for the village fire. I could swear that I heard the voices of children and, at last, all the sounds of an awakened Burmese village in the early morning, and the distinctive sound of a Burmese girl, treading backwards and forwards on the board that shells the rice-paddy free of its husks, for the morning meal.

And then there was silence, and suddenly I heard someone stirring, and saw the flame of a lighted lamp, and could see the silhouettes of my servants moving in front of it. I dropped back, pretending I was asleep. My man would be bringing me a cup of tea in ten minutes. He would never wake me with a touch, for the Burman thinks that if a European is woken up suddenly there may not be time for his spirit to return from visiting his own land. He calls the spirit of sleep a butterfly which takes wing silently and slowly, and which must be given time to return.

I saw my servant approach, through my half-shut eyes, and watched him bump on purpose into something; then he coughed and scraped with his feet. I turned over, and he murmured to me, " The mist has lifted." I drank my tea at once, dressed instantly, and was only too willing to get away from that place in record time. There was no chatting among my men. The elephants loomed up like ghosts out of the mist, in silence, as they arrived to load up. I led the way along the ridge, with my headman following me. We did not say a word, until, after an hour's travelling, I realised we had reached the Upper Myaingyaung drainage, and it became clear that I was quite off the track. I halted then, and asked my Burman where the hell we had camped the previous night.

" That, Thakin, was the deserted village," was his answer.

I made no comment at the time, but that evening I asked my servant if he had heard any noises during the night.

" No," he replied, " we did not. But we were frightened this morning when we were loading your kit. One of the oozies said that your bivouac under the nyaung tree was where the Nats lived, but where we camped under the zeebyn fruit-trees was the site of the old village."

I asked what had happened to the people who lived there, and he said that he had been told they had been wiped out by cholera. My men had known that a village, called Ywasoe, had existed thereabouts, but had never found the site before.

" You found it. Say no more. You are lucky. The Nats like you, and you respect them as we do."

He said no more, purposely avoiding any further discussion, obviously holding something back. I was left with the feeling that I had not been alone with the

Nats of Ywasoe. Curiously enough, this strange incident made a recording of the pleasant village sounds of Burma that I can almost hear again at will, and transformed them into an unforgettable memory of Burma.

Chapter Nine

ELEPHANTS are good swimmers and extremely buoyant. When the oozie is going to cross a large river, such as the Chindwin or the Irrawaddy, with his elephant, keeping it under control, he fits a surcingle under its belly and over the withers, kneels on the animal's back and grips the rope in front of him, using a small stick, instead of his feet, to signal his " aids," behind its ears. In this position he is on top of the highest point of the elephant.

Once they are under way and in deep water, it is most amusing to watch. For a time the elephant will swim along gaily, with a rather lunging action. Then, all of a sudden, the oozie will snatch a deep breath, as his mount goes down, like a submarine, into fifteen feet of water. The animal, for pure fun, will keep submerged, almost to bursting point, trying to make his rider, who goes down with him, let go.

But the oozie knows that an elephant can only stay under water for the same length of time as a man. So he holds on. The elephant, meanwhile, is doing a fairy-like dance on tiptoe along the bottom, while the poor old oozie is wondering if he will ever surface. Suddenly both reappear, blowing tremendously and taking great gasps of breath.

In crossing a wide river, where the elephant has to swim a thousand yards or so, he may drift as much as four hundred yards downstream. He does not make any strenuous effort to make the crossing where the river is narrowest, or to reach a particular point on the opposite bank.

Although elephants are such good swimmers, they are not infrequently drowned, a fact which I can only put down to heart failure. The Burmans, however, always attribute the loss of an elephant, when swimming, to the Nat Shin, a water-snake which no one has ever seen. The bite of the Nat Shin produces instantaneous death. A jungle Burman will tell you that a Nat Shin is just like a yay shin, only enormously larger. A yay shin is an unpleasant pale-green object, like a bootlace, about nine inches long and pointed at each end. It is very active in water, but when one pulls it out, looks like a fine strand of seaweed. One can tie it into as many knots as one likes, and it will have untied itself within five minutes of being dropped back into water. The yay shin is disliked for the practical reason that the water in which it lives is not fit to drink. But it seems uncanny to the Burmese, and they all accept the existence of its bigger, more deadly, brother, and give thanks that they have never had the misfortune to see one.

When elephants have to be moved long distances by water, they are frequently taken on rafts, or on river barges, which are towed alongside a paddle-steamer. Getting elephants on to such flats needs endless patience. First one has to find a leader which the other beasts will follow, and then one has to camouflage the gangway with tall grasses, or palms, on either side of it to a height of ten or twelve feet.

The flats usually have steel decks, which get terribly hot in the sun, and if elephants are standing on them for twenty-four hours, their feet swell to such a size that the fetters or chain hobbles have to be removed.

Once I had to ship two flat-loads of twenty elephants from a river station on the Irrawaddy. I was assisted by a very capable Anglo-Burman, and we started work at dawn, but had only got one flat loaded by noon. The irate old skipper of the paddle-steamer was due to leave at two p.m. and to proceed up river on a three-day trip, tying up each night to the river bank. By five p.m. we got the last elephant on board the second flat, and the skipper's temper was as bad as mine. Just when I thought my job was finished and the skipper's had begun, he blew the steamer's siren—of all the damn fool things! And at the same time the enormous side paddles started to churn alongside the loaded flats full of elephants, on either side of the steamer.

The captain's shock was greater than mine, as sixteen elephants trumpeted and roared, drowning every other sound. I think he thought half of them had broken loose and were boarding his steamer and after his blood, whereas only sheer terror kept them in their places. He had to reckon with me, however.

These particular animals had been transferred and marched from the Salween, via the Mawchi–Taungoo road, and had had about enough of it. All our tempers were on edge. We eventually got them settled down and under way, and put in an hour's steaming before tying up for the night. Leaving my Anglo-Burman Assistant to check up that all chains were secure and to supervise the hand feeding of the elephants, I made for the saloon to make it up with the skipper over a peg.

At nine p.m. I visited both flats, and found all remarkably quiet, no sound but a flapping of ears and the occasional movement of a foot, rattling a chain. At midnight I was still yarning with the skipper in the little saloon, when my Assistant arrived to say that a young tusker had collapsed. His doing so had caused little or no commotion among the others. As far as I could discover, he had fallen down dead beat, from fatigue. To get anywhere near him, one crawled through a forest of elephant legs.

After I had given him half a bottle of brandy, without results, I decided there was nothing more I could do but let him lie and wait for the dawn. I went back to the saloon for a night-cap, but my Assistant was still unhappy, and went to have another talk with the elephant-riders. I had gone to my cabin when he came back, looking very shy, to say that the Burman oozies wanted to put a temple candle for each year of the elephant's life round the prostrate body, and might they try it?

The theory was, that when all the candles were alight but before they burned out, the animal would get on its legs. My reply was: "Yes, by all means. Buy twenty-one blinking candles, but don't set fire to the ship!"

That was the last I saw of him that night, but at dawn he came to my cabin to say, "It's worked, sir. The

animal is up. But you were one year out in his age.
We had to do it a second time and use twenty-two
candles!"

He was so sincere that I did not like to say what I
thought, which was that the elephant was a young
animal which liked sleeping with the light on. When I
went to see him he was certainly up, bright, and eating
banana leaves. My Assistant little guessed that I had
probably worried far more about him than he had. As
regards sleep, elephants are rather like horses. They
get most of it standing up, and they will only go down
when they think that, for a brief period at night, all the
world is asleep. It is an uncanny period in the jungle
night, and, for some reason, never seems to come at just
the same time two nights in succession.

I have sat up with several elephants throughout the
night, purely to find out when they did sleep, and for
how long. The time is never the same, but it is always
at that eerie hour when even the insects stop their
serenades. It never lasts longer than half an hour if the
animal is fit, but while it lasts he sleeps very soundly.
For an hour previously the elephant stands absolutely
motionless without feeding. There is not a flap of the
ear or a swish of the tail. It seems as though he were
intently listening for any sound. Then he seems satisfied
that all is well, and down he goes in a slow, silent movement, as if overcome by some unseen jungle god. In
bright moonlight it is a most beautiful but uncanny sight.

A full-grown elephant has little to fear in the jungle,
unless it is protecting a calf, yet one can always notice
that it is on the alert for uncommon sounds or scents.
An elephant hates being startled, but it is startled only by
things which are not part of its normal life. A prowling
tiger will not worry a tusker elephant. He knows that
no tiger would ever attack him in the jungle.

Elephants and ponies do not get on together. Not
only are ponies frightened of elephants, but the elephants
sometimes become so scared of ponies that a whole train
of them will stampede at the sight of one, with the result
that oozies are injured, gear is smashed and camp pots

are broken. I was once away from my district for ten days with a severe attack of malaria. During my absence my Forest Manager toured my area and visited a training camp of which I was particularly proud. Fourteen calves had gone through the crushes, had been named, and were being put through their daily paces.

When I received a copy of the Forest Manager's report, I found to my astonishment that he was extremely critical of the training of these calves, which had been nervous and disobedient when he was inspecting them. His remarks almost brought on another attack of fever, but I did not stop to take my temperature. I at once went back to my forest, and travelled direct to the training camp. I felt certain there must be some explanation. Two marches from the training camp I was met by my trainer, Maung Chit Poo. I told him at once how displeased I was that he had failed to show my babies satisfactorily during my absence. But he was too loyal to question the Forest Manager's criticisms. I sensed that he had something to tell me, but that I must wait and find out indirectly what was in his mind. Nevertheless, there was a feeling of unpleasant tension during our two marches back to the training camp. I inspected the calves on the evening of my arrival, but only ten of the fourteen paraded. They were perfect. Not one of them had a mark on him from training, all were well under control, and each of them took a tamarind ball from my hand as sweetly as a puppy will take a tid-bit from its master.

It was disappointing that four of them were missing from the parade, but I accepted Maung Chit Poo's excuse that the oozies did not get their orders to parade early enough, and not all had been in camp. I gave orders, however, that as each of the four came into camp, it should be brought over to my camp, without waiting to bring all four at once. Not one of these calves had arrived by dusk. My camp was pitched on the site which had been used by the Forest Manager during his visit, in a large clearing, which was well laid out for the purpose.

E 2

I sent for Chit Poo, dropping the polite prefix of Maung when I greeted him. It was obvious that he was worried, and had something to tell me, but that he could not bring it out.

I suddenly asked him sharply: "What is your game, Chit Poo? What is wrong?"

He gave me a broken-hearted look and answered: "Please, Thakin, come out of camp to look at them. They are only fifty yards away, on the elephant track. But we cannot bring them in to camp."

"Why not?" I asked. "Don't be so foolish; they are only babies."

"They are not babies. That is the trouble," he said.

I at once went to see what was the matter. But the green light of evening was already going, and it was becoming too dark to inspect elephant calves. When I had walked about twenty yards I spotted some pony droppings on the path. I hit one of these with my stick and at once said to Chit Poo: "Take the calves back to camp. I will see them to-morrow." I knew well enough that the calves would not pass the spot where those stinking animals—ponies—had camped, only ten days before. Chit Poo realised that I had discovered the real trouble, and that it mattered little what he told me.

Suddenly he dropped on his knees and exclaimed piteously: "How can I be expected to parade trained calves in the presence of a white man, a white woman and three of their dogs, with two ponies shaking their coats only twenty yards away?"

Using a term which exalted his position I replied: "U Chit Poo. You are not expected to do so. Go back to camp, and don't worry about it any more."

That evening I tried to write my report, and tore up a dozen sheets of paper, wondering whether I dared criticise my superior. Next morning I wrote a report ending with Chit Poo's words which I inserted as my own, and gave the presence of the ponies as the explanation of the restive behaviour of the calves. My report came back to me after a month of anxious waiting. In the margin the Head Forest Officer had written in red ink: " You never know, you know."

I did not forget this lesson, although before I left Burma I had inspected calves in the presence of my own wife, my assistant and his wife, with three children and four dogs running about, and a wireless set mercilessly bawling out Bow Bells. But I made allowances, for I knew how the baby jumbos loathe such conditions. Bad as they were, it would have been worse if we had had ponies.

Quite apart from the dislike of elephants, ponies are out of place in the jungle. In the cold season it is quite possible and pleasant to ride them, but the anxiety experienced on account of tigers scarcely makes it worth while. Tigers have a passion for ponies, and the only way to keep them off is to keep fires up all night, and to have syces or attendants with lanterns sleeping with the ponies.

Ponies know immediately when there are tiger round the camp. There are few camps in the deep jungle where tiger pug-marks are not as common, along the banks of the creeks, as are water-rat footprints in the mud of a Thames backwater. Naturally, there is perpetual anxiety, and the fear of the ponies is most distressing. Those who have handled horses in a burning building can best imagine what it is like. When tiger are about, ponies shiver continuously with terror, their eyes become staring, they appear hypnotised; and nothing one can say or do will calm them. One thinks that at any moment they will stampede into the black night of the surrounding jungle, but they remain shivering and glued to the ground on which they stand. No lover of horses who has watched this, for night after night, without being able to help, will willingly take his ponies into deep jungle again.

The dislike which elephants feel for ponies is exceeded only by their hatred and fear of dogs. In fact, a dog is one of the few animals at which an elephant will lash out with its trunk. I can remember once that a group of six travelling elephants had arrived in camp and were waiting to be unloaded. One of them had on its back a basket containing four lively fox-terrier puppies, just at the age when they are most mischievous, but not able to keep up on a journey. Their mother, Twigs, who was one of the principal figures in my camp at that time, was sitting beside me on a fallen tree, waiting to join her precious family when they were unloaded, when suddenly there was a shout of " The puppies are out," after the basket had been put on the ground.

There they were, walking around under the bellies and among the legs and feet of the six elephants, quite fearless and thinking it great fun. The elephants were stupefied. They hunched up their backs, rolled up their trunks and put them out of harm's way in their mouths and lifted their feet up like cats on hot bricks. Not one of the elephants made the slightest attempt to injure a puppy. On the contrary, they were doing their best to avoid hurting them. Poor little Twigs was watching all this, shivering with excitement and terror, and at last, unable to stand it any longer, she broke away from me and dashed out, hoping to retrieve her puppies. With one yelp she stampeded five out of the six elephants. Only one young tusker hit at her with his trunk. Luckily he missed, or he would have broken every bone in her body. Twigs rushed back to me for protection, with the elephant following her up. But on seeing me he turned and bolted after the others, as I had an alpine stick with a spearhead in the ferrule. There was definitely some natural instinct which forbade the elephants injuring the puppies. But they would have taken delight in killing Twigs, whom they all knew by sight and hated.

In spite of this hatred, almost every jungle camp has two or three dogs in it. They are useful as watch-dogs or guards and also as scavengers. Dogs are seldom used for hunting in the jungle, as they soon fall victims to panther if they once leave the main elephant timber-dragging paths. It is a very common occurrence to hear that a camp dog has been taken by a leopard. One usually enquires if the dog's carcase has been found, as if so one has a good chance of bagging the leopard, by sitting up over it the following night. In nine cases out of ten, however, the leopard gobbles up the dog at one meal and leaves nothing for the next day.

I have never known a dog and an elephant make friends. Elephants will eventually become accustomed to certain dogs in camp, and dogs learn not to bark at them and always to keep out of reach of the slash of a trunk or the kick of a leg. The hatred of elephants for dogs cannot easily be explained. It is possible that they are afraid of dogs biting their trunks, though I do not think such a thing can ever have happened. Sometimes it has occurred to me that it might be an instinctive dread of hydrophobia, which has been recorded in elephants, and which is the dread of everyone who keeps a dog in camp, Burman and European Assistant alike.

Nevertheless practically every European Assistant keeps a dog, and I have almost always had one myself. The elephants hate them, and one is always losing one's dog, owing to leopard, tiger, bear and snakes. The tragedies of lost dogs are often an Assistant's first experiences of real grief.

It is easy to ask why, under such conditions, do you keep a dog? But I know of no other existence where a dog is so necessary as a companion to share every moment of one's life and to drive away loneliness.

In my years in Burma I had many: Jabo, Chin, Juno, Bo, Sally, Karl, Basso, Rhoda, Cobbler and Molly, to mention but half of them, ranging from a Burman pariah, Chow, Bull Mastiff, Alsatian, Bassein Fishing Dog of Bloodhound extraction, to a Red Cocker Spaniel and a Labrador, the last of which shared the war years with me, as the mascot of the Elephant Companies. Each of these few, named here, was as different in character as in breed; each was obtained in different circumstances, and came by his death in a different way.

Jabo chose me, not I him. His name means Piebald in Burmese, and he was something between red and white in patches, with a bobtail, for at some time, when he was a puppy, a Burman had slashed at him with a jungle knife, or dah, and cut his tail off. He was a powerful dog, built for the jungle, deep ribbed and deep chested and with small, well-shaped feet for his size.

I had reached camp with my elephants with a violent bout of malaria on me. While I was waiting for them to be unloaded I called for a deck-chair, and sank into it and dozed off, oblivious of my surroundings, until I should be able to crawl into my camp bed.

Suddenly I was startled, almost to death, by the shock of what seemed to be the coldest thing on earth being pressed against my fevered body. It was a dog's cold nose, and as I sprang forward I saw a dog wagging his hindquarters at me in default of a tail. I was new to the Burmese jungle and in one of my first bouts of high fever. The Cornish cliffs had never seemed so far away, and all my gratitude went out to this friendly, sympathetic creature. By the time my camp was pitched we were close friends. I was feeling too ill for anything but bed, but I called my servant and asked for a glass of whisky, sugar and boiling water before I tried to sleep. In a few moments the Burman had brought the kettle, and as he was mixing my drink Jabo thrust forward his head inquisitively. The servant called out: " Get out, Jabo," and turned a stream of water from the kettle on to him. There was a yelp of pain and a curse from me.

" You uncivilised devil! What do you mean by it? " I exclaimed, and ordered him to prepare food for Jabo twice a day so long as the dog would stay with me, though I was beyond eating anything myself.

That evening, when I had sweated out my fever a bit and was feeling like death warmed up, Jabo came to lick my hand again, but he was painfully nervous and badly scalded. My servant brought him a whole boiled chicken with rice in a wash-basin, which he put beside my bed. I tore up the fowl with my own hands and mixed it in the rice, so that he should learn my smell. I hoped that he would sleep in my tent with me; but he never did, and always disappeared at dusk. I kept that formerly ownerless, roaming dog that was known in all the camps, five years, and never once did he sleep in my tent. He was too wise, for he was terrified of leopard, and always went to sleep in the midst of the elephant-men, or the camp servants, for better protection. Jabo became a character well known in the Chindwin jungles and riverside stations, where he had the reputation of being the father of more illegitimate puppies than any other dog in Burma.

He would be ashore from a river launch as soon as the mooring-rope, to search for a lady love before the siren sounded. He was usually last on board, but he almost always just made it before the gangway came up. If, however, he found a bitch, he would let the launch go without him and take the next one either upstream or down, according to the direction in which I had gone.

He always turned up, though he was often three days late. His end came when I was away, ill with fever, on two weeks' leave. I had left him with my head elephant-man, who greeted me when I got back with the news that poor old Jabo was dead. " A Nat Shin took him when he was following a canoe, swimming across the Chindwin at Yuwa."

I had to accept this story, though reluctantly, for one has to accept everything relating to the gods or Nats. The Nat Shin is the cursed water spirit, and even more mythical than the jungle Nats themselves.

For some reason unknown, then, I could not forgive that Burman. I did not believe that a Nat Shin had killed Jabo, or could kill him, though I have more than once had to accept the tale that a Nat Shin has taken an elephant swimming across the river. I sacked the fellow.

Two years later a young Burmese girl told me the true story, as all girls will on certain special occasions.

Six of my elephant riders, led by the one I had dismissed, were crossing the Chindwin for a gambling bout in a village on the opposite shore. They were overloaded in their canoe, but Jabo wanted to visit that village also, for his own ends, and, although told, in no very sweet tones, to stay behind in camp, he followed them swimming, and drew close to the canoe, as though bent on climbing in. The head Burman feared he would upset them, and gave him a crack on the head with the paddle, to make him keep off. The paddle must have stunned him, or split his hard old skull, and Jabo sank, and was not seen to rise again.

The girl told me how the elephant-men had hunted for days for Jabo's body. That showed me that they had not meant to' kill him. So I sought out the man responsible, and made him confess the whole story. He told me all, in tears; I forgave him and took him on once more.

Jabo was no ordinary pi dog. He was a grand companion, though he was no protection, since he would never sleep in my tent or hut. He knew the courses of my evening meal as well as any of my servants, who brought them fifty yards from the cookhouse. He would come with the soup, watch it being served, go back, to return again with the joint, and once more go back, to return with the savoury. But he would not travel those fifty yards after dark, except in company of a servant, for fear of leopard.

A dog that sleeps in one's hut or tent is a protection from dacoits, but is a great worry. For only if it is fenced in behind chairs and boxes under one's camp bed can one feel reasonably sure that a leopard will not take it from under one's very nose while one is asleep.

One Assistant had his black cocker spaniel snapped up by a leopard, when it was sleeping, chained up beside his bed, in his bamboo hut. He did not wake until it was too late to do anything. The chain was broken, and both had vanished. He could find no trace of his dead pal next day, but determined to try to have his revenge. So the next night he borrowed a dog from the elephant-men, fed it, and tied it up to his office box beside his bed. Then he put out his lamp and sat up in an upright chair in one corner of the room, determined to wait all night if need be.

The familiar sounds of chatting ceased in his servants'

camp, the glow of the fires died down, the sound of the brook seemed to increase slightly in the night and the heavy dew began to drip steadily in an incessant ping, ping, ping, from the leaves overhanging the roof of his hut.

A porcupine called, " Pyoo! pyoo! " A samba deer " belled " to call its mate, an occasional elephant bell sounded from across or down the stream, an owl cried, " Zee-gwet, zee-gwet," later followed by the mellow hoots of his bigger brother—calls which the Burmans associate with death and ill-luck.

The Assistant's chief worry was that he might shoot his bait-dog instead of the leopard.

The hour of stillness arrived, when all sounds seemed to cease. Even the stream seemed to stop babbling. Then there was a sudden tension in the room in which he could feel his heart pounding. The dog suddenly tore at his chain, pulling the heavy specie box to which it was tied across the bamboo floor.

The Assistant raised his shotgun, loaded with buck-shot, and switched on his torch; on the bamboo steps in the doorway stood a leopard, blinded by the light. He fired both barrels, and it fell, mangled and dead. In a moment the camp was stirring with lights and his servants were uttering exclamations of delight. One of them, who had always prepared his spaniel's food, ripped up the white belly of the leopard and disembowelled it; then he opened the intestines and pulled out a black knot of the curly coat of his master's beloved spaniel.

This was too much for my friend, who turned away and ordered his people back to bed, telling them to take the terrified camp dog with them. He told me that he cried himself to sleep that night, and that he thought it had done him good. He moved camp next day, with the leopard's carcase on one of his elephants. I met him at his next camp, and while we were talking after a day's work an elephant oozie and his wife approached us. They were a rather older couple than most camp Burmans, and real jungle-dwellers. The man was holding a baby honey-bear in his arms. It was quite small—about the size of a coffee-pot. They squatted down side by side in front of us, she with her shoulders bare and her tamain tucked across above her breasts.

I asked him where he had got the little creature, and he told me that the tree-fellers had killed its mother three weeks before, and that she had mauled Maung Chit Poo. The mother bear and her cub had been hidden in the branches of a teak-tree they were felling, and, just as the last strokes were being given and the tree was about to fall, had dropped among the tree-fellers. Maung Chit Poo's son had rushed to his father's help and hit the mother bear on the head with his axe, killing her outright.

" Would you like to have the baby, Thakin Galay? " he asked my friend, for they had heard of the loss of his spaniel.

It was a charming expression of sympathy, which they did not put into any other words.

" No," my friend and I both said together.

The little bear seemed to understand, and began to make queer babyish squeals and fumble about; and, with a perfectly simple and natural movement, the Burman passed it to his wife, who put it in her lap, while she untucked her tamain from under her arm, and fastened it again with a tuck in round her waist, exposing two perfectly shaped breasts. Then she lifted up the little bear and put her nipple in its mouth.

When we had thanked them again for the offer of their pet, they rose, bowed and departed with the bear cub still at her breast. She had been feeding it three or four times a day, filled with all the Buddhist pride that they were doing something of importance in their lives, by preserving life, and convinced that their action would put them on a higher plane in Nirvana.

There was nothing unusual in this. The jungle women will suckle baby fawns and any young creature which inspires them with pity. " It deserves pity " are words often on their lips, and their pity at once moves them to succour and keep alive the orphan. Thus they will adopt new-born tiger or leopard cubs, and bears, not hesitating to save the lives of the hated enemies of their menfolk, which would become dangerous if they were reared. There is a wonderful gentleness in these jungle people.

No woman, however, would nurse a snake, if snakes could be taught to suck. The Burman thinks all snakes are better dead, a view which is justified by a legend of Buddha. Disease came into Burma from the north, down the Chindwin River. Buddha slew it near Meegya-ungyay (the Crocodile Water), cutting off its head, which lay in Lower Burma, and leaving its tail in Upper Burma. The head was venomous, and, for that reason, there are few poisonous snakes in Upper Burma, whereas Lower Burma is full of them.

With the example of Buddha to fortify his hatred, the Burman has no sympathy with any eccentric European who keeps a snake as a pet.

I have been told the story of one *jungle salt* in the Pyinmana Forest who did keep such a pet. She was a seventeen-foot python, whom he called Eve. She had a silver collar and chain, and he took her on all his tours in a basket, carried on one of his elephants.

Eve did little except sleep and eat, at longish intervals. She lived entirely in his hut or tent, at his headquarters, finding warmth during the day between the blankets of his bed, and at night getting what warmth she could from her master. But he kept her lying outside his bedclothes.

In the end familiarity bred contempt of danger. One cold night when her master was asleep, Eve glided under the bedclothes, and lay beside him, seeking not love, but warmth. While he slept, she gradually twined her coils around his body. The Assistant woke to find his legs and hips in a vice-like embrace. The more he struggled, the tighter Eve drew her constricting coils. His yells for help brought his camp servants running to his bedside, but he was not released until Eve had been cut into several pieces.

The Burman who told me the story gave it a moral twist of his own, by saying that women are safest on the other side of the blanket, and that snakes are best dead.

Snakes such as hamadryads and Russell's viper are common, but are seldom seen in heavy jungle, as they usually avoid man. But an extraordinary coincidence occurred to a friend of mine and myself, as each of us was chased by the same snake within a period of two years. Brian wrote to me from the Upper Kanti, describing how he had had the unpleasant and rather terrifying experience of being chased by a hamadryad snake at the confluence of the Big and Small Kanti Creeks, where a game-track led up to the ridge from a ford, where game habitually came down to drink.

The snake had suddenly slid down out of a large clump of bamboo. The Burman with him gave the alarm, and the snake chased them along the track, for at least fifty yards. The Burman, of course, insisted that it was a Nat snake.

Two years afterwards I was just leaving the same creek junction, and had just begun to climb up the game-track: I had quite forgotten the incident which Brian had described, when suddenly my Burman shouted a warning. I saw a large black hamadryad slithering down a bamboo clump and coming for us. By the time it had reached the ground I had overtaken my Burman, and we were in flight. It chased us, but I do not think it followed us for any distance. I am afraid I did not stop to look back until I was almost at the ridge. There was no question that the incident occurred at the exact spot where Brian had been chased two years before. It occurred during the same month, in the hottest season of the year. My conclusion is that it was the spot always used by a pair of hamadryads for breeding. The Burmans heard all about both stories, and no doubt a magnificent legend of a Jungle Nat by now attaches itself to the spot.

Strangely enough, the Burman who was with me at the time was bitten by a poisonous snake some months later. In those days I was quite ignorant of the proper treatment for snake-bite, and employed exactly the

worst methods. I first made him drink a bottle of
whisky and then lanced the place where he had been
bitten on the leg with a razor blade, making criss-cross
cuts, like a Union Jack. I then found I could not stop
the bleeding, and spent a most anxious night, thinking
he was going to succumb to alcoholic poisoning, loss of
blood or snake-bite. Fortunately he survived both the
snake-bite and my treatment of it.

So far as I know, elephants don't worry about snakes,
though the oozies believe that a number of elephant
calves die of snake-bite. I have had this reported to me
many times, but in no instance could I find any proof.
The Burmans believe that the hairs of an elephant's tail
pull out very easily after it has been bitten by a snake.
But, as this has also to be proved, I was never able to accept
it as conclusive evidence that an elephant had been killed
by snake-bite.

There is a widespread belief that an elephant is really
terrified of a mouse. The idea makes an obvious appeal
to the human love of paradox. But, if it is true, I can
see no reason for it. It certainly cannot be because
the elephant is afraid of the mouse getting inside his trunk,
since, with one snort, he could eject it like a cork from a
popgun. However, many women are terrified of mice,
with as little reason. After all, most fears are imaginary,
and there is no reason why elephants should be immune
from such terrors.

Elephants are not, however, usually frightened by
natural phenomena without very good reason. They do
not mind thunderstorms in the way that dogs do, and
they remain calm in the face of forest fires.

Forest fires are not by any means as terrible in the
jungles of Burma as they are described as being in
other parts of the world. Practically every mixed
deciduous forest area in Burma has an annual spring-
cleaning of fire, during the latter part of April or the
early part of May. It is sometimes due to spontaneous
combustion of the rotting leaves of the preceding autumn.
The result is usually a carpet fire of leaves, dead twigs
and fallen branches, which does not involve the living

trees themselves. These carpet fires travel very slowly against any breeze there may be, at a rate not exceeding two miles an hour. Once they have started, they fan out, and become a narrow ribbon of flames, usually quite low, but occasionally catching hold of any tree with dead leaves or dry branches within their reach.

The only areas in which one gets really fierce raging conflagrations are stretches of dry kaing grass. But, as this grows by water, the stretches of grass are usually intersected by creeks, or by the beds of dry streams, which form natural fire-lines, barring its progress.

Elephants have no fear of the carpet type of fire. Domesticated elephants can be marched straight at the line of flame and through it. Their lack of fear and their immunity are due to their weight—for the weight on their pads extinguishes any burning leaves they tread on, and, as long as they keep moving, the under side of their pads will not scorch or blister.

It is a different matter in conflagrations of kaing grass. These fires travel fast, and elephants and all other wild animals recognise the sound and smell of fire immediately, and at once cross the nearest creek. Their understanding of wind direction, and how it will make the fire travel, is far greater than man's.

On many occasions I have set areas of kaing grass on fire on purpose, so as to clear the ground for a new growth. It is quite unnecessary to try to clear animals out of such areas before setting fire to them; directly they hear and smell the fire, the animals move out, at a steady pace, without any panic or excitement. In fact they remember what areas have been burnt earlier on, and return to them. Within a very short space of time, after heavy showers have fallen, the blocks of blackened, fire-swept swamp become emerald-green with the fresh young grass.

I have only once seen elephants really frightened by natural phenomena, and that was due to their realising that they were in a gorge where water was rapidly rising in a spate. Rain was coming down as though it would never cease, and in the distance there was a rumbling of thunder, which added to the anxiety.

I had decided to take a short cut through the Kanti Gorge. I was travelling with eight young pack elephants, and it would save us a climb of two thousand feet from one watershed to another. After passing down the gorge, I meant to move up a side stream. It was during the month of September, and I was almost at the end of my tether. I had been on my own since the previous May, with daily fever, and I was making my way back to jungle headquarters, where I should at least get a week in the same camp. My spirits were high, the oozies were whistling and singing, and our circus was travelling in Indian file down the hard, sandy bottom of the stream.

Both banks of the gorge were sheer rock, to a height of about thirty feet, with dense overhanging jungle and bamboos along their tops. The gorge was three miles long, and the stream was about ankle-deep when we started down it. By the time we had gone a mile one could hear the unmistakable sound of a heavy thunder-storm breaking in the headwaters of the stream. The elephants showed their nervousness by half-turning round. An elephant cannot see behind it by merely turning its head; it has to half-turn its body. The bore of water eventually overtook us, after which there was broken water well above my knees, and it was lapping under the bellies and round the flanks of the smaller female calves.

For a time it seemed as though the water would rise no higher, and we were making good progress. But, by some instinct not shared by man, the elephants knew there was more water coming down. They began what would soon have become a stampede, if they had not been hindered by the depth of the water and kept under partial restraint by their riders. It became a terrifying experience, as there was no possibility of turning back, and no hope of getting up the sides. During the last mile all the elephants began bellowing; that, with the sound of the torrential rain, and the raging muddy water around, made it seem a pretty grim situation. I

kept expecting to see one of the calves lose its balance
at any moment. At the end the water was up to my
armpits, and I was holding my rifle in both hands above
my head.

I never knew a mile to seem longer. Bend after
bend came in view, with never a sign of the mouth of the
creek I knew, which would provide for our exodus from
the black hole in which we floundered. Logs were
floating past, and, though I had no time to be amused
then, I noticed how the elephants' hindquarters seemed
to have a magnetic attraction for the logs that floated
down and overtook us. Just as a log was about to strike
its hindquarters, the elephant would swing its rear end to
one side, giving the log a glancing blow, so that it
cannoned off like a billiard ball from the cushion, and
passed on to the chap in front—and so on all down the
line.

We were fortunate really, as the smaller animals
were just afloat when we went round the bend to go up
the side creek. Moreover, the side creek only came
down in spate half an hour after we had started up it.
If we had met the combined spates at the confluence,
all our kit would certainly have been lost.

The elephants scrambled up the first feasible bank
after turning in off the main river, and at a general halt
they seemed to look at me as if to say: "And you call
yourself a jungle man!"

Chapter Ten

SAVAGE elephants are as rare as really wicked men, but those that are not savage sometimes give way to moments of bad temper. They are particularly liable to do so when they are in harness dragging a very heavy weight. Their most tiresome and dangerous habit at such moments is to pick up a large stick or stone with the trunk and throw it with great force and accuracy at some onlooker, particularly at someone in authority, whom they guess is responsible. One has to be prepared to jump, and jump quickly, when this happens.

A young European Assistant of my acquaintance visited the London Zoo with his mother and his sister on his first leave home. They went straight to the elephant house. After explaining all about the female elephant on view, he was emboldened to suggest: " Shall I make her sit down? "

His mother and sister were delighted at the idea, and the onlookers were most impressed.

" Hmit! " he shouted, in close imitation of a Burmese oozie.

The elephant merely swished her tail and tickled her mouth with imaginary bananas.

" Hmit! " he shouted again, and, as the elephant ignored him, he grew angrier and more determined with the disobedient animal. " Hmit! hmit! hmit! "

At last the elephant condescended to notice him, swinging her head round, cocking her ears, and eyeing him with an expression as though she were saying, " So you come from Burma, too, do you? " Then, with lightning swiftness, she seized a lump of her dung the size of a cottage loaf and slung it at the young Assistant. It missed him, but it knocked a feather out of his mother's hat and exploded against the wall behind them. No one laughed, but the elephant house was soon empty.

Savage elephants—whether male or female—are rare, and the few exceptions are usually of a savage temperament from birth. Of course, during the musth period all males are of uncertain temper. My interpretation of musth is that it is an instinctive desire in the male elephant to fight and kill before mating. His blood is up, and his brain is affected. The mere act of mating does not cool his passion. He would rather fight for his chosen mate before he wins her, and drive off and kill an intruder during the time that he is making love.

The great majority of cases in which oozies are killed by their elephants take place when their charges are on musth. For some unknown reason, the animal may then suddenly attack his rider, first striking him with tusk or trunk, then crushing him to death with a knee, when he is on the ground. A vicious young animal will throw his rider, and then attack him on the ground. Once he has done this he is classed as dangerous and given a metal bell, as he is likely to repeat such an attack. For three years he may never show a sign of viciousness— then suddenly he will catch his new rider off his guard, and so kill his second man.

Strange as it may sound, there is very little difficulty in finding a new rider for such an animal. Many riders take pride in riding an elephant known to be dangerous, and take such a job in a spirit of bravado. Such men find life easy; they care nothing for anything or anyone. They are usually opium-eaters, but in spite of that they work well. Every village girl knows them by name. But, though they gain in reputation and importance, they do not get spoilt, as they are not paid much more for such work than the ordinary riders.

In addition to the rider, a dangerous animal has a really good type of spearman attached to it as an attendant, whose duty is to cover every movement of the rider when he lies entirely at the mercy of the elephant—undoing his fetters, for example. Although the spearman carries a spear, the secret of his control is by the eye. He keeps his eye fixed on the elephant's. The two men together are usually sufficient to keep a savage elephant under control.

The temperament of a nasty-tempered elephant is somewhat like that of a Burman. The animal loses its temper and kills, and realises too late what it has done. In just the same way a Burman will lose his temper about some trivial gambling debt and will draw his dagger and stab his best friend—ten minutes later he will realise with most bitter regret what he has done.

I have known one case of something that seemed like remorse in an elephant. He was a tusker who killed his rider. But he guarded the body, and would let nobody get near it, for a whole week. He grazed all round it, and charged in mad fury at anyone who came near. When the body had quite decomposed he wandered away from it, and ten days later was recaptured, without any difficulty, and behaved quite normally. He was not on musth.

An animal named Ah Noh (a Siamese name) killed nine riders in a period of fifteen years, but there was never any difficulty in getting a new rider for him. He was peculiar in that he always killed his man with his tusks, actually goring him to death. He was never in harness unless there was a rider on his head and two spearmen, one on each side, with their spears at the ready.

It was finally decided to saw his tusks right off to the lip, or as near as possible to the lip. This involved over-powering him completely, and a description of it would make very painful reading, as it was cruel. But the job was done, under my supervision, and we cured him. The two great nerves were almost exposed by the sawing. They healed in a remarkable way, for the tusks did not grow again, but formed a rosette of ivory at each end. He was one of those exceptional and magnificent animals which are rarely seen, either in the wild state or in captivity. One could walk up to him and give him a banana, and he was so beautifully behaved one would think butter would not melt in his mouth. I have come across him feeding alone in the jungle many times, and have stopped to admire him. He never made the slightest attempt to attack me.

The wickedest elephant I ever knew was called Taw

Sin Ma (Miss Wild Elephant). I never knew her when she was a calf, but she cannot have been greatly loved, to have earned herself a name like that, and she must have been very truculent in the crush. She was about twenty-five years old when I first knew her, and there was nothing in her recorded history which gave any explanation of why she should just loathe every European she saw. She had never been operated on, and could never have been ill-treated by a European. Even when she was had up for inspection she had to be chained to a tree, and when one was a hundred yards away would begin to lunge and strain at her chains, in order to attack one.

She recognised a European by his appearance quite as much as by smell, because she would attack a Burman rider if he were wearing a khaki shirt. I had a nasty experience with her, when she first attacked me on sight, and then chased me, following my trail by scent for four miles, from one catchment area over the watershed to the next. It was terrifying.

I met her by chance, when I was walking from one camp to another. We came on her suddenly, and she went for us at once. The Burman I had with me stampeded in one direction, and I in another, and for two miles I was not sure whether I was on the right track back to the camp I had left. There would have been no hope for me if her hobbles had snapped or come undone, unless I had found refuge up a tree. But I knew well that if I had done that I might have had to stay there for twenty-four hours or longer. As she was hobbled, my pace was a little faster than hers. She wore a brass danger bell around her neck (docile elephants wear wooden bells). Often it sounded from the bell as though she were nearly up to me, at times as though she had cut me off. Of course, I know that sounds in the jungle are deceptive, and play tricks; but it was not pleasant. This experience gave me the first opportunity I had ever had of trying out a trick for delaying a pursuing elephant, by dropping an article of clothing, in the belief that the animal will halt and attack it, and so give one a chance of gaining ground.

I first dropped a haversack, but I heard no check in the sound of the clanking bell on the elephant hurrying after me. When I had climbed to the top of the ridge I halted for a few moments, to locate her whereabouts. Then, after going as fast as I could along the ridge, I chose the steepest place for my descent, hoping she would hesitate to follow, and there I dropped my khaki shirt, for her to savage, or to chew to her heart's content. But I had no sooner reached the small spur reaching to the drainage area below than I heard an avalanche of crashing trees and bamboos, and it needed very little imagination to visualise Taw Sin Ma sitting on her haunches and tobogganing down the steep incline, much faster than I had done. My shirt had not delayed her a moment. Perhaps she was holding it in her mouth, to chew after she had first caught me. On I plunged, trying to remember to act on the law of the jungle, that one must never hurry and always keep cool. Once one breaks that rule every thorny bush that grows reaches out a tentacle to impede one, to tear and scratch, or even trip one up. I thought of discarding my once white, and very wet, vest, but I thought that if I was eventually treed, I might need something on. My relief was great when I met two men, busy with a crosscut saw on a fallen teak-tree. But I had only to shout out the words: "Taw Sin Ma!" and they joined me in my flight, without asking questions. They soon took the lead, and as I followed I at least had the satisfaction of knowing I was on the right track to camp and safety.

One of them got into camp, well ahead of me, and gave the alarm on my account. When I got in I met a chattering group of elephant-riders and their families, all of them doubled up with laughter, or smacking their hands on their hips in mirth at the sight of me—all, that is, except Maung Po Net (Mr Black as Night), who tucked up his lungyi skirt, as he prepared to go out and meet his "pet."

There was no alternative but to join the Burmans in their joke—for I often wanted them to share in mine. So I joined in their laughter and their hip-smacking.

Within an hour a rider came back with my shirt and haversack, quite undamaged and not even trodden on, and Po Net rode Taw Sin Ma back into camp. The expressions on both their faces seemed to indicate that the same incident might be repeated next day. It did not, as I at once issued twenty-five feet of chain, for Taw Sin Ma to trail behind her, whenever she was at large, grazing, in addition to her hobbles.

As far as I know, she was the only animal we never inoculated against anthrax. She was the type that never gets it!

Some riders teach their charges tricks that give a wrong impression of the real disposition of the animal. Bo Gyi (Big Man), a young elephant, which became well known, always charged his rider, as soon as he appeared to catch him and bring him to camp. But at ten paces the animal would stop dead, and sit down for his fetter to be undone, as gentle as a lamb. Any other rider would bolt when the elephant charged him. The secret, that it was just a matter of standing one's ground, was only discovered after the rider who had taught him the trick had been killed by a bear. The elephant was at large for a month after his rider's death; nobody would face him. Finally a reward of three hundred rupees was offered for his recapture. A young village lad turned up one day, saying he could capture him, but asking if he would get the reward, since he was not one of my riders. I told him that of course he would. Two days later he came into camp riding the animal and smiling gaily, and was paid his three hundred rupees. Two of my own men had gone with the lad, and had watched the whole procedure, from a hiding-place near by. The secret had come from a young Burmese girl, a former sweetheart of the dead rider. The young lad was her new lover, and no doubt boy and girl found the three hundred rupees a useful start in life.

After a strike among eighty elephant-riders, in the early days, at a time when there had been political agitation in the neighbourhood, I was left with the job of capturing what appeared to be six savage elephants, simply because none of the men left with me knew the tricks that had to be employed with each animal. These tricks were just the result of habitual methods employed by their riders. In some cases the approach had to be made from the near side, in other cases from the off, or from in front, or behind, or when the animal was sitting, or standing. The approach to each animal had to be learned separately.

The last one to be caught was Toe Hline (The Destroyer). I got the information of how to catch him by bribing the rider who was on strike, through an agent of my own, who confided to the rider a long story of how he wanted a job so as to get enough money to marry a certain girl in camp. If he could catch Toe Hline he would get that money reward and the job of riding him.

I watched this recapture with great relief, as Toe Hline had a bad reputation for tearing down jungle rice godowns (store-houses), and he had taken up his grazing quarters near my jungle hut, which was by no means substantial, being built of bamboo, with very flimsy posts, and it looked just like a godown. The volunteer to catch Toe Hline was " attacked " twice, on getting within one hundred and fifty yards of the animal. It looked pretty hopeless, but I soon discovered that these " attacks " were merely a method of getting the elephant and the rider in full view of each other. Once this had been achieved, the rider designate sat down on his haunches and began calling in a very persuasive voice: " Hmit! Hmit! Hmit! Hmit! " This went on for at least fifteen minutes, with the elephant taking no heed, but just going on feeding, keeping one eye on the rider, all the time. Quite abruptly, he stopped feeding, and stood perfectly still. Then, slowly moving his head towards where the rider sat, and, setting his ears forward inquisitively, he decided to " Hmit."

Even then it needed great pluck for the rider to go up to him. As he advanced, he repeated the same word, and, bending down, unfastened the fetter, which is normally done when the animal is standing up. Then

he climbed on the elephant's head and said : " Htah ! "
Toe Hline rose, and proceeded to camp, and I proceeded
to get myself a peg, to celebrate the recapture of the last
elephant. I had them all equipped with eighty new
riders, and the strikers were left wondering.

The rider married his girl and got his money reward.
Then Po Lone, the original rider, who was the pleasantest
of rogues, came in to say that now he had enabled his
friend to win the reward, and get his girl, he would like
to ride his old elephant again himself. He got him, for the
two riders had fixed it all up between themselves, while I
thought I was breaking the strike. They are lovable
rogues.

Young calves, if they have not been properly trained,
are apt to get savage if not well handled afterwards.
One particular calf, named Soe Bone (Wicked Bone)—
the name of the creek where he was born—delighted
in chasing me whenever he got an opportunity. I
thought at first it was only rough play, but my head
Burmans assured me it was not, so we decided he was
not too old to learn his manners. " Shoot him in his
toe-nails with roasted rice," was the suggestion. So I
emptied two cartridges and, after filling them with
rice instead of shot, I wandered out of camp to find Soe
Bone. He was in a sandy creek, throwing wet sand
over his body with his trunk, and was under a bank,
only three foot high.

" Hullo, little chap ! " I said, greeting him.

" Little chap to you," he seemed to reply, and charged
me on sight, as though determined to see me off.

I stood my ground, and gave him a left and right in
the forefeet, so as to sting his toe-nails. Did it stop him?
I nearly lost my precious shotgun as I made my getaway.
He was up that bank with his fetters on almost as quickly
as I could turn to run. And did he love me next time he
saw me?

" What's the next move? " I asked.

" Oh well, we'll put him back into a crush and cane
the little devil."

A substantial crush was made, and into it he was en-

ticed and trapped.   My head Burman came to fetch me,
carrying in his hand a six-foot whippy cane.

At least a dozen Burmans were there to witness the
caning of this naughty schoolboy, as even Soe Bone's
own rider had no use for this tiresome game of chasing
people.

I was asked to give him the first twenty strokes.   And
what a behind it was to whip!   I went to his head first,
and showed him the cane.   He showed me the whites of
his eyes, as if to say: "Wait till I get out of here," but I
changed his mind for him, and he squealed blue murder.
Then everyone present, except his rider, was ordered to
give him half a dozen, whereas his rider was permitted
to stay behind and give him lots of tid-bits, after we had
all gone.

I saw him next morning being loaded with some light
kit as we were moving camp, and he looked rather
ashamed of himself.   Suddenly he saw me, carrying a
stick, and, instead of pricking his ears, as he did when he
was going to chase me, he gave one shrieking trumpet and
bolted into the jungle for his life.

Shortly afterwards I left him for another forest, and
did not see him again for fifteen years.   By that time he
was a magnificent beast of twenty-five, and quite docile.
I won't say that he had forgotten, but he had certainly
forgiven me.

One of the most remarkable incidents I ever had with
savage elephants concerned a young Shan woman of
about twenty.   I was sitting in my hut near the camp one
evening, very worried over a seriously injured spearman,
Maung Chan Tha, who had been gored that afternoon
by an elephant named Kyauk Sein (Jade-coloured Eyes)
while he was trying to save the life of the rider, Maung
Po Yin, who had been killed instantaneously by the
elephant, who had then attacked the spearman.   The
animal had gone on musth, and was at large in the
neighbourhood of the camp.

I was discussing with my head Burman how we were
going to get the wounded spearman away to hospital.
To put him on an elephant would kill him, as he had a

F

serious abdominal wound and a broken leg. To carry him on a bamboo stretcher to hospital would take five days, and was the only alternative.

Suddenly, quite unannounced, a tall, fine-looking girl walked into my bamboo hut, and I immediately recognised her as the widow of the dead rider. She was not wailing, or weeping, or carrying her youngest child, which is the custom on such occasions, nor did she kneel and sit before me, in the customary manner. She just stood erect and in a firm, unemotional voice said: " May I have a dismissal certificate from you for my husband Maung Po Yin, who was killed to-day by Kyauk Sein ? "

" Yes," I replied. " And your compensation, if you will wait till to-morrow, as I am busy arranging to get Maung Chan Tha to hospital." I added how grieved I was, and, in sympathy, asked her if she had any children.

My head Burman answered, instead of her, that she had none, and then, addressing her as though he were most displeased with her for coming to see me in such an unceremonious way, said :

" You can go now. I shall be coming back to the camp presently."

She moved quietly out of the room, a tall and graceful figure.

When she was out of earshot I turned to my head Burman and asked : " Is that Po Yin's wife ? "

" Yes," he replied, " but she takes more opium than Po Yin did, and that is the reason why she has no children."

I was very much surprised, as it was the first time I had ever heard of a Shan girl taking opium. I was even more staggered when my old Burman said in a quiet voice, " Give me ten ticals of opium to-night, and she will recapture Kyauk Sein to-morrow, because she has often caught him for Po Yin, when he was in a heavy opium bout."

I gave him the opium he asked for, but I went to bed that night with a very disturbed conscience. To add to my troubles, Chan Tha died before dawn.

I met my old Burman very early the following morning, but I asked him no questions, and waited to see what the day would bring forth.

By ten o'clock, however, he came to me saying:

"Kyauk Sein is coming in, with Ma Kyaw riding him. Come and look."

I could scarcely believe my eyes when I saw Kyauk Sein passing through the camp, with the Shan girl riding him, oblivious to everything, and her eyes fixed straight in front of her. Her long black hair was hanging loose down her back, and she wore her blue tamain girdled above her breasts, leaving her beautiful pale shoulders bare. Again I did not interfere, and by noon I was informed that Kyauk Sein was securely tethered to a tree, as is customary for elephants on musth.

That evening Ma Kyaw was brought to me, to receive the compensation due to her. She was dressed in her best, wearing a multi-coloured tamain, a little white coat, and a flower in her jet-black hair. She knelt and shikoed three times, and then sat down in front of me. She kept her eyes lowered, looking at the mat she sat on, and she toyed with a matchstick in her right hand, as though she were drawing something.

After paying her the compensation due to her for the loss of her husband, I gave her an extra bonus for re-capturing Kyauk Sein. When I told her this, I could see a wisp of a smile at the corners of her mouth. I then wrote for her a certificate, such as is customarily made out for all men killed in accidents. These certificates are for the benefit of the Jungle Nats, who require them before admitting the spirit of the dead rider to their domains. The certificate ran, "I hereby give leave to Maung Po Yin, rider of Kyauk Sein, to go where he wishes, as he has been dismissed from my service," and I signed it.

When I had risen from my table and given the money and the certificate into her hands, she wiped away two crocodile tears, did three shikos with her hands, got up and went quietly out into the dusk, back to the camp, three hundred yards away, on the other side of the creek.

I was only left guessing what the future developments would be for another twenty-four hours, for then, when I asked my old Burman about finding a new rider for Kyauk Sein, he told me:

"Oh, that is all arranged. Maung Ngwe Gyaw is an opium-taker, too. He has ' taken on ' (not married) Ma Kyaw, and they tell me that the biggest opium-taker of the lot is Kyauk Sein, the elephant. Another ten ticals of opium would be useful."

By that time I would willingly have given him twenty, if he had asked for them.

I do not believe to this day that the girl took opium, but she was a resolute character, and the elephant Kyauk Sein knew her well enough to take opium out of her hand. He probably knew the smell of her hand, because she was the wife of his rider. I think she completely stupefied the animal before she caught him.

The ways of the jungle are strange, but all is not savage, hard and cruel in it. For every savage elephant that attacks or kills his rider there are ninety-nine that are docile and friendly.

Chapter Eleven

I FIND it hard to realise now, after living for twenty-five years in the jungle with the most magnificent of all animals, that for the first three and a half years my eyes were blinded by the thrill of big-game shooting. I now feel that elephants are God's own, and I would never shoot another.

However, it was as a result of those three and a half years that I reached my present views, and because of my experiences then that I developed as deep a reverence for the jungle and all the jungle creatures as anyone possibly could.

Of course, the big cats are a nuisance. There are too many tigers and leopards in the jungle—so many, indeed, that the few which are shot make scarcely any impression on their numbers. Quite apart from seeing them, when sitting up for them in a tree over a kill, hoping to get a shot, the European Assistant almost invariably has some memorable incident in his career, when he sees tiger in more natural conditions. I once jumped into a creek, ten yards from a tiger that was lying down eating a freshly killed samba deer. He was magnificent. I could not jump back from the boulder I had alighted on to the bank behind me. For what seemed quite half a minute we stared at each other, and he snarled at me. Then he jumped up and, with the most graceful movements, bounded from boulder to boulder up the creek. He whoofed twice as he went, as though disgusted that the stench of a white man should interrupt his lunch.

Willie, whose reception of me when I first arrived in the jungle will be remembered, first came out to Burma in the early years of this century. Although he belonged to a good family and was a good shot, he arrived with very little equipment, for I fancy he had exhausted his father's purse and patience before he was sent East.

If he was anything like his son, Willie's father must have been a formidable disciplinarian in his day. On Willie's arrival he was at once invited to a big shoot, at which high jungle-fowl were expected. Poor Willie had to confess that he had not got a gun. However, as it was obvious that the lad was very keen, one of the party took pity on him and lent him a small-calibre rifle, saying it was possible that the beaters might put up some ground game, and that Willie might get a shot. He was told, however, that he must not fire in front of him towards the line of beaters, but must wait until the game had passed through the line of waiting guns. The first two beats were most successful, with numbers of high birds, which were brought down brilliantly by the guns. But poor Willie did not get a shot.

The third beat was a blank. Not a single jungle-fowl rose to meet the line of waiting guns, and the beaters were almost up to them and had ceased rattling their sticks on the bamboos, when there was the crack of a rifle, and Willie's neighbours were horrified to see that he had disobeyed instructions, and fired in front of him, towards the beaters.

"What the hell do you think you are doing, young man?" demanded "Growler" Moore, going up to him in a fury. "What on earth are you firing at?"

"I saw a tiger," said Willie.

"Tiger? What d'you mean, tiger? Don't talk nonsense!" shouted Growler, intent on ticking off the offender.

"Well, there it is, and it's dead," said Willie.

And there, twenty yards from them, was a fine tiger, with a bullet through its head. Willie could not make out why the other guns made such a fuss about it when they came up and inspected it, for he had assumed that tigers were a normal part of the bag in a Burmese jungle-fowl shoot.

Although I now dislike the thought of shooting big game, I can still recall, and live over again, the thrill when I was young enough to take any opportunity that offered which gave me even chances of life or death.

I remember how for two whole months I spent day after day near the mouth of the Manipur River, trying to get a solitary wild bull elephant—and every day was hard, and ended in disappointment. He was well known by the name of Shwe Kah, which my elephant-riders had given him.

These words are used to describe the pose of a Burmese girl's arms and hands when she is dancing: a pose in which the forearms and the hands and extended fingers are gracefully curved upwards and outwards. In the beautiful and perfectly symmetrical tusks of this wild elephant my riders had seen the same lovely upward and outward curve. Shwe Kah had gored two of my tuskers badly, and had continually worried my elephants. He was far too bold for the liking of my riders, particularly when they were catching their beasts deep in the jungle. Many of them had seen him, and they described the dimensions of his tusks outside the lip, by stretching both arms out horizontally, to show their length, and by encircling their legs above the knee with the outstretched thumbs and forefingers of both hands to indicate their girth. Some tusks!

I had numerous opportunities to bag other wild elephant at that time, but I was set on getting Shwe Kah. I saw him twice, but not in a position for a shot. I then went on leave for a month, knowing I should be back in the same area during May, the best month in Burma for big game.

If I got him, Shwe Kah would be my fourth elephant, and I had learned quite a lot about tracking and all that big-game shooting entailed. One night during my leave, a very pleasant Sapper Major joined our small party at the bar of the Maymyo Club (now no more). While we were chatting, he mentioned that he had just purchased a rifle from someone going home, and that he was more than keen to bag an elephant before he left Burma. It was a case of finding him somewhere where he could shoot. I did not like the description of his purchase. It was a magazine rifle with a high-velocity bullet, but on the small side. My opinion was (and is) that a double-barrel breech-loader 400–450 was the right weapon for Burma big game. This difference of opinion led to a hot argument, as it usually does, but we ended up such good friends that finally I said: "Can you get a month's leave, from the twenty-fifth of April, as I am going back for a tour of jungle camps, during which I hope to get some big-game shooting in my spare time?" He jumped at it, but, to make it quite square, I explained that I would do all that I could to put him on to the track of a decent wild tusker, but that it must be understood that Shwe Kah was to be mine only. This he fully appreciated.

He had never done any big-game shooting, and he was thrilled with the idea of the trip, even apart from the chance of getting an elephant. He was a man of thirty-seven. I was just twenty-six. I worked out that he might expect to get ten days' actual shooting, and that, with any reasonable luck, working from my little jungle headquarters, he ought to bag an elephant, and stood a good chance of getting a bison and other game.

He joined me on the appointed date, and we set off, poling up the Myittha River in a country dug-out. One evening we had a bathe after I had been out with a rod. While I was drying my feet, he said: "Lord, I wish I had feet like yours!"

Laughingly I replied: "Why, have you got corns?"

"No," he replied. "But I have eight hammer toes."

Looking at them, I saw eight tightly clenched toes, in spite of his feet being flat on the boat boards. I howled with laughter, and asked him how on earth he thought he was going to trek all day through the jungle. He was quite honest, and said he had hoped to sit quietly in one spot and wait for the game to go by. This rather damped my hopes that he would have any great success. But he was quite happy, as he was much enjoying all my routine work of inspecting elephant camps.

When we reached Sinywa (Wild Elephant Village), late one evening, I was told by my men that Shwe Kah was about, and had been seen the previous day, two miles away, on the other bank of the river. My shikar companion insisted on accompanying me the next day, without his rifle, purely to see what would happen. He had a morning which quite cooked him, but he saw two female wild elephants, and was thrilled to the marrow of his aching toes.

We eventually got on the tracks of a big tusker, which I imagined to be those of Shwe Kah. These led us back to the Myittha River bank, where it was quite obvious that during the night the animal had crossed the river, to the side on which we were encamped. It was then well after noon, and was sweltering hot. As we should pass near our camp, I suggested that we should have a cup of tea and something to eat there, and then continue our attempt to find Shwe Kah. My friend was all for the cup of tea and the cold Green Pigeon pie, but candidly admitted he was far too cooked to leave camp again, but said he'd excuse me if I went.

I had just eaten a first mouthful of pie when a Burman arrived to say there was an enormous wild tusker, believed to be Shwe Kah, not three hundred yards from their camp, a mile away from where we were.

Without any hesitation, I was off. No tea, no pie—I left my companion resting his weary bare feet on a box by our camp table. As I left, he graciously said: "I'll leave some pie for you."

By three p.m., under a sweltering tropical sun, I had got near enough to this wild elephant to hear an occasional flap of his ear. There was no other sound, as he was browsing in elephant grass, twelve feet high, through which I had ventured, following up his tracks. I knew that the river bank could not be far to my left, I knew only too well that if he were suddenly disturbed he would stampede back, direct on his tracks. I therefore decided to get off them into the tall grass on one side. There I rested my rifle against a small tree, and wiped the sweat from my face and brow. I took a quick swallow from a water-flask, as that was probably the last refresher I should get. I was determined to get a shot that afternoon.

I was suddenly alarmed by realising that my presence had been detected by the elephant, probably, as so often happens, by scent. There was a never-to-be-forgotten noise of the animal cracking the end of his trunk on the hard ground—it makes a sharp, clear, metallic, ringing sound, owing to the trunk being hollow. Then there followed that awful silence. I had no alternative but to stand my ground. Both of us were left guessing, but the elephant broke first, and made away from where I was standing, whereupon I made direct to where I imagined the river bank to be. It was closer than I had realised, and I reached it where the tall kaing grass grew to the very edge, which was eight feet high above the water, and had recently fallen in. The edge was unapproach-able without risk of further collapse, but not many seconds passed before I heard a tremendous splashing, and through the tall grass I saw a magnificent tusker elephant, crossing the river fifty yards below me, moving at a fast ambling trot, the splashes of water covering his body.

Without hesitation, I jumped down the eight feet, landing in three feet of water, but sinking into the mud to the tops of my boots. I was bogged. It was now or never for a shot. I decided on a heart shot, as he was moving quickly, water splashing, and I was unsteady.

Crack! He was quite seventy-five yards away when I fired. He stumbled a bit, recovered, and then swung round, like a polo pony, and came back on his tracks, not twenty-five yards below me. He was wild with rage—so wild that he did not see me. I was stuck, and had no hope of regaining the bank. As he climbed up, where he had slid down a few minutes before, I realised that he was mortally wounded, and noticed that his tusks did not appear as big as those of Shwe Kah, nor as tilted.

I gave him another heart shot, and there was no mistake this time. He collapsed stone dead against the top of the bank. Before I had extricated myself from the mud, my gun-boy, who had remained behind in a tree on the bank, went off to inspect him, and came rushing back to me yelling: "Amai! (Oh Mother) Amai! You have shot a Kyan Zit."

I was far too excited and occupied to appreciate what he meant. It was about half-past four in the after-

noon, and sweltering hot. I well remember my feelings
when I realised that I had not bagged Shwe Kah, as I
so much wanted his tusk as the trophy of my last wild
elephant. For I could not get a licence to shoot another
for a year. However, all my disappointment vanished
as soon as I saw the head of the magnificent beast I had
shot. For he was something very rare, and was already
causing great excitement among all the elephant-riders,
who had come rushing along from their camp.

" Kyan Zit! Kyan Zit! Kyan Zit! " was all they
could repeat as if one of the strangest myths of the jungle
had been proved.

I could not have been more astonished if I had shot a
unicorn. The words Kyan Zit describe a rare type of
elephant tusk, that has grown in rings or corrugations,
like the sections of a piece of sugar-cane. The Burmans
speak of such an animal as such a rarity as to be almost
mythical, but in existence, and they believe that a Kyan
Zit is a king of elephants, to whom all other elephants do
obeisance, in terror of his strength.

The tusks were corrugated, in rings, from the tip to
the lip where they entered the head; after they were
extracted the corrugations were found to continue, but
faded out gradually, right up to the socket and root. A
photograph of the tusks was afterwards published in the
Bombay Natural History Journal, but no explanation of the
cause of their formation was forthcoming. It was not a
malformation, as the rings were symmetrical in both
tusks. I have never seen comparable tusks amongst any
of the thousands of captive elephants I have known in
Burma.

I rested on the leg of the dead beast and had a drink
of water, and looked at him with a mixture of excitement
and remorse, and I asked myself what had the King of
Elephants with the Kyan Zit tusks done to me?—What
had I done to him?

Long discussions followed among the riders standing
round and admiring the rare tusks. A head man
arrived from camp to supervise their removal with small
axes and sharpened knives. Then the women of the

camp arrived with children and babies in arms, all to be shown Kyan Zit.

Up to this time I had not allowed any of them to touch him, as I knew that once those Burmans started on a dead elephant they combined the qualities of Americans after souvenirs and vultures after flesh.

I then heard someone yelling my name. It was my guest, who, on hearing my two shots in camp, had just hopped off his camp bed and, without waiting to put on his shoes, had come along, with two or three of the men from my camp. Hammer toes or no hammer toes, he wanted to see the result of those two rifle-shots. When he emerged from the tall kaing grass he nearly collapsed with surprise.

" Lord, how magnificent! " was his only remark, as he opened up his camera and took several snapshots.

Not till he had finished did I get the chance to explain that it was not Shwe Kah but Kyan Zit—and I explained the whole story, as we stood beside the tusks.

" Oh! I am sorry! " he exclaimed.

But I assured him that I was more than content. So pleased, in fact, that our next job must be for him to bag Shwe Kah, as he was now his game. My guest was beginning to be a little doubtful about having to take on anything the size of such a monster, but I told him he could borrow my rifle for the job, which seemed to relieve his mind a little.

I had not noticed that he was barefoot, until I suddenly looked down.

" Good Lord, man! Your feet will be blistered to hell! " I exclaimed.

So I sent back to camp for his shoes, and for tea and sandwiches for myself, and we settled down to supervise the removal of the tusks, taking also the hairs from the tail and one forefoot, as the Kyan Zit had the most perfect feet and toe-nails I have ever seen on an elephant. The toe-nails looked as though they had just been manicured, and the oil sweat-glands between the nails showed that he was an animal in his prime. The forefeet were perfectly circular, and my shikar companion was quite ready to take a heavy bet that twice their circumference was not equal to the animal's height at the withers. He was astonished when I measured it up and showed him that it was.

By this time the human vultures had started operations. Whole baskets of meat were carried off to camp, to be dried in the sun. There was enough to last them many months. It was my Burman hunter's perquisite to have the two aphrodisiac snips, which consist of the triangular tip of the trunk and the tip of the penis, also the big nerves out of the tusks, which are a native medicine for eye troubles, as well as a coveted aphrodisiac.

By the time we had removed the tusks and the forefoot it was almost dusk. More men and women from Sinywa village had arrived, to carry away meat. It was a really savage-looking party, with a lot of jokes and chatter. My Burman hunter came in for a great deal of chipping and cross-chat from the girls on the subject of his special perquisites.

As dusk fell we left them to it and went back to camp. Before we went to bed I had many things to tell my guest, as he was thrilled with all this, and was one mass of questions. The last thing he said to me, after I had done what I could for his poor feet by anointing them with Zam-Buk, was: "You know, I am so enjoying this that I don't mind if I don't shoot anything."

I had work to do the next day, and left my guest to watch my men cleaning the tusks and the forefoot for curing.

That evening news came into camp that there was a small herd of wild elephant feeding in a swamp area three miles from camp, and that it was more than likely that Shwe Kah was hanging round.

Next morning my guest insisted that his feet were not fit for marching that day, but I overcame his objections by saying we would ride an elephant of mine as far as the swamp, so as to have a look round, though I did not think it sounded very promising. The swamp was about half a mile wide—of tall, dense kaing grass, flanked on either side by fairly open jungle with big trees.

On the west side there were all the signs that the herd had entered the swamp during the night, and about half a mile to the north there were tracks of two solitary and separate bulls, which had gone in also. Either of these tracks might have been those of Shwe Kah.

We talked it over with my hunter, and agreed that very little could be done in this dense swamp area, but that if my guest remained on the west side, and we stampeded the animals from the east, he might have the luck of a novice in seeing a tusker pass him.

I explained everything, and placed my guest in the fork of a large tree, fifteen feet from the ground. His farewell remark was to whisper: " What a host! This is what I call a sitter." I left my rifle and gun-boy with him, and skirted the whole swamp on my own elephant, with an expert rider.

It was two hours before I got into position on the eastern side. I had warned my guest that he would have a long wait, and that he was to take no notice of any calling or talking he might hear. I moved up and down on the edge of the swamp, from north to south and back again, speaking as loudly as I could to my rider. Unfortunately, my elephant was completely silent as it strode up and down, as there was no fodder for it to snatch at whilst walking.

Presently I heard a wild elephant " chirping," at short intervals. It is a beautiful note of warning, rather than a signal of real danger, as though to say: " Keep in together. There are voices from the east side."

We halted our elephant for a short time on high ground, and from its back I could overlook the sea of kaing grass covering the swamp.

My elephant, Chit Sia Yah (Lovable), who was trained to stand a rifle-shot fired from his back, stood facing west, with his ears cocked forward, listening. He could hear something that we could not. Then my rider pointed to the sea of kaing grass, and said in a quiet voice: " See the grass tips moving. Wild elephant are closing in."

I was particularly anxious that they should move

west without any panic or stampede, so we remained perfectly quiet for fifteen to twenty minutes.

It was all most exciting to watch—there was silent movement without a sound. Here and there I could see the grass stirred, as though by a fitful breeze, though there was not a breath of wind.

Then from the very centre three or four elephants' trunks appeared above the sea of kaing. They kept moving from side to side in an uncanny fashion, like cobras poised to strike.

My rider whispered: "They have scented either you or the other Thakin on the other side."

Without hesitation, I gave a series of shouts, in which my rider joined. This left the herd in no doubt as to our position. One animal trumpeted, and then the whole herd began moving west towards my guest in the tree. It was like watching a silent, slow roller, as the herd moved in a body through the tall grass. One could see it going down, as they moved steadily, not in a stampede, but in an organised stream. Their leader had undoubtedly decided to leave the swamp, which was a small area and a poor hiding-place, as it was surrounded by open jungle.

It seemed an hour before they passed out of sight and hearing, but really it was only ten minutes. Then there was an overpowering silence, while we waited to hear a shot. Even my elephant seemed in a state of tension, and to be expecting it. I had very nearly come to the conclusion that all the elephants must have passed either to the north or to the south of my guest in his tree, when two rifle-shots echoed through the jungle. I began to move towards him on my elephant, when "Crack! crack!" came another couple of shots, shortly followed by two more.

I began to wonder whether my guest was having a stand-up fight with Shwe Kah, or whether he was shooting down the whole herd—males, females and calves—and was also wondering if there would be any rifling left in the barrels of my precious rifle!

Suddenly Chit Sia Yah, my elephant, pulled up,

motionless. I then heard, and immediately afterwards saw, a magnificent bull elephant with a pair of finely shaped tusks about three hundred yards away on my left, moving rapidly into the jungle behind me. I thought it was Shwe Kah, and that beginner's luck had not favoured my guest.

Complete silence reigned once more. The pageant was over as far as we were concerned on the eastern flank. But what was happening on the west?

I yelled and shouted to my friend, but could get no answer, although I knew he was within hearing. I was still uncertain if there were a wounded animal in the sea of kaing grass, and did not dare to take Chit Sia Yah through it until I knew. One thing I did know, and that was that my friend would not come down from his perch if he had only wounded an elephant.

Finally I could not wait any longer so, dismounting from Chit Sia Yah, I told the rider to wait till I called, and started to cross the swamp on foot, heading towards my friend. The going was fairly good, as it was the month of May, and therefore fairly dry, and the wild elephant had made a wide trail through the tall, heavy grass.

I occasionally halted and called, forgetting my rider would follow up, so I had a severe shock when he appeared behind me. I halted him, as I thought that if my guest had downed all the beasts he could in the wild herd, he was quite capable of finishing off his day's sport by shooting Chit Sia Yah by mistake. The track I followed was that along which the herd had avalanched, leaving a roadway fifteen to twenty feet wide through the kaing grass, as though a reaping-machine had gone through it.

Finally I came out, calling to my friend before I did so, and found him sitting twenty yards away in his tree.

" Why the hell can't you answer? " I asked him.

" You told me not to," he replied, adding: " But look out, I've shot an elephant."

I did not know what that meant, or stop to enquire, but dashed forward to the protection of the nearest big tree. From there, however, I saw a magnificent dead tusker on the edge of the kaing grass directly in front of my friend. The shape of his tusks left no doubt that he was Shwe Kah.

" He's dead, isn't he? " I shouted.

" I think so, but I'll make certain again," replied my friend, and gave the carcase another couple of rounds.

" For God's sake have some respect for my rifle," I shouted, and then Kya Sine, who was with him in the tree, called to me in Burmese :

" It has been dead nearly an hour. It must be cold by now, but he won't let me come down the tree."

I went up to the dead elephant, and saw the largest and most magnificent pair of tusks I have ever seen in Burma. My guest was so thrilled by all that had happened to him that he could not get it out, but Maung Kya Sine gave me a wonderful description. The whole herd of twenty-two animals had walked directly under their tree, and they had had a circus view of them. According to Kya Sine, my guest had the rifle at his shoulder the whole time, pointing it in turn at every animal with the least sign of a tusk. As the parade was coming to an end, Kya Sine spotted the back of an enormous beast which was following up at the tail of the herd, and indicated by nods and shrugs that my friend must wait. My guest had then dropped the rifle from his shoulder, thinking he had lost his chance, when this enormous tusker had appeared and halted with his head projecting from the kaing grass.

My friend dropped him first shot and wisely gave another. But, being determined not to let him rise again and escape, he began to try to get a heart shot. I had discussed this with him, telling him it was often more advisable than one through the brain. It was, however, an impossible shot from the angle at which he was up the tree. My gun-boy went back to camp on Chit Sia Yah to give the news, and soon the scene was the same as that we had watched two days before when I had shot Kyan Zit. My friend had quite forgotten his blistered feet and hammer toes, as we went back to camp. He spent the next two days with his trophy, while I continued my daily work. On his fifth day in camp I sent him off to hilly jungle, in spite of his feet, to see if he could find a bison. Before they left, my gunboy told me that he knew the whereabouts of a bull. They reappeared by noon. My visitor had again had the most phenomenal luck. He had come across a bull bison, which was lying down chewing the cud, like any dairy bull in an English meadow, and he had bagged him. I rather regretted this, as it would have given him a real shikar thrill if he had met the great beast face to face, for it stood five feet ten inches at the withers.

My visitor left me to return to his unit, in a country dug-out, piled high with elephants' feet, tusks measuring six feet two inches in length, a bison's head and two hoofs, not to mention all sorts of curios that he had collected in camp, such as elephant bells, rings and bracelets of elephant's hair, and bamboo gongs. He waved good-bye to me, with a smile spreading from ear to ear, and wished he might return.

He never came back, and with his visit my own biggame shooting came to an end. I never shot big game again, and never catered for others who might want to do so.

Nevertheless, though I dislike it now, I have no regrets in regard to those early years. For it was those years that laid the foundations of a love and understanding of the jungle and the elephants in it. I shot four elephants; but on the other side of the account is all I have tried to do for hundreds of their fellows. I fought for their wellbeing for years, and fought with them during the years of war.

PART TWO

Chapter Twelve

DURING the open season of 1925–6 I had to run a shoot for General Sir William Birdwood, as he then was, the Commander-in-Chief, India, and his staff on the Upper Chindwin River. I met him and his party at Sittaung.

Burma was at that time under India Command, but the significance of the Commander-in-Chief trekking into India from Imphal to Tamu on foot can scarcely be linked with the subsequent events over the same track, eighteen to twenty years later.

As far as I can remember, the trek took him five days, during which time he made every member of his staff swim in the coldest mountain streams imaginable. The track was then a six-foot ungraded bridle-track; it had, apart from any strategical importance in the future defences of India, a political interest, as at that time the question of the separation of Burma from India was very much to the fore.

Opinion in Burma was strongly against any development of this road to India. It was pointed out that a good road might serve as a backdoor entrance through which a flood of undesirable Indian immigrants might pour. It would be more difficult to control than immigration by sea. The road would have no value as a trade route, and it was concluded that it would be of no advantage to Burma.

The whole of the Burma Campaign from 1942 to 1945 depended on the existence of this route. For there are only two ways of reaching India from Burma—by sea, and by this, and one or two other mountain tracks leading from the tributaries of the Upper Chindwin into Northern Assam. In other words, there is an impenetrable mountain barrier running down the Burma–India frontier, which completely seals off the valley of the Irrawaddy from Assam; and there is no feasible coast road along the Burmese seaboard province of Arakan. Thus, to reach India from Burma overland, one has to go up the Chindwin as far as Kalewa, go up the Kabaw Valley to Tamu, and cross the mountains into Manipur and the Imphal plain.

The strategic importance of the road is therefore immense. But so long as it was believed that Britain had undisputed command of the sea, the strategic importance of the road was subordinate to the political disadvantages to which it might lead.

The impression I gathered from General Birdwood at that time was that he favoured the improvement of the road, as a strategical communication of great importance. He had enormously enjoyed trekking over it, as during the trip he had escaped entirely from the world of red tape and official receptions. He obviously felt as though he were a subaltern again on a month's leave. Lady Birdwood came by sea from Calcutta to Rangoon, and then proceeded to Mandalay, where she painted some water-colours, and later on joined her husband on the Chindwin.

The object of the shoot was to get duck and geese, and there was no question of big game or elephant.

I remained with the Commander-in-Chief and Lady Birdwood for two days, having at my disposal the Bombay Burma Corporation launch *Chindwin*, which had been suitably victualled. It made a very enjoyable break for me.

Little did I guess then that during the war years of 1942 and 1944 I should lunch informally with Lord Wavell when he was Commander-in-Chief, and dine informally with Sir Claude Auchinleck when he was Commander-in-Chief, on the same road between Burma and India.

The Japanese invasion was not the first time that the Kabaw Valley and the bridle-track from Tamu to Imphal had been a scene of war, and of all the miseries that go with it. As far back as the sixteenth century this route was used by the Burmese General, Ba-Yin-Naung, to lead his army from Burma to Manipur.

Again in 1812 the Burmese King Bo-Daw-Pa-Ya annexed the Kabaw Valley, after intervening to decide the succession to the throne of Manipur.

It is one of those valleys which impress one either as a miniature paradise or as a green hell. During the years I have lived there, in peace and in war, I have known it in both aspects. The Manipuris and Burmans look on it as an ideal grazing ground for their cattle and buffalo herds, during the hot and dry seasons of the year, when pasture has been dried up elsewhere. And in the cold season it is a sportsman's paradise. The wild jungle-fowl provide almost ideal high driven birds, and the gin-clear waters of its streams abound in mahseer up to eight pounds in weight. But in the monsoon it becomes a squelching swamp, generally overgrown by heavy unhealthy jungles.

In describing the withdrawal of the British Army in 1942, the Chief of Staff said that " death dripped from every leaf." That phrase might damn it for ever, but, visiting it to-day, one would not guess that his words had ever been true. Nor would one find many signs that the largest British Army of the Second World War, the XIVth Army, had fought its way down it.

In 1938 I was at home on leave and, as war seemed imminent, was for some time undecided whether I should return to Burma and my elephants. However, I finally made up my mind to go back, as I thought that if war did come, Japan would join our enemies, and that I should be of more use East of Suez than in the West.

With the outbreak of war in 1939, teak became as important a munition of war as steel, and all those employed in its extraction were regarded as engaged in work of national importance. Vast quantities of it were shipped to England during the first period of the war. When the Italians came in, supplies of timber were required in the Middle East. India's demand for teak alone was greater than could be supplied from Burma, and work in the forests was accelerated. Elephants were required for the extraction not only of teak, but of other kinds of timber as well.

After the Japanese came into the war, India's demands increased still further, and vast projects were put in hand after December 1941. Practically every officer concerned with teak extraction was away in the jungle in the three months which followed. Many of them were accompanied by their families. Their only link with developments in the war was by wireless. In spite of the rapid advances of the Japs, everyone was confident they would be held at Singapore and in Malaya. However, things were going so badly that a hurried warning was given by the Bombay Burma Corporation that it might, as a private firm, have to arrange for the evacuation of its European officers and their families from the Upper Chindwin into Manipur, and thence to Assam. A scheme for this was therefore prepared. If we had not had elephants for transport, it is unlikely that the scheme would have been put forward.

At that time I was on tour with my wife and family in the Shan states, right up the Shweli River.

By the same mail runner I received a confidential letter, strongly advising that all wives should return to headquarters, and a telegram instructing me to proceed to Monywa, on the Chindwin River, and to be ready to proceed beyond. I had no knowledge of the scheme for evacuation, but knew the country so well that I guessed what might be coming. My first thoughts, however, were that my instructions might be due to internal troubles in Burma. By forced marches with elephants to the river, followed by two days' voyage downstream in my own launch, we reached the Irrawaddy. I little thought that I was saying good-bye to my Shweli elephants.

At Mandalay I found that the conditions, to which one had become accustomed since the war, were unchanged. But all wives and children, except those who were members of the Women's Auxiliary Forces, had proceeded up the Chindwin. There was great tension, and the wealthy Indians were already on the move.

I was instructed to go direct from Mandalay to Monywa, but I decided to go first to my home and headquarters at Maymyo, for one night, to dump my camp kit and

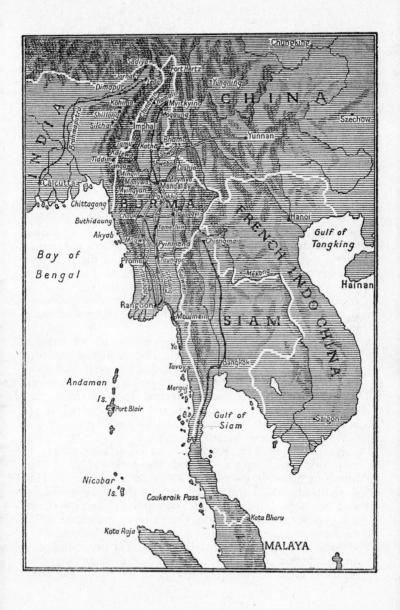

collect the light kit my wife would require while up the Chindwin. I felt sure that even if she were forced to leave Burma, I should have an opportunity of returning to Maymyo myself.

Even at this stage the trains to Monywa and the steamers to Kalewa were crowded by Indians. The Bombay Burma Corporation had been the first to move all the European women and children of its employees up the Chindwin, from which they could get a good start if the worst should happen. A few of the more far-sighted Government officials had privately made the same arrangements for their wives. The Government had formed no plans to deal with such an emergency. The Bombay Burma Corporation was severely criticised at the time for its policy of partial evacuation of women and children. But it had the excellent effect of stirring the Government to action, at a time when the situation was becoming grave. Quite apart from the fact that the policy of women and children first was the right one, it relieved the married men among the employees of their heaviest responsibility, and greatly increased their usefulness.

At Monywa I overtook the second batch of women and children. The first batch had travelled up the Chindwin River by launch, as far as Mawlaik, where it had been decided to assemble, to await a final decision. It had been my intention to return from Monywa, but when I reached it I was instructed to proceed to Mawlaik on the launch, in charge of the second party.

When I reached Mawlaik, and had handed over the party in my charge, I was instructed to stay there, to help organise preparations for the trek to India, via Manipur State, in case it finally became necessary. If it were decided on, I was to accompany the party of women and children with elephant transport. The elephants were not for them to ride on, but to carry their food and a minimum of camp kit and their personal belongings.

From that time forward the elephants began to play an important part. Geoff Bostock, the senior member of the Forest Staff up country, ordered all elephant

work in timber extraction on the west bank of the Chindwin, north of Kalewa, to be stopped, and the elephants
to be used to assist evacuation wherever possible. It was
February 1942.

Rumours had spread that a road was being hurriedly
constructed from Imphal to Kalewa, for the use of some
phantom army which was coming from India to check the
rapid advance of the Japanese on the Sittang River on
which we were falling back from the border of Malaya.
Some people believed these rumours. Work had in fact
been begun on the road, from the Kalewa end, and on to
Tamu, from where the ranges of hills towered up to the
west—an effective bottle-neck. Elephants were used in
road-making, dragging timber to the bridge sites. The
riders and elephants worked very hard for long hours, but
with great willingness, and were quite unperturbed by the
stream of Indians going past them.

Other elephants were being used to start a shuttle
service to carry aged and sick people from Sittaung on
the Chindwin to Tamu. There was a Forest Assistant
in charge at each of the temporary camps at which
they stopped on the way. Other elephants were being
used to carry up rations for the evacuee rest camps. In
the final stages the Bombay Burma scheme was handed
over to the Government, together with the Forest Staff
and elephants necessary for its operation.

The elephants and their riders continued on the work
until the end of April, after which date there was no water
left to water the animals. Those working on the Kalewa-
Tamu road stayed there, until the retreating Army in
Burma crossed the Chindwin at Kalewa, on its way out.

Our women and children were to reach Tamu by
forest paths, as I thought that it would have created
chaos to have travelled on the main track, with elephants
among the packed crowds of refugees. I left Mawlaik
with Bostock on 14 February, 1942, in charge of a party
of twenty women and fifteen children, with a train of
elephants. The second party, under Parker and Jones,
left with twenty women and twelve children, two days
later. There were, altogether, forty women, twenty-

seven children and one hundred and ten elephants. The reports sent us from Tamu were that it would be impossible to take elephants beyond that point. However, I was certain it could be done, even if it meant destroying them at the end of the trek, after we had reached the Imphal Plain.

In general, Bostock's job was to look after the women and children, and mine to manage the elephants. Both of us were married, and our families were with the party. Parker was also married, with his wife in the party, but Jones was a bachelor and, no doubt, glad to be put in charge of elephants only.

Fortunately, during the whole of the trek from Mawlaïk to Tamu, over the route we took, there was ample fodder. We were thus able to tie the elephants up by night, and their riders were able to cut enough bamboos, branches, grass, etc., to hand-feed them. The camps from Kalewa to Tamu were well off the beaten track, and were pleasant places for the women and children. For me they were rather a nightmare, as the elephants were continually breaking loose at night, and I felt the responsibility. We reached Tamu in six marches without any incidents except one bad stampede of elephants at night, when it was lucky no one was killed. The spirit of the women was remarkable, as every one of them had had to leave a comfortable home and abandon all her possessions at a few hours' notice. The novelty of roughing it in camp kept them from brooding over their misfortunes. Their chief worry was that their husbands were remaining in Burma, no scheme having been organised for withdrawing them, even with the Army. I got very exasperated on being told by several women that I was lucky to be in charge of them, and I found it more and more difficult to return a polite answer.

Tamu had become a congested bottle-neck, filled with thousands of Indians, all wondering how they would negotiate the next fifty miles, along a rough bridle-track, and over mountains five thousand feet high. During the one day we halted there I thought it necessary to throw out all the tuskers and proceed with only thirty-two female elephants, all of them between twenty and forty-five years of age. Kit and personal luggage were cut to sixty pounds per head, as sufficient supplies of food had to be carried. A head Burman was killed on our arrival in Tamu. He was standing ten yards from me at the time, taking an air-travel suit-case, covered with labels from voyages in more civili ed quarters of the globe, from an oozie sitting on an elephant's head, when the animal suddenly attacked him. I privately thought we were extremely lucky to have got so far with nothing worse happening, but the camp was greatly upset for the rest of the day.

From Tamu onwards the women became less talkative and their tempers more strained. However, I don't think any of the women in our two parties travelling on foot, but with elephant transport for kit and food, could describe the journey as anything worse than uncomfortable at times. For others it was a hellish nightmare, which became worse and worse as time went on.

I had many worries with the elephants, but the oozies remained serene. At one camp eight refugees had died of cholera and the elephants had to drop one thousand six hundred feet down from the ridge before they could get water. The women and children, however, camped on the ridge, although the ground had been fouled under every tree by the hordes who had preceded us.

We pushed on, although we were warned that it would be worse ahead. The warning proved only too accurate. The elephants were without water or fodder for thirty hours, except for twelve wild plantain stalks each, which were cut for us by some Lushai Chins from a Chin village. This just saved the situation. The elephants had to be tied up directly we reached our bivouac, and they could do no foraging for themselves. It was a big undertaking to have embarked on a sudden march, with women and children, without any rehearsal. However, every day things became better organised, and a routine was established.

Before dawn the children were pulled out of their blankets, and the camp resounded with their pathetic wails. They wondered why they were there, and what it was all about. Then, after they had been given some food, they set off on their long and weary trek with Bostock in charge. I remained behind, and supervised loading the elephants. When I had seen the last of the elephants fall into the line of march, I set off at a rapid pace, to overtake the party of women and children, and forge ahead to pick the next halting place about nine miles farther on. The presence of water was usually the reason for my choosing it.

On the third morning, when I was passing the party, and trying to make a cheerful remark to each family as it trailed along, my wife called me back, as though she had something important to say to me; but it was to show me something. In her hand she held half a dozen wild white violets. It was a tremendous thrill for us both that she should have found them growing at five thousand feet, among the mountains of Manipur, and for a moment we were able to forget all that this march meant to us, leaving Burma and our home. The sight and scent of those fresh, perfect little flowers was a wonderful stimulus to my morale, as I walked on up the line of straggling children. Some were singing, some crying. The track was narrow, and the sides so precipitous that it was easy to roll any dead who collapsed in their journey over the edge and down into the jungle. But a tell-tale stench lingered, and at such places mothers hurried the children on, leaving their questions unanswered.

At Tengnopal the country ahead to the saddle appeared a little less trying to the elephants; and the two young Assam tea-planters, who had just arrived to set up some sort of rest camp for the hordes of refugees, told us that things were not so bad ahead to Palel. It was, however, between Tengnopal and the saddle that the elephants met the first of the bulldozers, monsters which were to become their workmates in the months and years to follow. It was what was known as a D4, which had been sent forging ahead to reconnoitre the track which was later to become the Burma Road. We had all heard rumours that some phantom engine of war lay ahead of us, but late one night Major Murray Lees came to see me in our camp, in order to ask me what was likely to happen next morning, when his baby bulldozer encountered my train of elephants, going in the opposite direction. I was quite as scared that his bulldozer would make my elephants stampede, as he was that they would charge his mechanical pet and hurl it down the precipitous slope, or khudside, with their tusks. I was careful not to give away, in our discussion, that my fears were more realistic than his.

Since we seemed to hold equally strong cards, we compromised, and decided that he should start up his bulldozer at dawn and jockey it into a position which would allow my elephants room to get by. The track where it was working was the width of an ordinary single bed, and was cut out of the side of a precipitous slope.

I went ahead to have a look at my first bulldozer, and thought that if anyone ever deserved a knighthood it was the subaltern who was working it. I watched him for ten minutes, expecting that he would crash two thousand feet with every bladeful of earth, stones and shrubs his machine excavated and pushed over the edge. I found a spot where my elephants could pass round his machine, and work was stopped while they did so, leaving the engine idling. I have been informed that in one of the stages of D.T.'s the sufferer sees visions of green elephants with yellow braces. But I am sure that if elephants have D.T.'s, they see bulldozers. The look on the faces of both the elephants and the oozies riding them, as they sidled round this yellow-painted D4 bulldozer, with a British subaltern perched upon it like an oozie, while it blew out a blue diesel engine exhaust from its head, was that of sufferers in the most acute stages of D.T.'s, seeing things. When we reached the saddle, the roar of the larger bulldozers working up the hill could be heard, but we were able to avoid passing them, by dropping down to a foot-track to the plains from Sita. As far as the eye could see, it was marked by an irregular line of refugees, walking in single file, each with a bundle, or a child, on shoulders or head. From above it looked like a line of black ants.

We halted for an hour or so on the saddle, so as to get women and children well ahead. Eventually the word was given for us to push on, as within a few hours another larger tide of refugees was expected. I went ahead. I had been told that the track crossed many small ravines, which had been roughly bridged. There were dozens of them, and we had continual trouble in getting the elephants into the ravines and then out again, as the bridges were only made of the branches of trees, and none of them would have stood an elephant's weight. I watched all the animals pass alongside a particularly bad one, and as they went by gave orders that no one was to risk trying to cross over any bridge ahead. I then followed the last elephant, and stopped for a moment to speak a few cheering words to an unfortunate Anglo-Burman family.

Suddenly terrific yells and shouts burst out ahead of us, and, looking down the steep path, I saw odd refugees and stragglers jumping this way and that, bundles rolling into a ravine, and signs of chaos. Then I saw a riderless elephant, with its pack gone, coming up the slope towards me at a fast stride. Her ears were forward and she had an expression on her face which, I thought, meant that she was off back to Burma.

The path had cleared by magic, and I faced her alone, armed with an alpine stick fitted with a spearhead. I thought there would be an awful tragedy if I did not stop her, as there were hundreds of Indian women and children coming down the slope behind me. The valley below was ringing with shouts and yells. But she came straight at me, without hesitation, and only by hurling my spear at her and rolling down the khud did I escape being crushed. Only one of the deep narrow ravines behind me would check her.

I collected myself and my spear, and had regained the path, when I saw her come tearing back upon me at a high speed. Between us lay a deep, narrow ravine, which she must have crossed going up, though I had not seen her do so. To my amazement, I saw her " jump " it, with an action I had never seen an elephant make before, except a hobbled animal in slow motion. But there was no slow motion here. She was over the obstacle like a 'chaser over a brook, and I jumped clear of the track. I followed her down as fast as I could, and found she had been caught, and a batch of men were helping an injured oozie out of a deep ravine. He was in charge of the last elephant in the train, and it was obvious that he had disobeyed my orders, for fear of being left too far behind. He had tried to force his mount across the bridge, but she had refused, and had pushed it down with her forefeet, with the unfortunate result that the rider and pack went headlong into the ravine, while she kept her balance on the brink. Then, like a convict making a bold bid for liberty, she had stampeded up the hill, hoping to return from the barren hills to a land of bamboos. She stood quietly to be saddled, and went on with her work. She is the only elephant I have ever seen jump something wider than it could step across, but she must have hurt herself in doing so, as she went dead lame on both fore pads within two days. But by then the trek was over.

All the way to Palel, in the Imphal Plain, we could hear the bulldozers, coming up the new road they were cutting from that end. But was it for an army to march into Burma, or to help an army march out? The news from Burma was very grave. From Palel we were able to get motor transport to Imphal, but instead of destroying my tired and run-down elephants, I decided to march them back again, as there was more work for them to do. There was quite fair fodder and water for them near Palel, and while Bostock and I took the women and children to Dimapur, on the Assam Railway, the elephants had a well-earned rest for five days.

It was a relief to see the families off by the train on the Assam-Bengal Railway, and after we had waved good-bye, Bostock and I returned, against the tide of evacuees, to Palel and our elephants. The second party did not use elephants for the hill section from Tamu, but engaged Chin coolies.

The Assam tea-planters were travelling in the same direction, coming up with thousands of their coolies to help in constructing the road, while others were putting up relief camps for the increasing numbers of homeless Indian refugees.

We were asked if on our return journey we would take supplies, by elephant, for a projected camp for evacuees at Konkhan and build it when we got there. This we did successfully, and when we had completed it and stocked it with food we went back to Tamu and Burma.

The elephants all got back, none the worse for their journey to Manipur, and at once went on to help in the work on the Kalewa-Tamu road. The riders were still game to carry on, though by that time they realised that the fall of Burma was imminent and that India was threatened.

In this terrible upheaval big men became petty. I do not wish to blame anyone, for the struggle against odds was appalling. One night there were two thousand four hundred Indian refugees in Tamu, and only eight sacks of rice to feed them on. But the more I saw of men during those last days in Tamu in 1942 the better I liked my elephants. I don't want to criticise others, for I have no doubt I was criticised myself.

I made one final bid to get two hundred elephants out, but it was too late. I was told that if I had carried on with my plan I should have congested the one remaining walking-track for the wretched Indians, and so have caused even greater hardship and greater loss of life.

Mr Justice Braund, of the Allahabad High Court, did much stalwart work in those dark days, and in an article on the evacuation over the Manipur road said: " It was an affair of ' tea ' to the rescue at one end, and ' teak ' to the rescue at the other. But for the help of the planters, the Indian Tea Association and the men of the Bombay Burma, it would never have been possible."

There are few occasions in life when one is in such a

tight place that one is unable to help others. But I can record two incidents, which happened when I moved out for the last time as an evacuee myself. I left Tamu on 9 April, 1942, under a scorching midday sun, carrying all the kit I possessed, and leading a friend's faithful old Labrador—for I had lost my own dogs. As I turned a bend where the track took off for the first ascent into the Manipur hills, I found two sobbing little Indian children, a girl of about seven and a boy of about four. Against the bank lay an Indian girl mother, aged about twenty, dying of thirst, hunger, exhaustion and grief. I could do nothing less than give her a drink out of my water-bottle, and in her eyes I read gratitude and a terrible question: "What will happen to my children?"

While I was looking at her, in despair of doing anything, the change came suddenly, and a moment later I realised that I was left alone with the responsibility of these children, and that every man and woman coming up the road was fighting for his or her own life, and many of them would be lucky if they could save themselves. I could not carry one child, even if I were to leave the other. Something made it impossible for me to go on, and so I turned back instead. Providence came to my aid, for within a mile I met a jeep—one of the first jeeps we had seen on that road. It was being driven by a Staff Captain, whom I had met a few days previously in Tamu.

I stepped out in front of him, blocking the track, and taking the risk that he would drive over me or send me spinning down the khudside. But he recognised me, and pulled up. Then he greeted me with the words: "Can't be done, old chap. If I pick you up, I'll never get through, and I have to get over the mountains before dark."

I told him I would rather die by the roadside than be seen in such a car, or take the risk of being driven by him, but I begged him to take the two children, packed under his kit in the back, and to drop them at the evacuee camp at Imphal. I was determined he should take them, and I think if he had refused I would have tried to shove his car off the road, down the khudside. But he did not, and when I had loaded the two children and watched them being driven off, there was a lump in my throat. Then I plodded on after them with a lighter heart, while the noise of the jeep grew less and less. When I had crossed the mountains for the second time, I went along to the evacuee camp at Imphal, and found both children being properly looked after in the Orphan Section.

But before then I saw many heart-rending sights, when I could give no help. At one of the wayside camps, which would obviously be washed away when the rains broke, a young Anglo-Indian spoke to me. He was sitting in a ditch near the camp, with his wife and a little girl of six huddled beside them in a blanket. They all seemed ill, and had that look that one sees only on the faces of refugees and lost animals.

The man's voice sounded as though he were delirious with fever, as he asked me if I had passed a little boy of eight, lying dead on a blanket. Without waiting for me to answer, he poured out his tragic story. He had carried his son, who was dying of pneumonia, until his wife had collapsed and could carry the little girl no farther. Then he had abandoned his dead, or dying, boy, to carry the little girl and enable his wife to continue. He was haunted by the fear that the little boy wasn't actually dead, and might have been saved. By the end of the trek over the mountain both the man and his wife were casualties with pneumonia, and I discovered that when he spoke to me he had been describing what had happened to them five days before. So there could have been no question of turning back.

That road was full of tragedy and tears. But it was rapidly becoming a road. We met the bulldozers coming down, clearing a real road to Tamu, just in time to enable the Army to get out from Burma. When the elephants saw them they must have felt their day was over—but if so they were wrong, for they were needed in all the stages of the campaign.

The first army lorry reached Tamu from Manipur just before I started to walk out, and for a time the Army tried to clear the road of evacuees before the retreating troops arrived from Burma. I remember one big lorry passing me, loaded with forty people, and as it reached the bend I saw it fail to turn, and take a headlong dive, keeping upright for an amazing distance, before it was shattered on a tree. I went down to help. There were four dead and any number of broken arms and legs. This sort of accident was always happening.

When I was climbing to the saddle overlooking the Palel Plain, on my second walk out, a staff car going towards Tamu along the newly cut roadway pulled up. A Major-General got out, spoke a cheering word to me, and admired my Labrador. The wise old dog wagged his rudder and looked eagerly at the car, as if asking him to give us a lift. The General told his A.D.C. to turn his car round, at a perilous spot on the edge of the precipice, and took us as far as where the old bridle-track diverged from the new road, overlooking the Palel Plain. There the General dropped us with the words, " Au Revoir." His farewell words came true, for within six months I was serving under him in the Army at Tamu, when he was commanding the 20th Indian Division.

Chapter Thirteen

With the fall of Burma the demand for timber in India became of increasing importance, and I was employed until the end of October in making timber surveys in Bengal and Assam, and in helping to raise a labour corps for timber extraction, for the Assam Government. If I could have laid my hands on a hundred of my timber elephants, I have no doubt my war job would have been the extraction of timber in Assam. But I could not, and I felt a gnawing ache to get back to those we had left behind in Burma. I knew well that, once we advanced down that new road, elephants and their oozies would play a big part.

Luckily I was not the only person to think so. In October 1942, I had a letter from the General Officer Commanding, Eastern Army (which later became the XIVth Army), asking me to come to see him, in order to discuss elephants, my knowledge of the Chindwin forests and the topography of Burma.

I did so, and, at his personal request, I joined his staff as Elephant Adviser, though at that time the Army had no actual elephant for me to advise him on. On 8 November, 1942, I was posted to 4th Corps Head-quarters, then at Jorhat in Assam. I was quite a novelty at 4th Corps Headquarters. I could speak Burmese, I knew the roads, rivers and railways of Burma, I knew the Irrawaddy river area and, most marvellous of all, I knew the jungle tracks! Intelligence Branch secured a room in which to instal me, as a living ready reference library. No doubt they intended to allow me out for a breath of fresh air at stated intervals, but on one of these airings I greatly shocked them, and indeed the whole of Headquarters, by going direct to the Commander.

"Might I disturb you for five minutes, sir?" I asked.

"Yes, sit down. What can I do?"

" I want a jeep of my own, and I want to get down to Tamu to find out if there are any elephants not yet in the hands of the Japs."

I got my jeep within three days, a feat which had been regarded by everyone as an impossibility, but even that was easier than getting out of the clutches of Intelligence Branch. Eventually they let me go, on the understanding that I might be recalled at any moment to meet an important personage.

I was free again, this time with my own jeep, and on my way to Tamu I got in contact with the Forward Division Headquarters, and from the General Officer Commanding got permission to pull out Harold Browne, a great friend of mine. I had known Harold from his first days as a Forest Assistant. He was a South African by birth and a man of magnificent physique, with broad shoulders and narrow hips, Scandinavian blue eyes, and hairy all over, like a gorilla. On his arrival in Burma he had taken to the jungle like a duck to water, and he never minded the loneliness of the life; indeed, he often preferred to be alone, even when he was on leave, though at other times he threw himself into riotous parties and entertained lavishly. He was a man without vices, though certain of his characteristics almost ranked as such. One of them was always over-calling his hand at bridge or poker, another was an inordinate passion for crossword puzzles, and the third was that he was an impenitent practical joker. I remember at one gala dance at Maymyo he put sardine sandwiches into the handbags of all the women who were dancing, and had the audacity to sympathise with various girls who pulled them out when they stopped to powder their noses after that dance was over. He even went about saying: " Some awful cad must be at large." He had made the mistake, however, of putting one in my wife's bag; she instantly recognised his handiwork and exposed him. On a similar occasion he let loose an enormous number of mole crickets of the largest size in the ladies' room and on the dance-floor. They at once took wing and settled everywhere, exhibiting a particular fondness for seeking shelter for their silky bodies in the bosoms and down the backs of the girls wearing the lowest frocks. Panic reigned and modesty disappeared, as the girls' partners helped, with nervous fingers, to track down the bolder and more enterprising insects. Harold, however, had not waited to watch the results of his crime, but had gone off for a solitary moonlight swim.

Not long after he became my Number One officer he gave way once more to his propensity for practical joking. Part of his duty in forward areas was to pick up anything suspicious and send it back to Intelligence Headquarters for investigation. Sometimes when nothing turned up he used to scribble mysterious messages in Burmese on scraps of paper and plant them where they would be found and sent back. In this way he kept the wretched interpreters busy. But as these efforts produced no visible reaction, he came to me one day with a much-crumpled bit of paper on which something or other was printed in Japanese characters. I told him to send it back to Intelligence Headquarters, and he remarked with perfect *sang froid*: " I bet it will give that little schoolmaster who taught English in Tokyo something to scratch his head over." I had forgotten the incident when, about a month later, Harold brought me in a young Intelligence officer who had come up from Headquarters to speak to me. Unlocking an important-looking dispatch-case, the officer produced a sealed envelope, and from the envelope he extracted the scrap of paper printed in Japanese characters, which I recognised. I leant forward hoping to hear something of real interest. Browne, however, gave a howl of laughter the moment he saw it, and I then saw a piece of paper attached to it with the words written in red ink: " Advertisement for Eno's Fruit Salts. Ascertain who sent in this document." By laughing too soon, Harold had almost given himself away. In Burma bottles of Eno's used to be wrapped in an advertisement extolling their merits in various Oriental languages, and when he was taking an early morning dose, Harold had noticed that one of them was in Japanese. The Intelligence officer was more than suspicious, and I had to take the matter up on a much higher level than I should have liked before I could smooth it over.

It was difficult to talk to Harold Browne seriously, for though he was thirty-five years old he had remained a mischievous schoolboy who would not grow up. However, I did my best, and he regretfully abandoned manufacturing suspicious objects with which to plague Headquarters and pull the legs of the experts.

Harold Browne was one hundred per cent loyal to me as an officer and as a friend, and he would fight tooth and nail to secure fair play for our Burman oozies.

During the war the Kabaw Valley became his estate, and he was a wonderful host for the senior officers who visited my camp.

In the first months, before I got hold of him, Harold Browne had volunteered to remain behind as a liaison officer with No. 1 Brigade, and had done a sterling job of work for them between May and October.

During those months he was the only officer with a knowledge of Burma who kept in contact with the Kabaw Valley right down to the banks of the Chindwin. On occasions during his patrols he had used a few straggling elephants recruited with their oozies from villages to which the Japs had not yet penetrated.

During the rains of 1942 the Japs had not penetrated as far as Tamu even with patrols. At Lokechao we met the Headquarters of No. 49 Brigade, the then forward brigade.

Just before we arrived at Tamu, a young Anglo-Burman, named Goldberg, who had joined Civil Affairs, had accompanied a patrol to Auktaung, near Sittaung on the Chindwin, in an endeavour to make contact with a party of Burmese with forty elephants which, it was said, had been ordered to march to Mawlaik by the Japanese.

The headman at Auktaung turned out, unquestionably, to be working for the Japs, and he had ordered the oozies of these elephants to march them to Mawlaik. The officer in charge of the patrol—quite rightly, I think, in this case—showed him no mercy, while Goldberg, on his own initiative, went and talked to the Burmese elephant-riders. They were due to march next day, to join the Japs, but Goldberg, who knew many of them, persuaded them to march as hard as possible to the Upper Teelaung Creek and then head west for Tamu. There were more elephants than there were oozies, and it had been planned to leave these behind, if they had joined the Japs. But, on hearing that we should be at Tamu to meet them, the oozies' women volunteered to ride the riderless elephants and bring them along. They set off by night, and showed great boldness, as the oozies and their families ran a big risk of running into Japanese patrols in the jungles of the Teelaung Creek, which were a No Man's Land, but which Japanese patrols visited more frequently than ours did.

It was wonderful to be able to welcome these oozies in Tamu. This batch of elephants was the nucleus of what eventually became No. 1 Elephant Company, Royal Indian Engineers.

There was sufficient timber-dragging gear to equip twenty-five of them. Some of the others were trained calves under twenty, only fit for transport work, and the remainder were either thin and out of condition, heavy with calf, or with babies at heel, and would, from an Army point of view, have been better out of the way at that time.

Experiments had been made by an Anti-Aircraft Bofors Gun Regiment with an adaptable platform that made it possible to break the Bofors gun down sufficiently for transport on elephants. I was ordered to experiment and report on the type of gear necessary for loading it on elephants. It did not take long, for we found that the standard pack, known as the Siamese pack, would take the gun. It was also found that the Burmese oozies and their attendants could load and unload the elephants very quickly without assistance. The gun-crews did not, therefore, need training in loading elephants. A section of eight elephants took one gun, with the spare barrel, reserve ammunition and all the kit of the British gun-crew, without difficulty.

These experiments were not followed up. Had the necessity arisen, the elephants would have provided invaluable transport, for they could have negotiated the most precipitous forest tracks over the hills, where no mechanical transport could have been taken.

The elephants used in the experiments remained quite unperturbed seventy-five yards from where the Bofors gun was firing. This was the only foundation for a tale the Gunners told the Infantry—that we had plans to have elephants in close support of the infantry, each with a gun fired off its back!

A signal I sent to the Commandant Royal Artillery, that I was supplying a certain regiment of anti-aircraft gunners with " eight good weight-carrying females, for experiment," was interpreted in many ways, which I need not go into in detail. Such hopes were disappointed when the female elephants turned up.

At this early period an incident occurred which made my plans of getting in touch with my former elephant-riders in the No Man's Land between Mawlaik and Tamu far more difficult to realise. A patrol had gone down to Yuwa, unfortunately without Goldberg, and had shot the only village elder of any importance there, U Nwa.

This was a great blow, and a set-back to all my hopes.

U Nwa was a Burman, aged sixty, who had worked in the closest contact with Europeans engaged in teak extraction in the jungle for forty years. He was possessed of all the instincts of a gentleman. His name was known to practically every Burman from the Upper Chindwin down to Mandalay, and it was never mentioned without the word " Auza " cropping up, a word which is not easily translatable. " Authority with labour " is the nearest I can get. U Nwa was a born leader of the Burmans. He was always naturally at ease with Europeans, and was completely without any inferiority complex. At the time of the evacuation he was believed to be wealthy for a jungle Burman. He had twelve thousand rupees in the Provident Fund, and private savings in the hands of his wife, who was one of the leading traders in Yuwa.

U Nwa had remained quite unperturbed by visits of Japanese and British patrols to his village.

The only reason for suspecting him was that he had not fled into the jungle when a British patrol arrived. U Nwa was bewildered by all that had happened during the last six months, but he had never doubted our promise that we should return, and had been waiting patiently for someone to arrive. He came up to welcome the British, but, to his amazement, found that not one of them could speak Burmese.

U Nwa was tied to a tree at ten o'clock at night, and shot at dawn.

The effect of this action was electric. The news at once spread back to the Japs, who were employing jungle Burmans and elephants in every way they could, and of course it was a piece of heaven-sent propaganda for them.

But no time was lost in ensuring that the officer responsible got no more chances of going out with patrols. Luckily Tommy Thomas of the Burma Civil Service was at Tamu, and both he and I put in red-hot reports on the incident.

Only someone who, like myself, has had the difficult task of making contacts with the Burmese elephant-riders during the two years of stalemate on the Burma-India border can possibly realise the lasting consequences and repercussions of this disastrous beginning to our work. The dearth of Burmese-speaking British officers in forward areas in those days of late 1942 and early 1943 was a tragedy. It was due to the disastrous " reconstruction " organised in the Simla Hills, which took away many qualified men from where they could be most useful.

A journalist who visited Tamu in November 1942, described it as " a city of the dead," but in reality it was a jungle village, in which hundreds of private cars, lorries and buses had been abandoned by refugees, since the road came to an end, and they could take them no farther. When I had last seen these cars they were all empty, and their owners were struggling to climb the mountain side.

But now, when I came back, I saw that these abandoned, derelict cars were filled with grisly figures, unbelievably emaciated, with rags still clinging to them here and there. Some sat rigid in the seats, some were tumbled into shapeless heaps, some were bent, some bowed, some sat behind the steering-wheels, gazing through the windscreens from the empty sockets of their skulls.

These were our rearguard from Burma, unfortunates who had reached Tamu after the withdrawal of our Army, when the monsoon had broken; unfortunates too worn out to tackle the mountain crossing in the floods and without food; unfortunates who had no hope left and, unable to find other shelter from the torrential rain, had climbed into the deserted cars and died in them, six months ago.

One landmark which stood in Tamu for some time, untouched, was a military ambulance, with four stretcher beds, each with a skeleton lying on it. Something had gone wrong with the engine, and the retreating Army had abandoned it, transferring any casualties it may originally have carried. Four poor wretches had found shelter in it, and perhaps had even felt that they were luckier than their neighbours, in being able to lie down, at full length, on well-slung stretchers to die.

Harold Browne eventually rid us of that gruesome reminder of the previous summer, by setting fire to it. He made away with hundreds of similar ghastly sights, all along the trail, by the same method.

In such surroundings we pitched camp at Moreh, close to Tamu, to wait for the coming of a new army. Occasionally we saw one of our patrols going out.

Almost every day representatives of all sorts of different Army services visited us, but all of them had to return to their headquarters at Imphal every night. One of the first to arrive was the Commandant Royal Engineers of the forward division, who called on me at our camp at Moreh to ask if we could help with elephants, to drag a few logs, and assist the sappers in building a bridge over the Lokechao River at Moreh, as a brigade was to move forward, but could not possibly do so until it had been bridged. I replied that of course we could, but asked what kind of bridge did the sappers mean to build, and where were they? Blue prints, pink prints, and even white prints were produced from a pigskin portfolio. My first impression was that I was being shown a design for the new Ava-Mandalay bridge! All these plans were merely to cross a river four feet deep and two hundred feet wide, full of fast-flowing, clear water. He told me the sappers would not be able to get up for some time, as they were busily engaged on a hill section farther back, but that timber was required in readiness.

I picked up a pencil and drew him an "elephant bridge," and after making a rough calculation of the number of logs that would be wanted and the number of elephants available, told him it would take me fifteen days to complete it without any assistance from the sappers, and that it would take anything in the Division on wheels or tracks.

"What class will it be, and what width?" asked the officer.

"First class, and twelve foot wide," I answered.

"No, I mean what tonnage vehicle will it take? The Chief Engineer wants it to be twenty-two foot wide."

"What is your heaviest load?" I asked.

"About ten tons."

"Well, I will guarantee it will take a twenty-ton load, and you can tell the Chief Engineer that he can't have it twenty-two foot wide. When we've finished this bridge, we'll build another one for vehicles going in the opposite direction. In any case there would not be enough timber for a twenty-two-foot bridge at the site you've chosen. But we'll find another site nearby, for the second bridge. Moreover, Indian drivers are safer if they have a bridge to themselves—from what I've seen of our lorry-drivers, we shall do better without two-way traffic over rivers."

The Commandant Royal Engineers put his plans away reluctantly, and was obviously somewhat doubtful about these new methods of bridging rivers. Then he said, "It's O.K. by me, but I must be getting back, and will see the Chief Engineer and let you know the day after to-morrow."

Before his jeep was out of earshot I was giving orders to my head elephant-man to arrange for the felling and logging of trees, four to six feet in girth with boles twenty-five feet long. All the riders were to make dragging harness for twenty-five elephants.

Browne had the work under way before ten o'clock next morning.

Shortly after this the Brigadier of the 49th Brigade arrived to have a look at this circus camp in front of him. He had come out of Burma, in command of a Scottish regiment with the Burma Army. I explained the whole thing to him, and he cheered me up a lot by saying: " Don't worry a damn about anyone. Build your bridge, and if the sappers want another, they can build another." It was then the second of December, and he told me confidentially that the bridge would be needed by the nineteenth.

Actually the whole of his brigade transport passed over that bridge on the fifteenth. The elephants were of great interest while they were building this bridge, and many visitors to Tamu came forward to watch them.

On 20 December, much to my annoyance, I received a signal to return to Corps Headquarters at Jorhat in Assam for another conference on the carriage of Bofors guns on elephants. This started up another war on the subject of whether elephants were transport or bridge-building animals. Fortunately, on Christmas Eve I went into the Planters Club at Jorhat, and there I met Stanley White.

He was, until the war, a River Captain of the Irra-waddy Flotilla Company. His job, buoying the Chind-win River, brought him into contact with the Bombay Burma staff. Our Forest Assistants often travelled on his launch, and he shared their interest in jungle life, and, as he was a very keen shot, joined in all the shoots up and down the banks of the river.

White and I were often referred to as " the long and the short of it," as White was not more than five foot four inches high. He was a powerfully built, square-shouldered little man who could keep up with the best of us on a long trek. He delighted in dressing himself up like a Christmas tree, carrying a gigantic rucksack, with an enormous revolver-holster hiding half of one side of him, and an outsize in jungle knives bumping up and down in its sheath over his fat little stern. White always walked like a sailor, with a salt-sea roll. He was a typical Scot, with a sense of humour which sparkled in his blue eyes. He had a very large fund of general information, and if by any chance there was something he did not know, he could bluff so well that he was seldom detected. I once heard him telling an innocent Colonel in the Royal Veterinary Corps how to castrate an elephant, and White was so glib and so convincing with his nonsense that I was quite impressed myself.

He spoke fluent Hindustani and good Burmese, and was thus a very useful interpreter at Corps Headquarters. During the evacuation of Burma and the final period of " scorched earth," White did a great job in scuttling launches up and down the river. He was naturally intensely eager to get back to his river, and soon after joining me became known to everyone as " Chindwin White."

I had not known him particularly well before the war, but we had many interests in common, and as he was a great friend of Harold Browne's, we soon became as inseparable as the Three Musketeers.

White shared the greater part of the rest of the Burma Campaign with me. We sometimes got separated, but, as he was exactly the man I wanted, I left no stone unturned to get him back on the job I knew he could do best. I got the very best out of him, and he stuck to me.

Harold Browne and Chindwin White made a grand team. Their intimate knowledge of all Burmans was extraordinarily useful.

They had the same love of practical jokes, and had one trick in particular, which they often brought out if they thought it would perturb some visitor to our camp.

They would start an argument in Burmese, which at first amused visitors who did not understand a word. Then their faces would grow grimly serious, and English words would creep into the dispute—unpleasant English words and phrases which are not often employed by one man to another. For they translated freely the foulest Burmese abuse of each other's families and particular relatives.

One night they started this, after having several drinks, and, though I had heard them at it before, it seemed to me they were getting a bit hot. They were sitting on opposite sides of a long bamboo table with a hurricane lamp in the middle. Each was holding a tin mug full of rum and limejuice in his hand, and they took turns, one sipping his drink and glaring over the top of his mug, while the other treated him to the foulest abuse.

Suddenly Chindwin brought out a grossly offensive remark about Harold Browne's sister, and I felt he had gone too far. Mothers and aunts are fair game, but I felt this remark about Harold's sister was beyond a joke —and Harold seemed to think so, too, for he dashed the contents of his mug in Chindwin's face. There was a dead silence, and Chindwin sat for a moment with his eyes tightly shut, while the precious rum and lime-juice streamed down his face. Then he suddenly flung the contents of his mug in Harold's face, and, grabbing the hurricane lamp in his other hand, swung it at Harold Browne's head. There was a crash of broken glass, and the lamp went out. I felt sure Harold had been badly hurt, but peals and peals of laughter came from them both as they sat in the darkness, and a convivial evening followed after we lighted up again, much to the relief of our visitors, who had thought that they were witnessing a very ugly scene.

Chindwin White always tried to give the impression that he thought everyone he met was a bloody fool, but he had most loyal feelings and a real respect for anyone who really knew his job, and for such people he would work his fingers to the bone.

When I met him at Jorhat he was a round peg in a

square hole, and he pleaded that the obvious place for him was with me up at Tamu.

I much enjoyed a convivial Christmas Eve with him, but on Christmas morning I decided that Intelligence Branch would be a useful lever with which to extract him from his square hole. I put it up to them, and got the answer: " The very man we want immediately."

Within an hour I had got him into my cage, and we were busy on a job of work passed on from the Commander. This kept us busy for half Christmas night, but we finished the bottle and finished the job about simultaneously, and then sang a carol. White was soon christened " Chindwin White," while I was commonly known as " Sabu," which changed later on into " Elephant Bill."

Chapter Fourteen

My one idea was to get away to Tamu again, taking White with me. This led to another battle with Intelligence Branch. It ended by my telling them that the only information I possessed which might be of use to them was the female elephant's period of gestation. I have reason to believe that they took this personally, as an obscure reflection on themselves.

On White's being asked the depth of the Chindwin River opposite Sittaung, he replied that it all depended whether the tide was in or out; at which a young Intelligence Officer exclaimed: " Oh, is it tidal up there? " As Sittaung is fifteen hundred miles from the nearest tidal stretch, the innocent question gave us an advantage which we pressed. However, we remained friends with them, and for a long time we made use of the Intelligence Office as a haven whenever we visited Corps Headquarters.

I think that even Intelligence Branch would admit we gave them some valuable information, which was lost or mislaid a dozen times, before it was eventually made use of three years later, by which time an elephant cow might have had a second litter.

I was just about to get away when the Commander sent for me and told me he wanted me to stay on at least another two days, as a visiting Brigadier wanted to see me. I suggested that White should also be called in, if any information about crossing the Chindwin were wanted. I was told I might take him with me if I liked.

On 3 January, 1943, I was told to wait in the anteroom of the Commander's mess at nine o'clock. White was with me. The mess was empty, and I had just picked up a magazine when a sullen-faced Brigadier came in, wearing only one ribbon—the D.S.O. and bar.

He threw his hat into a chair, and said, as though he were angry:

" Are you Williams? "

" Yes, sir."

" Well, come on. Have you got the key of the War Room? "

" Yes," I replied.

With that we moved off to the Commander's War Room. The Brigadier went in first, and, as I followed, White gave me a dig in the ribs from behind, from which I gathered that he guessed that my reaction had been that I was not going to be bullied.

Wingate, the name of the Brigadier, at that time meant nothing whatever, except to those of the Higher Command. He kept me for two hours, standing in front of a very well-illuminated wall-map, on a scale of half an inch to the mile, and he stood directly behind me, with a pointer in his hand. His questions were abrupt, and my replies equally so. He had ignored White, with such rudeness that whenever he put a question concerning the Chindwin River I turned round and asked White to reply.

Wingate's manners were almost intolerably aggressive, but within an hour I was deeply impressed, and within another half-hour I was completely absorbed in what was obviously the general plan. I felt that if I did not go with him, the whole damned shooting-party would get lost in the Burmese jungles within a week. Most of it was.

Part of that story is told in Bernard Fergusson's beautiful book, *Beyond the Chindwin*.

While I was being questioned in detail, on jungle, streams, mountains and valleys, and my answers written down, I was making up my mind what I would reply if I were asked to join this wild-cat expedition, as I fully expected to be at the end of the interview. But the question never came, and I only afterwards found out that Wingate had been told that he could not have me, and that I was to continue with my job as Elephant Adviser, which lasted throughout the Burma Campaign.

The thing which impressed me about Wingate was the thought behind each of his questions. Pointing to some high ground on the map—a hill I knew—he would ask: " Could troops live on that hill during the monsoon, and make it a strong-point, if they had to? "

" All depends how many, sir. It is practically impossible to dig in, as it is mostly solid rock, only covered with very sparse jungle. It might water twenty-five men, but no more. Mules could not get up and down."

" Could mules get down that creek? "

" Definitely not. Elephants could. But mules could take this ridge away to the east, by following Forest Department boundaries."

" Right. I want that information later."

Before he went away, leaving us to lock up, I asked him if he was likely to require any elephant pack on either side of the Chindwin. A decided " No" was his reply.

White and I went off to Tamu next day, and discussed Wingate for most of the way.

When we got back we found that during our absence Browne had completed three more bridges—one going north to Myothit, one south to Witok, and one east towards Sittaung. White was to go off on a reconnaissance to Sittaung. By the end of January, 23rd Division had its Headquarters at Moreh, near Tamu. I found that the Brigadier of 49th Brigade had laid out Tamu and its surrounding roads and bridges, and had named our first bridge " Williams Bridge," and the second " Browne Low Bridge," with large placards bearing their names beside them. They stayed there, and the names stuck. Even the local Burmans used them, but I found it embarrassing. Later that season I saw Wingate's columns pass through Tamu. A personal friend of mine, Peter Buchanan, was with one of them. His exploits are recorded in *Beyond the Chindwin*.

Unknown to anyone but him, I arranged for elephants to help his party over the Tonhe track, to clear it for mules, and I provided twelve pack-elephants to help him as far as Tonhe. His was the only Wingate column that got its complete equipment as far as the Chindwin.

Wingate's own column got half-way from Tamu to the Chindwin, and came across a Burman, Maung Chit Gyi, building a bridge, with four elephants. He ordered him, at the point of his revolver, to remove their harness, and then loaded them up with everything that he would otherwise have left behind. Sticky bombs, boxes of grenades and other heavy equipment were tied on anyhow with rope. These four elephants did the journey to the Chindwin, with far less trouble than the mules, and Wingate was so satisfied that he swam them across the Chindwin with their full loads on. One badly loaded animal overturned in deep water, and was lost.

However, he had not gone far on the other bank when, greatly to his surprise, he received a signal ordering him to send my elephants back. One went astray, and only two came back with Maung Chit Gyi. However, the stray one eventually swam across the Chindwin on her own, and rejoined her companions, with a fine story of adventure, if she chose to tell it.

Wingate only used one or two stray elephants on the east bank of the Chindwin during that campaign. In fact, his column came across very few, and gained no information concerning the herds left behind.

Two months later, parties of Wingate's expedition were recrossing the Chindwin, north of Yuwa as far as Homalin.

Malcolm Freshney, returning with his party—which included some Karens, who had come out with the Burma Army in May 1942—met two Karen elephant-riders in dense jungle, about fifty miles east of the Chindwin. They said, when questioned, that they came from an elephant camp with twenty-nine elephants and forty-nine Karens, who were in hiding from the Japs, and that they had been there for six months. The Karens are a particularly loyal hill tribe. These two men were very friendly, were Christians and very pro-British, so Freshney decided to spend a night in their camp. There were two English-speaking Karens amongst those at the camp, and in the course of conversation they told Freshney that they had worked under me in the Moo and Shweli

Forests. When he told them that I was at Tamu, three of them asked to join his party, as far as Tamu, so that they could see me.

He brought these three Karens along, and they were of immense importance to Intelligence Branch. One of them had travelled since the Japanese invasion as far south as Toungoo between Mandalay and Rangoon, in Lower Burma.

The Divisional Commander then gave help, in providing an escort to return with these men to their camp. I knew the country well enough to plan their route there and back when they would make an attempt to bring their elephants back to us across the Chindwin, and through territory occupied by camps working for the enemy.

Two young officers who knew Burma—Jonah Jones and Robin Stewart, both in an Intelligence Branch—reached Tamu at that time, and they both volunteered to go with the Karens and make the attempt. Browne was unfortunately not in camp at the time.

Wingate's expedition had, of course, stirred up the Japs, and their patrols were becoming increasingly difficult to elude, for they were following up tired parties of Wingate's men, or trying to intercept them during their withdrawal.

Stewart and Jones covered the fifty miles on the other bank of the Chindwin in two days, relying on their own irregulars, and leaving the escort party half-way, to cover their rear.

I had asked for two platoons to cover the Chindwin crossing, as at that time Pantha was occupied by the enemy, and our crossing was to be made just above Yuwa, at Kadun. Jones and Stewart performed a remarkable feat on the return journey, marching twenty-nine elephants, with forty-nine attendants and their irregular escort, fifty miles back to the Chindwin in two days, reaching the river at six p.m. There were no women with the party. Jones reached the river a few hours before the main body, and met a small party of Burmans, which was obviously a Japanese agent's scouting patrol from Pantha. They did not engage, but made off south towards Pantha. White was in charge of eight Lundwin country boats, for ferrying the escort and men. The two platoons of troops which were supposed to cover the crossing had not turned up. There was only a section of Indian troops, which was obviously considerably rattled. The forty-nine Karens were unarmed.

From the time of arrival until dark every effort was made to swim the elephants. But the animals were all too dead beat from their march to face the swim, and not one leader could be found among them. A decision was eventually made to tie up all the elephants on the east bank and to ferry all personnel across and sleep on the west bank. The expected platoons to cover the crossing had still not arrived.

All was quiet on both banks of the river during the night. At dawn White set off with his eight boats full of oozies and a small escort from the west bank to the east. Now that the elephants and men had rested, there was no doubt that they could cross without difficulty. White was in the leading boat with the head boatman holding the paddle-rudder, and two other Burmans rowing. The other seven boats were strung out at irregular intervals, and packed with Karen oozies.

When White's boat was about seventy-five yards from the east bank, a Japanese officer rushed on to the bank shouting, " Banzai! banzai! " and then took cover behind a tree. At the same time Japanese machine-gun, rifle and mortar fire opened on the boats. A few shots were fired in return, but several of the leading boats at once capsized, and within two minutes everyone was in the water. Three sepoys and one Karen were killed, and two Karens were wounded. Everyone else swam successfully back to the west bank. White considers that he owed his escape to the Japanese concentrating their fire on his topee, which floated away downstream, whilst he was swimming under water. He had never realised that a man could hold his breath for so long. The Japanese had been brought up from Pantha during the night and, finding our elephants unattended, had laid an ambush for the morning.

The Japanese showed great folly in not holding their fire. If they had waited until the boats were ten yards from the shore not one man of the party would have survived. Their shooting was also extremely poor.

It was not until 1945, after our general advance down the Chindwin, that I heard the true story of the fate of these elephants.

A dacoit Burman from Pantha, who was with the Japanese, and was one of their agents, told them that as they were Karen elephants, no Burman would risk unchaining them. He therefore advised shooting them for their ivory. Fourteen were shot before some Burmans arrived, who said they could manage the remainder, all of which were young animals. Only one of these was eventually recaptured, after the Japanese had been finally defeated.

The whole incident, which with better management would have succeeded, was most unfortunate. I may add that it did not end there for those who should have provided the platoons to cover the crossing of the river, and had not done so.

Seventeen elephants were captured during the hot weather of 1943, bringing our strength up to fifty-seven animals. They were first employed in building bridges along the three roads in the Kabaw Valley, and later in making these bridges double width. By that time the elephants had established their reputation in the military mind as bridge-builders and road-makers of immense value.

There were patrol clashes with the enemy throughout the hot weather. We had only two brigades guarding the gateway from the Kabaw Valley to Imphal, so they were rather thinly spread out over the ground. Straggling parties of Wingate's columns were still coming back, through the screen of the 23rd Division, protecting the Tamu-Imphal road. The Japanese had been becoming more aggressive farther south, from Kalemyo up towards Tiddim in the Chin Hills.

The Mango showers of April gave the troops some idea of the effects of rain in the Kabaw Valley.

The 17th Division of the Burma Army on their withdrawal up it, the previous May, had nicknamed it " The Valley of Death," because they were following the tragic trail of refugees, who were dying in hundreds along the road from exhaustion, starvation, cholera, dysentery and smallpox.

But the name stuck, and had an unfortunate psychological effect upon the health of the troops holding it later on. Actually malaria was no worse in the Kabaw Valley than in any other forest valley in the wet zone. But it had gained an evil reputation, and did not live it down until the 11th East African Division went down it, before the end of the 1944 monsoon, and showed that it could be faced with impunity, even in the worst weather.

I was living in our established elephant camp at Moreh, but I made periodic visits to Corps Headquarters in Assam. As a result, I was one of those who were kept informed of the general position. Only those who have had the experience of keeping up the morale and confidence of their men when privately aware that we were carrying out a strategy of mere bluff, which might at any time collapse, can understand the difficulties and embarrassments I went through at this time. In May 1943, I was called to Headquarters and told to write an appreciation of the elephant situation if all troops were withdrawn from the valley before the monsoon broke. My appreciation was expressed in very few words:

" The elephants must remain in the valley, and Browne and I will stay there with them. All we need is six months' rations for the riders and ourselves. We will keep the elephants ready to make their escape to Imphal, if the Japanese patrols come up far enough to threaten us."

The value of the elephants when our troops re-entered the valley after the monsoon was over was fully realised. But I was not willing to take them out and upset the morale of my Burmans, by making them take part in another retreat by our Army. I was also doubtful whether I should be able to get the elephants back again at the right time, as directly our Army started to come back, the road would be packed with faster mechanical transport.

My proposal met considerable opposition, but I eventually got it sanctioned, and was told to make my own arrangements. Luckily I had plenty of time, as the withdrawal of the 23rd Division had not started.

Just at this time the inhabitants of Tamu and the surrounding villages in the valley gave a celebration pwai to welcome the return of our Army. They had been a little slow in organising it, and, unfortunately, had timed it when we were on the point of abandoning them again. After I had taken an extra tot of rum, I danced with the Minthami, or Princess of the Show, and towards the end of the evening U Po Sine, my head elephant-man, was presented with a beautifully engraved sword by the Commander of 23rd Indian Division.

It was a great night for the Burmans, and a cheery one while it lasted, but I went to bed with the bitter knowledge that the valley would be empty of troops again within two months, at most. As it fell out the withdrawal was delayed for a fortnight owing to events to the south-west, in which the 17th Division was involved. The monsoon broke early, and caught the 49th Brigade still in the valley at Witok. Within two days all motor transport was bogged. There was a small break in the rain, and then the vehicles were able to start crawling back. But they could never have done it except for my elephants. All along the road there were urgent requests for help, and the elephants were pulling the army lorries out of the mud like champagne corks out of bottles. Two or three lorries were wrecked owing to drivers starting up their engines, in order to help the elephants, by spinning the back wheels. But they found themselves and the lorry being taken for a fifty-yard stampede into the jungle, ending up with the lorry hitting a tree or over-turning, or the elephant's chains snapping and releasing him from the jungle devil he was towing.

Besides pulling lorries out of tight places, the elephants

laid causeways of logs in the mud in amazingly quick time, while whole convoys waited to pass over them. Elephants could not be hurried in their work, but they could, and did, work overtime until the job was finished. After seeing the last vehicle over the Moreh causeway, the Brigade Major walked along the logs to tell me that all the motor transport were out.

The elephants were standing near, in the fast-fading light, and gazing, with what I thought was bewilderment and disgust, at this new kind of jungle demon, the motor lorry. What the oozies thought of the withdrawal of our Army, I don't know. All I could tell them was that Browne and I were staying behind with them.

Those really were, I think, the bloodiest rains that two Europeans ever weathered in Burma. There were weekly Gurkha patrols through our camp, and elephants were used throughout, on a shuttle system, to get them across that quagmire of a valley. The Gurkhas were grand little men, but, fit as they were, they often came back after a patrol of anything from eight to twelve days staggering with exhaustion and fever. No quinine or mepacrine was being issued to them at that time, owing to the mistaken order that only a doctor could administer it!

Our elephant camp was the first camp they reached on their way home, and for the last three marches they always rode elephants. The sick men had to be brought back on elephants, and in that swamp those that were still fit could not keep up with them. So we provided enough animals to carry all of them. Their rations were sent down, on a separate shuttle system, as far as Mintha, throughout the rains. No elephant or oozie ever let them down.

I found it rather a heartbreaking job at times trying to teach not only Indian soldiers, but also British officers, that an elephant is an animal which needs quite as much care as a mule. It was far more valuable at that time, as mules would have got bogged at once in the quagmire of mud.

At last, in desperation, I issued general notes on elephant management. In spite of that, elephants were still kept tied to trees for hours and hours on end, waiting at rendezvous points for patrols, instead of being allowed to graze on nearby fodder. As a result their digestions were upset for no good reason. Animals were also loaded in any fashion, with no attention to balancing the loads. The Gurkha, who is a jolly little man, thought it very funny to be riding an elephant, and it was quite common for me to catch as many as six of them on the back of one animal, with their rifle-slings looped round the animal's ears, as though on a hat-stand. On several occasions when I caught them doing this they would slide off over the hindquarters *en masse* and bolt into the jungle, to hide from me, like school children caught climbing apple-trees. I finally got my way, by a resolute refusal to supply elephants to any troops who would not co-operate in treating them properly.

The whole subject also led to a battle between the Royal Indian Army Service Corps and the Royal Engineers, partly to decide which of them could obtain priority in the use of elephants, and partly to determine the perennial military question of whether elephants were a branch of transport or of sappers. To those who knew conditions in the Chindwin areas and what lay ahead of us, it was a foregone conclusion that elephants would ultimately be used as sappers. However, in those early days it was a case of trying to be of the greatest use to both parties, and please them both.

Although the position was obvious to anyone working with elephants in the field, the problem was far too difficult for General Headquarters to decide. Elephant Companies were raised later on, and such questions as their war equipment and war establishment were involved, and the question of their status dragged on until after the war with Japan was over; and I am by no means sure that it is settled yet. I see now that I ought to have invoked precedent, and called up the ghost of Daisy, in the Royal Engineers, in 1895. At the time I was concerned only in getting on with the job and keeping the animals fit. I had no time to spend months arguing on paper in an Indian depot over Elephant Companies. But it was lamentable that our work should have suffered owing to the inability of someone to cut through red tape, or for the sake of what was a purely academic question, in a paper organisation.

The elephants, however, were not the chief sufferers from this lamentable incompetence. After burying eight men and two officers in my own little private cemetery, and making the teak crosses for their graves myself in my hut in the evenings, I became so frantic about the idiotic order which prohibited their taking quinine that I secretly supplied each patrol as it was going out with sufficient supplies of it for any man going down with malaria. Even so, I had to make fourteen crosses by the end of those rains. Twelve of them were for men whose lives had been thrown away for no reason.

It was an eerie camp. Most of the time there was nothing between us and the Japanese but dripping jungle. My oozies were, however, in contact with all the small villages scattered up and down the valley. I had implicit faith in them as a screen which would give us early warning of the approach of any Japanese patrol.

Some changes took place in my party. Chindwin White went off to take up a job on the Arakan front, and C. W. Hann, an Anglo-Burman, joined Browne and me.

In July the log bridge over the Lokechao was swept away like matchwood, but a small Bailey bridge, which had been put up well above the gorge and over it, remained.

We had several scares, for the jungle is a land of rumours. But the Japanese made no attempt to interfere with the road-head at Tamu, and my elephants were kept busy doing everything possible to prepare for the re-entry of the Army. But when?

Chapter Fifteen

WE prayed that in October 1943 we should launch the offensive to recover Burma. Elephant Camp became a hostel that autumn, where everyone dropped in. No place was ever visited by so many specialists. We remained a hostel until the following March. There was a field telephone connected, and we became a general information bureau as well. I was constantly being rung up and told: "An important person is arriving to-morrow at ten a.m. Apart from other things he would like to see the elephants at work. Will you put him up?"

Apart from the cheery company, the interest of it all provided me with the best memories I have of that camp. Everyone who stayed there will no doubt remember the friendly arguments over the camp fire. There was no red tape. The General Staff must have been told a dozen times at least how and when to retake Burma! The earliest of my visitors were, however, malariologists and tank experts.

For me it meant spending whole days in jeeps, going right down the valley, as there was no way of imparting one's knowledge so well as on the ground. The malari-ologists tried to damp my enthusiasm by telling me that the lwins (small open marshes which occur in dense jungle) could not be breeding-grounds for malaria mosquitoes, as they were still and stagnant waters. But they found no answer when I told them that it was not still water, but that there was movement owing to seepage from one lwin to the next. The fauna and flora in the Kabaw Valley are completely different from those of Manipur and Assam, and the habits of the mosquitoes, and even their species, might differ. My final argument was that no jungle wallah and no Burmans would ever camp near lwins, and that, as for elephants, they avoided them like the plague.

Before the malariologists had taken their departure,
in came the Brigadier of a Tank Brigade, to have a cup
of tea, and then to be taken round to visit the various
types of jungle, and to learn that most of the common
big trees were shallow-rooted and that a tank could
push them over like ninepins. A simple little fact, but
of some practical value. Then came the R.A.F., then
Radar, then the Artillery. Besides these, the camp was
never without at least one Sapper. With all these
visitors, I led a busy life, quite apart from looking after
my elephants. Everything pointed to the Army's
coming back quite soon. Souvenirs of tips of elephant
tusks and hand-made pipes in teak, with ivory mouth-
pieces, made by the oozies were in great demand—
these gave out but not the curry and rice.

The mud of the monsoons was fast drying in the valley,
and before the motor transport of the 20th Indian
Division arrived to take the place of the 23rd, a sufficient
number of elephant bridges had been constructed over
the rivers, creeks and nullahs to allow the brigades to
fan out over the same fair-weather tracks which had been
used before—north to Myothit, east towards Sittaung and
south to Witok.

Elephants were still occasionally used for pack, but
only to help in fording rivers, for it had become quite
obvious to all that their chief function was in building log
bridges.

I still had difficulty in persuading troops to handle
elephants in the proper Burmese fashion.

The good humour of the oozies when working with
Indian troops was the greatest help, and conditions
never became unworkable. The oozies were not enlisted men. When the sun was boiling hot and the elephants needed shade and fodder, the oozies just went
off with them where they could find it. They did not
care a damn whether it was a Jemadar Sahib or the
Officer Commanding a Field Company who was trying
to stop them. The demands for elephants here, there
and everywhere were more than I could cope with.
A large percentage of them were busy in bridge-building;

others were wanted to help with patrols and others dragging logs for building native boats. At that time I never had more than seventy-eight elephants. They had become accustomed to traffic much sooner than I ever imagined that they would. However, there were a lot of accidents before all drivers of motor transport learned to slow up before passing elephants at work.

There were casualties from the animals fighting, owing to our restricted quarters, and my finest male elephant, Bandoola, killed two other tuskers.

A Gurkha sentry heard a wandering elephant approaching his beat, and was fascinated by the tusks gleaming in the moonlight. He fired a well-aimed shot; the bullet entered just below the eye, passed through the cheek and after leaving a hole the size of a five-shilling piece in it, was deflected into the animal's chest. The bullet was extracted after an operation on the chest, and that elephant was back at work within three weeks.

This was the beginning of a new source of trouble, because once the habit started it would be repeated in any camp that happened to be disturbed at night by elephants. I began to get called to the telephone at all hours of the night, often from places many miles away.

" Hullo! We have an elephant here in the camp that is eating all our rations. Everyone is terrified of him. What are we to do about it? "

" Who are you? "

" Cascara " (or some such code name).

" Good Lord! but that is seven miles from here. He will have eaten them all before I can get to you. You had better let him carry on until he's finished."

" Right ho! But he is making such a hell of a row opening the bully-beef tins! "

Such was the humour of the sappers, and it helped a lot to make the combination of elephants working with an army in the field possible.

If I had been told three years before that elephants would be working alongside pile-drivers and bulldozers, I should never have believed it. If I had interfered it would never have worked. The oozies took for granted

H

that I expected it of them, so they made the best of it—and the elephants thought the same. This work was constantly within sound of gunfire, and we were all wondering what the next move would be, and waiting for it.

I cannot say I was altogether happy, for at the back of my mind I was always wondering what I could do with my men and elephants if the Japanese made a determined attack. I was continually being called up on the telephone and questioned on topographical points about jungles, hundreds of miles away, in the heart of Burma, but all I actually knew was that something big was due to start soon. It was tedious work, waiting for it, but at the end of December I had a stroke of good luck. Two days before Christmas, a friendly Corps Commander sent me a signal to report back from Elephant Camp to Corps Headquarters. I drove my jeep back up the Imphal road, every bend of which was by that time only too familiar to me. I reported, and gave the information for which I had been asked; then, just as I was about to salute and leave the room, he said jovially, " I've been given five days' leave to Shillong for Christmas."

" Grand, sir," I replied. Then, suddenly seeing how the wind lay, I added, " Three would do me."

" All right," he replied. " Take seven, and see the New Year in with your family."

In less than ten minutes after leaving his room I was heading west in my jeep, accompanied by Abdul, my unnecessary Indian Army orderly, who, for some reason unknown to me, had by Indian Army regulations always to be hanging around at my heels, even when I was in Burma.

I drove four hundred miles non-stop, and arrived in Shillong, Assam, on Christmas Eve, in time to find my wife busily employed in filling the four children's stockings. It was a wonderful Christmas, but the grey dawn of 1 January, 1944, came all too quickly, and at four a.m. I had to say good-bye. It was a cold, frosty morning up there in the hills, and the engine of my jeep seemed to purr with pride as I pushed down the hill road towards the plains of Assam. The headlights made the wall of jungle on each side seem a sad and sinister green. The wretched Abdul was sitting at my side, with his rifle between his knees, and he and I were lost in our own thoughts when, swinging around a bend in the road at thirty miles an hour, I had to jam on the brakes hard. For what at first glance looked like a calf was lying in the middle of the tarred macadam road. As I came to a dead stop, my headlights were focused on a magnificent male tiger.

He sat up suddenly on his haunches, blinded by the lights, but yet quite unperturbed. Abdul sat frozen in his seat, with his rifle unheeded between his knees. I felt as though I were sitting in the toy jeep that I had seen an excited child haul out of his stocking on Christmas morning. The tiger slowly stood up on all fours, and I felt myself shrinking into a toy driver. In a moment of inspiration I blew the horn, and Stripes turned his back, and I noticed his furry testicles sway slightly as he walked away in a slow quiet gait down the road, to disappear round the next bend.

When he had gone Abdul and I awoke from our trance, and I heard him working the bolt of his rifle to bring a cartridge into the breech. I gave him a dig with my elbow, which he understood—it was an un-flattering reminder that he could not hit a haystack, let alone a tiger. Otherwise he would never have been taken out of the ranks to be my servant.

I lit a cigarette, and sat thinking for a few minutes. If I shot that tiger it would almost serve as justification for taking another day's leave. But I made no move, and when I had given him enough time to slip away down the khudside I started off again on my journey. I had got into third gear and gone round another two bends of this picturesque hillside road, when I was once more faced with the same startling apparition. For there, lying in the centre of the black tarmac, facing me, with his pink tongue lolling out and his warm breath condensing as he breathed out into the cold morning air, framed against a background of green forest, lay this perfect animal, in his finest full winter striped coat. He was not twenty yards from us when we pulled up. It flashed through my mind that I must shoot or go back. I drew my .45 Colt from the webbing at my waist, and fired two shots, sideways, out into the jungle. I thought for a moment of taking Abdul's rifle and getting out, but thought better of it. Stripes remained unperturbed by my two shots. He slowly got up, and then, turning out of the glare of the headlights, broke into a gentle trot, until he had nearly reached the next bend. He then subsided into a walk, and looked back once at us over his shoulder. I have no doubt he was cursing us.

This time I waited at least ten minutes, lit a cigarette, and smoked it through. It was obvious that this tiger loved lying on the warm surface of the road, which still held some of the heat of the previous day, and was as reluctant to leave it as I had been to rise from my warm bed in Shillong.

I then followed him up again, and thought I had seen the last of him, when, after travelling about a mile, I overtook him once more. By this time I was becoming hardened, and did not pull up at once, but went on slowly towards him, slipping the clutch, roaring the engine, and keeping my finger on the horn. He got up again and turned broadside on to me, but before he slowly slipped over the khudside he turned his great painted head and looked at me, puzzled and angry, and I imagined he was growling out, " Curse this bloody war." I accelerated all I could as I went by the spot where he had disappeared, and so came back to Elephant Camp with mixed memories of Christmas trees and tigers.

At last, early in the New Year, the Army began to make a move. It seemed as though we intended to advance south, as every available elephant was put on to improving the main road from Tamu to Kalemyo. Bailey and Hamilton bridges and heavy road-construction mechanical equipment were arriving. Only a very few knew the true situation. The Japanese had been clearing the villages in their forward areas of all Burmese,

and there were many rumours that they were preparing
for an offensive up the Kabaw Valley.

Then one glorious evening something passed over our
heads. It was our first airborne troops and gliders—
Wingate's Chindits. Their passage made us believe
that they would be followed by something more. But
the expected army did not arrive. We went on building
the road. It had been decided to add log-timber abut-
ments to all the bridges, and the elephants were working
twice their normal hours, in order to keep ahead of the
sappers and have logs stacked in readiness for them at
every bridge. It seemed a case of working desperately
hard. The tanks were up, but there were only three
months left before the break of the 1944 monsoon.
Knowing the valley, I realised that it would need a
gigantic effort to make that road passable in all weathers.

I was sitting at my table one evening in March, when
the telephone bell went. I had just calculated that the
elephants had delivered two thousand three hundred
tons of timber at the road in three months. It was the
Divisional Commander speaking, not with his usual
cheerful personal touch, but giving me a grave invitation to lunch next day, to meet the Corps Commander.
I could tell that the invitation meant something very
serious. I walked across to Browne's hut, where, as
usual, he was poring over a crossword puzzle. He suggested a rum peg and at the same time remarked that I
looked tired. I accepted the drink, and told him that I
could not come to Hlezeik next day, as the Corps Commander was expected. We ate our supper early, and
talked about the Chindit gliders until bedtime.

At luncheon next day there was a tension, as though
something very serious were the matter. After lunch
the Corps Commander and the Divisional Commander
took me alone into a tent and said to me: " This is Top
Secret. How many days' warning would you need to get
all your elephants collected together, and how would
you get them out of the Kabaw Valley? "

My heart missed a couple of beats, in bitter disappointment at the idea that the troops were going to be withdrawn

again, and that this time my elephants would have to go with them. I got up and walked to the Divisional Commander's table, where there was a map. I knew the position of all the elephants in the valley, and could easily calculate that it would take five days to assemble all the animals. I suggested that there should be two rendezvous areas. The Corps Commander agreed, and ordered me to assemble them without delay. Details were discussed, and half an hour later they agreed that I could tell Browne my secret orders, as I pointed out that the success of this movement of elephants depended on complete co-operation, and that I should need his help.

Feeling very depressed and rather stunned by this development, I immediately drove off in my jeep to the elephant camp farthest away, and gave orders cheerfully for them to move up the valley next day. It was well after dark when I got back to camp. It was after midnight before I had explained everything to Browne and we had laid our plans for the following day. We fell asleep to the sounds of heavy gunfire.

For the next four days we kept out of the way of all our friends. But at this stage all our plans went well, and we even managed to get the oozies' women and children who were not already in the camp to come in from their jungle encampments.

On the fourth evening I telephoned to the Divisional Commander, to say that all elephant camps were assembled, with the exception of one which was centrally placed at Tamu. On the fifth day reserve rations for fifteen days were dumped at the assembly points. There were forty-six elephants at Kanchaung, eight miles north of Tamu, and thirty-three at Mintha twenty miles north of Tamu.

Rumours of Japanese activity on the east bank of the Chindwin and in the Kalemyo area, due south of Tamu, were now rife. My Burmans had realised by this time that there was something in the air. But they had no idea it would mean a move west, away from their beloved Chindwin. I was never in any doubt about their following me.

White, who had joined me again from the Arakan, was in charge of a shuttle service of country dug-out boats on the Yu River, which were manned by Burmese boatmen. He received orders to disband his Burmans and then rejoin me. However, without carrying out these orders, on his own initiative he packed eighty of his best men on to motor transport and sent them along, to live and fight another day. They turned out most valuable the following year.

I had put Hann in charge of the herd of forty-six elephants at Kanchaung, and had explained to him that he might be called upon to move suddenly, and told him to be in readiness.

Browne was to be in charge of the herd of thirty-three at Mintha. All the best animals which had been doing engineering work were at Kanchaung. All the young calves and thin or sick animals were at Mintha.

My Karens, who had lost their elephants when they were ambushed at the Chindwin River crossing, were at Elephant Camp with me. I formed them into two escort parties, one for Hann and one for Browne. On 16 March I sent Browne off to check up that Hann was ready to go on and visit Mintha, if he had time.

At noon the code signal to withdraw came over my telephone. I was further informed that the Japanese had crossed the Chindwin to the north of us, and were moving fast. Their patrols had already by-passed our troops on the Tonhe track.

I went off at once to Kanchaung in my jeep, and was lucky enough to find Browne still there with Hann. I told Browne to push on to Mintha to warn his party, and I explained to Hann, by the aid of maps, the route he was to follow.

Hann was rather staggered by these orders, but I explained to him that the only alternative was to shoot all the elephants. I told him to catch all elephants that evening and tie them up for the night, and then to push on as hard as he could at dawn. I then arranged that, with luck, I would next meet him in the Imphal Plain, with a supply of rations and our next orders.

My last words were: " *Au revoir*, and the best of luck. You can make it. You must. Don't worry if you lose any animals *en route*, but push on with your main body."

I went back to the main road to wait for Browne. He was back by dusk, and we returned to Elephant Camp with much to do there that night, as we had to be back at Mintha by dawn, where he would find his herd ready to move off. I had picked out his route. Although shorter, as Mintha is rather nearer to the Imphal Plain, it was over the most frightful mountainous country. We both had confidence in our men and animals, and believed it could be done, although we knew nothing like it had ever been attempted before. But this was War.

At midnight, after Browne had turned in, I received news that the Japanese had crossed the Chindwin to the north in strength, and were pushing forward over two main tracks, and also that a brigade of ours would be going up the north road beyond Mintha at dawn. This last piece of news cheered me a good deal.

There had been a roar of traffic all through the night. Browne left at dawn. Things were obviously moving fast, and when I saw Browne off I felt a presentiment that he would not find things at Mintha as we had planned. There was no news by eleven a.m., so I telephoned Brigadier, General Staff, at Corps Headquarters, to say that all was going well at Kanchaung but things were not going as planned elsewhere. I was then instructed to get back to Headquarters at Imphal myself, with my remaining Karens, in order to prepare for the arrival of the elephants. My elephant camp was to become Tactical Headquarters for an anti-aircraft, anti-tank regiment, which was already moving in.

The Head Burmans to whom I spoke were completely bewildered. But they took it like well-trained troops.

I was just about to destroy a pile of secret papers and maps, when I saw Browne coming into camp, covered with blood and bandages. Just when he was nearing Kanchaung, his truck had skidded, when going at forty miles an hour, and hit a tree head-on. He was in a hell of a mess as a result. Luckily, it occurred close to where

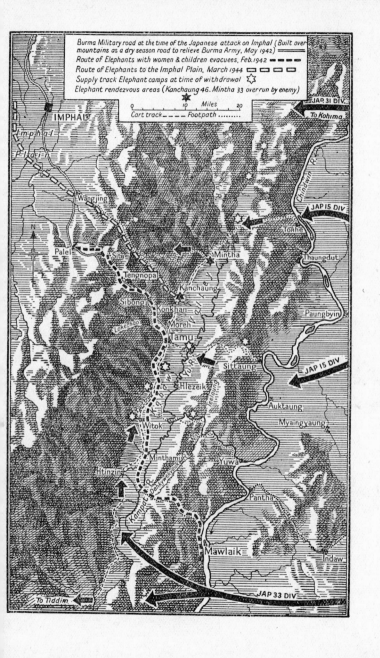

Burma Military road at the time of the Japanese attack on Imphal (Built over mountains as a dry season road to relieve Burma Army, May 1942) ═══
Route of Elephants with women & children evacuees, Feb.1942 ▬ ▬ ▬
Route of Elephants to the Imphal Plain, March 1944 ▢ ▢ ▢
Supply track Elephant camps at time of withdrawal ☆
Elephant rendezvous areas (Kanchaung 46. Mintha 33 overrun by enemy)

0   10   Miles   20
Cart track ─ ─ ─ ─   Footpath ....

IMPHAL

I-m-p-h-a-l
P-l-a-t-e-i

Wangjing

Palel   Tonhe
        Sita   Thaungdut
Tengnopa   Mintha
        Kanchaung
Sibong
    Konkhan   Paungbyin
    Moreh
    Tamu
                Sittaung
        Hlezeik
                Auktaung
                Myaingyaung
    Witok
        Minthami   Yuwa
Htinzin
                Pantha

                Mawlaik   Indaw

To Tiddim

JAP 31 DIV
To Kohima
JAP 15 DIV
JAP 15 DIV
JAP 33 DIV

Chindwin R.
Lokchao
Yu R.
Kampat R. Sanhwegyin R.

a west-country regiment was furiously digging in. The Medical Officer of the battalion gave him first aid, and Browne, very much cut about and badly shaken, tried to borrow another truck in order to push on, as every minute counted. He was told no traffic was to proceed beyond the sector he was in, let alone to Mintha, and that fighting was expected there within two hours.

Browne came back to appeal to me. I rang up Divisional Headquarters, and it was confirmed that a brigade was on its way up, so I told Browne we would change places. He should take over Headquarters and I would make an attempt to get up to the waiting elephants and set off with them. However, he begged me to let him go and try again, so I let him go.

I then heard that the movement of the brigade up the valley had been cancelled, so once more Browne could not get by. It was a good thing he was stopped, as he would have driven straight into the Japanese if he had pushed on. This happened to three Bren carriers an hour after Browne had come back and rejoined me.

It was pretty clear by this time that the Japanese had launched a large offensive. Our only hope was that the oozies at Mintha would have acted on their own initiative and moved west into the hills, when they heard our forward patrols engaging the enemy. However, this hope was disappointed. They just remained waiting at their posts, completely bewildered, as they had no orders. They had been cut off by Japanese patrols behind them before the main body of Japanese entered Mintha. We were completely cut off from hearing any news of them, but retained a faint hope we might come across them in the hills.

We made a gloomy departure from Elephant Camp that evening, leaving everything. A battle was fast developing on both sides of us. One could hear it to the south already.

Just as I was leaving, a serious young subaltern turned up, looking for me, saying he belonged to the Graves Commission, and could I please tell him how he was to get to Dahkywekyauk Wa, on the Yu River, in order that he might record the graves of men of the Northampton-shire Regiment who were buried there. I told him that it was not the moment to go there, unless he wished to remain there for ever, and that my experiences of Dah-kywekyauk had convinced me that it was the unluckiest place in Burma.

We listened together to mortar fire, and, as he still seemed uncertain what to do, I added: " Dahkywekyauk is eight miles beyond those mortars. Go back to Imphal and tell them I sent you back."

He gave me the plan of the graves, and I put it in my pocket, feeling certain that some day I should have an opportunity of finding them, either when I went down next year with an offensive, or after the war was over. Then I could see that they were recorded. My pre-sentiment came true.

As I climbed back towards Imphal, over the road from Tamu, I thought again about my experiences at Dahkywekyauk, and wondered why they should always have been so disastrous. It is a jungle creek, and its name means " The stream with knife-sharpening stones." I first went there in 1925, and as I entered it from the mouth of the Yu River my first impression was of a dark, dismal tunnel, leading into the jungle, shaded impenetrably from any ray of sunlight by vast canopies of leafage.

For two years, in that dismal spot, I fought, all on my own, against considerable odds. I was stabbed by a Burman there in 1926. I was so ill with mud sores and high fever in 1927 that the only way to save my life was to get away by boat. This meant shooting the rapids in a dug-out, which had never been done before during floodwater of the monsoon. My elephant-men risked everything to get me out, and succeeded. My favourite dog, Juno, died there. One of my assistants was accident-ally shot there. Another of them developed blackwater fever, and died shortly after we got him to Mawlaik.

That is a very brief list of some unlucky experiences there. But before I left in 1927 I did clear a hut site at the mouth of the creek, with a garden, from which I used to make sketches. I little guessed what use that habit of observation was going to be in 1943! Before the Northamptonshires had attacked the Japanese bunkers at Dahkywekyauk, in February 1943, I was able to sketch an accurate and detailed map for their Brigadier, even marking a tree, which I had planted to mark Juno's grave. That tree was the key point of the Japanese bunkers.

I made an impassioned plea, as an amateur soldier, that the attack on the bunkers should be launched from the hill and down the slope, instead of along the bank. It was the last and most important piece of information I could give them. But after I had listened, from a distance, to the air strike which preceded the attack, the news came through that our first attempt, led by a young officer of the Northamptonshire Regiment, had failed. They had attacked along the bank. That afternoon he led a second attack, this time from the hill behind it, and captured the enemy position brilliantly. He was killed, and awarded a posthumous V.C.

These thoughts filled my mind as I buzzed up the mountain in a jeep. The Japs were back, I was again on the run, and had lost touch with thirty-three elephants.

Browne and I spent the night at Palel in the Imphal Plain, arriving there after dark. The Japanese had launched their offensive. Perhaps it was just what our Higher Command had been expecting and praying for— or perhaps not. But my only concern just then was with the elephants on the march, and wondering what had befallen those we had left at Mintha. The worry of having lost thirty-three animals, and the uncertainty about the others, not to speak of what our next move would be, was very great.

The first news I got was that the Mintha elephants had never started on the march, but that the oozies had hastily dispersed them into jungle hiding-places, where they had their fifteen days' rations with them. This was a relief, as the Japanese would certainly have pursued them, and overtaken them, if they had moved off as a body. Had the Japanese captured them, they would have provided them with a transport column of im-

mediate usefulness. It would be some time before the
Japanese found all of them and assembled them for use.

It was five days before I got in touch with Hann and
his party. One march after passing through Sita, on the
main ridge, when all the elephants were already tied up
at night, Hann received word that the Japanese had
taken Sita. So they hastily loaded up, and pushed on
again till dawn. In our eagerness to hear news of Hann
and his party, Browne and I ran the gauntlet back to
Konkhan in our jeep. But everyone had their own
worries. All the troops were at action stations, and my
constant question, " Have you seen any elephants? "
was usually regarded as a most untimely jest.

I was known intimately, and always greeted with a
joke and a cheerful welcome, at Brigade Headquarters.
Now when I went into their dug-outs all was serious. I
stood silently listening to a telephone conversation
about a counter-attack which was just going to be
launched by a company of my old regiment in which I
fought in the war of 1914–18. And as I listened I
could not help feeling that I should have been happier
if I had been an infantry subaltern again, leading a
platoon to the attack, instead of worrying about my
elephants, lost in the hills, through which the Japanese
were infiltrating like yellow ants.

When the Brigade Major put down the telephone he
looked at me and said: " Sorry, Sabu. Your elephants
were mistaken for Jap elephant transport in the high
bamboo, and were shot up coming down the slope from
Sibong." He assured me, however, that he was speaking
only of a small party of six, and I realised that they were
animals which had been attached to a special patrol, not
part of those I had assembled for evacuation. But there
was no news of the main party with Hann. We were
told to clear out as fast as we could.

I eventually got in touch with Hann, when his party
was two marches from the Imphal Plain. I left Browne
to deal with him when he arrived, and went to report at
once to Corps Headquarters.

By this time we all knew that the Japanese had launched

an offensive with three divisions, one against our 17th Division in the Chin Hills, one against our 20th Division at Tamu, and one in the north in the direction of Kohima, which was met by our 23rd Division, then in reserve in the Imphal Plain.

The Corps Commander sent for me, and told me that I must march the forty-five best animals, which I had saved, to the north of the Imphal Plain immediately, and then continue west out of the plain, as they were on no account to be lost.

No one knew better than he what those orders meant. He agreed that I would have to accompany them myself, and reconnoitre a route out. The Bishenpur track to the Silchar-Surma Valley could not be used, as the 17th Division had been cut off, and the Japanese were expected to cut that track as their next move.

Transport was impossible to get, but I knew that my only hope of moving on was to separate the oozies and their families, and send the latter to a place of safety—that is, down the Kohima road to the main railway. That would relieve all of us of a great responsibility.

It was a case of the devil helps those who help themselves. I made no attempt to get military transport, which I knew was impossible, but went direct to Steve Sutherland, an ex-officer of the Burma Forest Department, who was in charge of refugee supplies. He gave me the lorries.

When the train of elephants, with the oozies and their wives and families, arrived to cross the main road at Wangjing, I met them with eight lorries. I explained to the oozies that I would see that their families were all right. I then put the lorries of women and children into the charge of a young Anglo-Burman named McVittie and told him to proceed with them at once to the Manipur Road Railway and report to what was left of the Evacuee Camp there.

Browne and Hann continued north-west across the Imphal Plain with the oozies and the elephants, camping in Manipur villages, and feeding the elephants entirely on village banana-trees. We calculated that it would take them another five days to reach the north-west end of the Imphal Plain, where I should meet them again. In the meantime, White and I were to do a reconnaissance of the route over the mountains to the west. The Barak River, which drains out into the Surma Valley in Assam, rises in Manipur, where it is but a stream. It is bridged at milepost 102, on the main Imphal-Dimapur road. The first move was to reconnoitre its headwaters for fodder. The country through which it flowed was terrific, and to follow it one would have to negotiate a series of gorges and waterfalls. But water would always be available.

At three p.m. that day I sat with White at the bridge by 102 milestone, and decided that we would attempt to follow the Barak River route. I knew it would be a hellish trek. In front of us there were mountain ranges five to six thousand feet high, with cliff gorges engulfing the river.

I had, however, three officers to help me who would undertake anything I asked of them, whether it appeared possible or not.

Before six that evening, however, the road was cut by a strong party of the enemy, at the very bridge on which I had been sitting with White at three o'clock that afternoon.

With the Imphal-Tiddim road also cut, and the Bishenpur track seriously threatened, there was now no recognised track left out of the Imphal Plain, except a foot-track to Haflong to the west, to join the Lumding-Sylhet hill-section railway. This track passed through a village called Tamelong. Over this track, which was scarcely a footpath, it had been decided to march thirteen echelons of six hundred Pioneers at a time, so as to reduce the problem of rationing, which would be a big problem if our army were surrounded and besieged in Imphal.

My problem was to get from the Imphal Valley into the Surma Valley in Assam, due west of us, but divided from us by a series of five precipitous mountain ranges, five to six thousand feet high, over a country about which

I knew nothing, except what I could gather from maps of a quarter-inch to the mile. Before dark I saw the Brigadier, General Staff, again, and explained that any more reconnaissances were out of the question. All I wanted was fifteen days' rations for ninety-six elephant personnel and *carte blanche* to get out as best I could. This he was not prepared to give me. However, the Corps Commander saw me again, and gave it, provided that I visited Tamelong *en route*, so that I could signal back that all was well as far as that. I also armed all my Karens with Sten guns and rifles.

The 17th Division broke through the Japanese block on the Tiddim road that day, and the very tragic news of Wingate's crash came through. With the 17th Division came sixty-nine women and children—mainly Gurkhas—who were refugees from the Chin Hills. They had been in the hands of the Japanese, and were a pathetic sight. Nobody had any time to deal with them, so I arranged with Supplies Branch that if they would fly out the pregnant women and old people I would attempt to take the others with me. There were sixty-four of them. I drew fifteen days' rations for them, and then took them in lorries to our starting point. I was far from popular with my party. Not only was I tying this millstone of sixty-four strange women round our necks, but I had, only four days previously, almost forcibly separated my oozies from their own wives and children, who were at least familiar with elephants.

I returned to Imphal alone, after dumping my cargo, in order to have a tooth extracted, as toothache would not help me on the trip, and to pick up a red parachute, for ground signalling to the R.A.F. This was someone else's idea—not mine. Finally, I said *au revoir* to all those who had helped me and my attempt to get out.

The parting words of the Director Medical Services to me were: " I'd rather stay here and starve, Bill."

During the short run back to my elephant camp I was alone with my old Labrador dog, Cobber. He seemed to realise that sympathy was called for, and, leaning over the back of my seat, gave my face one slobbering lick, and wagged his tail cheeringly. Then he stared ahead through the windscreen, with his tongue hanging out and a broad grin on his face, as if he were saying: " Next stop, Surma Valley."

In the back of my jeep was a royal present of a case of rum. Steve Sutherland gave it me, saying as he did so: " Say nothing, Bill. If there's nothing else you'll need on this Hannibal trek, you'll need this."

Final plans were discussed that evening in camp. We were to start at dawn on 5 April, 1944. It rained most of the night, and Imphal was in a state of siege next morning—what is known in the war histories as the Fourth Corps Box.

Chapter Sixteen

THE foothills to the west of Imphal Plain are treeless. From where we started there is a graded mule-track up to about two thousand five hundred feet, as far as Tamelong. Only one person saw us off on our departure: an R.A.F. pilot in a Harvard Trainer, who damned nearly stampeded the whole party of elephants, just as they were descending a very steep bit of the track. Whether he was just verifying the direction in which we were starting off, or whether he thought we were a horde of Japs, I can't tell. But he made off as quickly as he came, possibly because he realised how disastrous to us his presence would be, or possibly because he saw a few rifles being aimed in his direction! If our curses had any effect, he would have had a forced landing on his trip back.

We were a most extraordinary collection. I went ahead, with an armed vanguard of Karens, and when I looked back, down over the serpentine track, the collection looked like the " Lame Host," and we were strung out to such an extent that it seemed possible that the first of the elephants would reach his destination before the last of them got started.

Our total strength was forty-five elephants, forty armed Karens, ninety elephant-riders and attendants, sixty-four refugee women and children, and four officers in charge. From where I was watching them, the elephants looked like slowly moving moles, followed by a trail of black ants. The cheerfulness of the Burmans was a great encouragement, and, provided that we escaped being attacked by Japanese patrols, we felt confident we should make the Surma Valley sometime and somehow.

Our first halt was the Iring River, after we had crossed the first watersheds. There was good water and ample

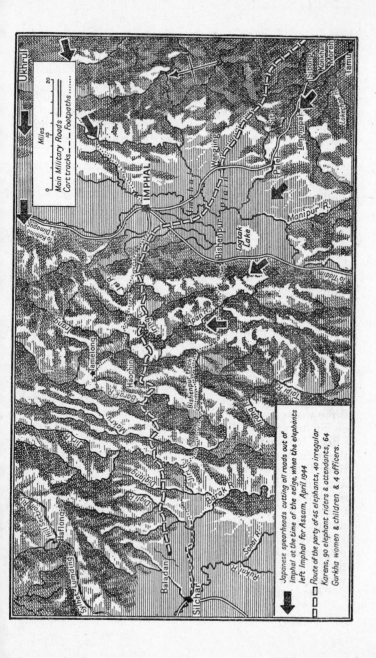

Miles
0   10   20

Main Military Roads ━━━
Cart tracks ━ ━ ━
Footpaths ·········

Japanese spearheads cutting all roads out of
Imphal at the time of the seige, when the elephants
left Imphal for Assam, April 1944

Route of the party of 45 elephants, 40 irregular
Karens, 90 elephant riders & attendants, 64
Gurkha women & children & 4 officers.

Ukhrul

to Kohima & Dimapur

IMPHAL

Wangjing

Palel

Tengnopal

Sibong

Konkhan
Moreh

Tamu

Lokchao R.

Manipur R.

Logtak Lake

Bishenpur

to Tiddim

Apanao

Haul

Jiri R.

Tamenlong

Haochin

Barak R.

Bishenpur R.

Iril R.

Ijibili R.

Ijibili R.

Leimatak R.

Digjang R.

Jiri R.

Makru R.

Barak R.

Sonai R.

Rukni R.

Silchar

Baladan

Haflong

Jatinga R.

Silchar-Lumding Rly.

fodder for the elephants at that halt. Half-rations were
issued to all, and even the lamest of the lame ducks got
into camp before dusk. That first evening, however, we
were overtaken by the first echelon of six hundred
Pioneers. They were carrying ten days' hard rations,
and it was obvious that chaos, if not tragedy, was going to
mark the whole of their route, as they could not cover the
distance in that time.

I was, anyhow, anxious to get my party off their
track as quickly as I could. I did not at all relish the
company of seven thousand eight hundred Pioneers,
and could visualise my elephants providing them with
a most welcome supply of fresh meat if we remained
with them. We were out of touch with any further
orders, and had only one remaining duty—to visit
Tamelong and send off a signal from there.

We therefore arranged that White and I should continue as far as Tamelong, and send off the signal, while
Browne and Hann should proceed due west to Haochin,
where we would rejoin them. However, we were still
two marches from the point where we planned to part
company, and during those two days I thought we should
get an idea of what we might expect on the trek.

The women and children found the marches very
exhausting, but on the whole they were marvellous.
When we started off in the morning there would be
three women and about four children riding on elephants,
owing to various ills. When we got in at night ten to
fifteen would be riding, the oozies having taken pity on
them, although pity was a luxury we could ill afford,
since the elephants were already overloaded with rations
and kit, and were making very severe marches. A few
elephants showed signs of feeling it. These had to be
nursed, by giving them lighter loads, which, in turn,
meant that the others had to be still further overloaded.
However, although every day the elephants would become
more exhausted, every day we were eating a portion of
their loads. That would make quite a difference after a
week of marching. Before White and I separated from
the elephant party, I gave orders that they should on no

account delay during their march to Haochin, and any rest and reorganisation of loading that might be necessary should take place after they had left it. For we were by no means out of range of Japanese patrols. I was to learn later that the very day on which the elephants left Haochin, a strong enemy patrol arrived in the evening and occupied the village, murdering a Political Officer, named Sharpe, who was following in the tracks of our party.

Tamelong was in the state of chaos which I had expected. A very young Political Officer, named Young, was in charge of thirty rifles, with one Indian officer. The fact that Sharpe did not arrive led eventually to a second tragedy.

The Pioneers were straggling deplorably. All the lame, the blind and the halt were just sitting there, and showed no disposition to push on. Young seemed to have been forgotten in the general confusion elsewhere, and was trying to manage against very heavy odds. I got a signal sent off, giving my intended route, and adding just what I thought of the Pioneer echelons marching out. This led to the departure of any further echelons from the Imphal Plain being stopped, and to an air drop of food for the stragglers stranded there.

White and I rejoined the elephants, as planned. The night after that we had to camp for the first time on a ridge, where there was only a trickle of water for the elephants. But it was just enough.

From Haochin onwards we had to face the unknown, and travel due west over whatever was in front of us, until we reached the Surma Valley. The point nearest us on the map was marked Baladan Tea Estate, high up on the edge of the valley. We made jokes about it, and decided we should find a bungalow with a very old tea-planter living with a very lovely young wife, and there would be buttered toast and a telephone. Then, slapping my Labrador, Cobber, on the flank, one of us added that he was quite sure that this ideal couple had a very elegant Labrador bitch who would appreciate him.

We were by this time five thousand feet up, which is

high above any normal " elephant line." In fact we were as high as Hannibal was when he crossed the Little St Bernard. The great beasts were painfully slow in climbing, and Browne had had difficulty, owing to some of the older animals nearly collapsing. It was magnificent scenery, which made a great deal of difference to us four officers, in spite of the hundred and one worries which continually beset us.

So far there was no doubt that there would be sufficient fodder for the elephants and, provided we could cross over a watershed each day, we should be able to find sufficient water for them at lower levels.

I had been given a compass by an Australian War Correspondent, who once spent a night at Elephant Camp, Tamu. It had originally been given to his father by Sir Alan Brooke, and it proved invaluable to us on that trek.

The cold, at the altitude we now were, brought on attacks of malaria amongst the women, and we soon had a number of fever patients to look after. There were heavy falls of rain at night, which made their lives miserable. In addition, there were cases of sore feet, dysentery, pneumonia and abscesses in the breasts. Some of the elephants were in need of first aid as well. But we could not let our invalids rest and recuperate; we had to push on. Every day we marched from dawn till after five o'clock in the afternoon, always in fear of a Japanese ambush.

From Haochin onwards we had to organise track-cutting and digging parties, each officer in turn starting off with a party, to clear the way ahead of the elephants. When, in climbing up from a creek or river, I had fixed on our reaching some particular point on that ridge from which to drop down into the next drainage area, I had to make certain that the leading party kept their direction to that ridge and did not drop into a side creek. Unfortunately game-tracks were non-existent, as there was very little or no game in those hills. Any small villages marked were usually non-existent also. This was because the people are nomadic agriculturists who move to new areas as they are cultivated for hill rice—and the land can be cropped only once in three years. When new areas are cleared in rotation the village moves on. The villages marked were, however, a guide, as we always found the headstones of the graves at the village site. The dead remained, though for the time being the living inhabitants had moved into another valley.

As we ate our rations, we could afford to carry more of the children, who had by this time quite lost their fear of the elephants. The mothers soon found that they need not walk beside the elephant, constantly expecting to have to catch a falling child. For the oozies were very good at looking after the children, and I rewarded them for their work with an extra cigarette ration. Thus the mothers were able to make an early start with the vanguard of path-finders. Many of the younger women even lent a hand with jungle-knives, clearing bamboos. I was constantly badgered by everyone for a day's rest. Then, on the ninth day of consecutive marching, the country decided the question for me.

We had reached a large creek with good fodder, far off the beaten track. It had been my day with the vanguard, and, as I reached the site for the camp a long while ahead of the elephants, I crossed the creek and went part of the way up the next ridge, so as to see what it was like for our start next morning. The map read as though there were a fault or escarpment running north to south, parallel with the creek, and on the west bank of it. The ridge I was climbing seemed the most likely to provide a way up to the top of the escarpment. I struggled up for about two miles of very steep climbing, through dense bamboo jungle, which would mean a very slow and exhausting climb for the elephants. Then I suddenly came out against a sheer rock face escarpment, three or four hundred feet high. My heart sank. I turned south and followed the foot of the cliff for a mile. There was not a single place where I could have possibly climbed it myself. There was no question of an elephant climbing a perpendicular cliff. I then came to a patch of old and very large bamboos, some of which had obviously been cut with a knife possibly a year before. This looked to me like the work of a Chin villager, who must have been there at some time, and who was more likely to have come down the escarpment, particularly as the map showed a deserted village on the ridge to the west of it.

Before I retraced my steps to camp I found a place where there had been a landslip in the escarpment. It looked a possible way for men to come down, but not at all the kind of place for elephants to go up. I marked the place with a large blaze on a tree, and went back to camp, exhausted. There could be no question of our turning back.

When the elephants and our party came into camp I was forced to announce that we would stay in camp for two days. The evacuee women and children actually cheered, and practically all the clothes they had on were immediately washed and hung up to dry, before the sun went down. I explained that there was a lot of hard work and serious trouble for us ahead. This was not because there was no path—we had not been following a path for many days—but because it was impossible to go on, until we found a place which it was possible to climb, and then dug a path up it. Next morning I sent Browne, White and Hann, each with a separate party, to explore the foot of the escarpment. Browne was to attempt to get up at the place I had found, Hann was to follow the escarpment to the north, and White to the south. I stayed in camp, and provided food for the party by blasting fish with grenades.

Much to my surprise, Browne was back in camp by noon. As I watched him crossing the creek I remembered his return to Elephant Camp at Tamu, after two attempts to reach the elephants at Mintha. Then I saw that among his party were two Chins, armed with spears, and I wondered if he could possibly have got up to the ridge. It was not long before I heard his story. He had climbed up the place I had found at considerable risk. It was, apparently, the route by which the Chins had gone up or down some time ago. But it developed higher up into a narrow ledge, with sheer cliff above and below it, until the top was reached. He knew how I hated heights, and said that I should have to be taken up blindfolded. He said also that he thought that unless White or Hann found something better we were stumped. He had, however, reached the main ridge above, and found the village marked on the map. On the ridge was quite a good path, which ran due south to join the Bishenpur track. This, however, was just the place we wanted to avoid, as, until we had crossed this path to the west, I thought there was quite a good chance of our running into a Japanese patrol. I wanted to keep out of trouble, not to look for it.

It was evening before White and Hann got back within half an hour of each other. They had found no place nearly as good as Browne's.

The only decision I made that night was to cut rations down still further. The strictest watch was set on our food dump. In fact, we officers slept on it, and I posted a guard over it during the day.

We spread the red parachute over some boulders in the bed of the creek, though we had seen no aircraft up to this time. Hann reported having heard a Harvard Trainer during the afternoon, but we had no wish to see our old friend again.

We agreed that the following day we should take our two head elephant-men to see the way by which Browne had got up. It was easy to understand, from the signs made by the two Chins, that there was no alternative route.

I was not actually blindfolded, but I preferred to crawl a good part of the way on all fours! I made sure of my hand-holds, knowing my feet could look after themselves.

Except for the one narrow and dangerous ledge round the face of the cliff, we considered that we could make it possible with two days' cutting and digging. Fortunately, it was sandstone. The question was whether elephants would face it. In some places it was so steep that the elephants would almost be standing on their hind legs.

Po Toke, who was not my head Burman, but in charge of a group of seven elephants, which included Bandoola, surprised us all by saying as we returned: "Bandoola will lead, and if he won't face it, no other elephant will. He knows how to close his eyes on the khudside, and won't put his foot on anything that will give. Moreover, if he should refuse half-way up, he can back all the way down, as he has eyes in his backside!"

Bandoola was a magnificent tusker, but with a bad name as being dangerous.

I don't think he really believed half what he said, but I took care not to give him an opportunity for re-tracting. All of us agreed what a marvellous elephant Bandoola was, and we left it at that.

Apart from the narrowness of the ledge, or shelf of rock, and the occasional, almost impassable, outcrops of rock, the whole of the inner wall of the proposed track had to be cleared of jungle growth. This would widen it as a path, and was in any case necessary for the passage of the pack carried on the elephant's back. White went ahead to the village with the two Chins hoping to raise a party of men to help in bamboo-cutting. He brought a dozen, all with good jungle-knives, and they started work from the top that afternoon.

Every fit man and woman in the camp, oozies included, was at work on that road by dawn next morning. We divided our labour force into four parties, each working on a different section. I took charge of the one nearest camp, so as not to be working where I might get giddy and fall over!

The good humour of even the evacuee women in tackling what was more than a full day's hard work helped enormously. In the evening I went up again. Far less crawling on all fours was necessary, and a lot of the jungle growth cut from the inner wall had been piled up on the outer edge, so as somewhat to hide the terrifying drop below. One day's work had certainly made a vast difference. All the same, I rather doubted if we could do it. I knew, however, that there was no possibility of turning back.

We continued work throughout the following day, and by evening the head Burman and Po Toke were satisfied that we could not improve it any more. If we could not do it now, we never could. There were two particular danger spots, where the track was only about three foot wide, with a wall above, and a sheer drop on the outside, with nothing to blind it. I could not help wondering whether the whole of this ledge might not collapse under the weight of forty-five elephants passing along it.

I had worked up old Po Toke to the pitch of thinking he was practically in charge of the whole adventure, and that all our chances of success depended upon his elephant, Bandoola.

I arranged that all the refugees were to wait until the last of the elephants had gone up the track. Needless to say no women or children were to ride, and invalids who were unable to walk would have to be carried up later. There was to be no talking among the oozies. Po Toke was to lead the way on foot, in sight of Bandoola.

I myself had pushed on ahead of everyone as soon as all the elephants were loaded up.

Only those who know how silently a train of elephants can march can imagine what an eerie start we made that morning. From half-way up, where I turned to look down into the valley, I could hear nothing but the burble of the water of the creek rushing over its boulders far below, and at intervals the distant thuds of gunfire, coming from the direction of the Bishenpur track to the south.

I sat and waited for two hours on that ledge, and thought over many things. Before I left Imphal I had given a scribbled note for my wife to a Spitfire pilot, who was flying to Calcutta. In it I merely said, " Starting to march to-morrow." I knew that this would set her wondering, now that the news of the Japanese offensive on Imphal was coming through.

I had stopped just two hundred yards above the most dangerous spot, at which we had actually cut a series of steps in the sandstone, each just big enough to take an elephant's foot. Once I saw Bandoola pass that, I intended to push on up the next stretch.

I thought that Po Toke would never appear—nor, in fact, did he. Bandoola's head and tusks suddenly came round the corner below me. He looked almost as though he were standing on his hind legs. Then up came his hindquarters, as though in a slow-motion picture. The oozie was sitting on his head, looking down, and seemed to be directing the elephant where to place each of his feet. Then he had passed that worst place. I caught a glimpse through the elephant's legs of old Po Toke following. Without a word I pushed hurriedly on. We had got Bandoola up at least half-way. I just prayed for good luck, but had no faith in success.

It was more than two hours before I saw Bandoola again, and then he was practically at the top, and all danger of his slipping or refusing was over. He was up, at all events, and my relief and excitement cannot be expressed in words.

Behind Bandoola came Po Toke, and after him a female elephant. As he passed me, Po Toke behaved rather like a pall-bearer at a village funeral who unexpectedly gives one of the onlookers a wink. He was intensely solemn, and did not utter a word, but he gave me a queer fleeting look, that was as good as saying: "Don't you worry. They'll all follow now."

He was right. They all did. I waited, and ticked off forty-five adult elephants and eight calves at heel go by. The back legs of some of the animals had been strained to such a point that when they halted they would not stop quivering.

Much as I hated having to camp on a ridge, where there was a well-worn track to the south, up which the Japanese might come, there was no alternative. It was dark by the time we had got the last of the refugee women up to the top. No day ever seemed longer.

I learned more in that one day about what elephants could be got to do than I had in twenty-four years. Po Toke's intuition had been perfectly right, and I am

certain that we should never have done it if we had led
with any animal except Bandoola.

Our camp on the ridge that night was the last one
where I put out pickets. From there onwards I felt no
fear of the Japanese.

Our next move was down to the Barak River. The
descent was almost as steep as the previous day's climb
up to the ridge, but there was no escarpment or ledges
of rock to follow. Again we had to have a day's rest, as
the elephants were feeling the strain, and had to be
allowed to recover.

From there we followed the course of the river; our
obstacles were mud and swamp, and very dense bamboo,
through which we had to hack a track. We should
never have got through if we had not been using Siamese-
pattern gear on our elephants. It is much stouter.

Time was now our enemy, and my chief worry was
whether our rations would last out. We still had a long
way to go, but from the map it looked as though we should
move into better country once we had reached the Digli
River. It was quite obvious that our trek would last
twenty days at least, and not the fifteen I had allowed for.
By that time we had two cases of pneumonia among the
refugee women, as well as other things. The only food
we four officers were getting, on which to do a day's
march, was chappattis made by the refugee women,
jam and half a cigarette-tin of rice in the evening. As
might be expected, our tempers were getting a bit short.
Cobber, my dog, enjoyed himself more than anyone, but
even he found the food dull. The Burmans were down to
half a cigarette-tin of rice a head per day, and were
feeling the pinch. They eventually petitioned me to
increase it. But I refused, and told them that it was my
job to get them through this march alive, and that I was
determined to keep three full days' rations as a reserve,
in case of some miscalculation. About this time we came
to a Chin village, and had some trouble over a pig. Po
Toke paid forty rupees for a village pig, but it escaped to the
jungle just before he could kill it. It was obvious that the
villager would get it back after we had gone, as these pigs

are left free to roam during the day, and come back to their pens at night. Po Toke naturally asked for his money back, and, just as naturally, the Chin villager refused to give it him. The dispute was therefore brought to me to settle, so I handed Po Toke a rifle and told him to go and shoot a wild one to-morrow instead. Before we left camp he had bagged two. Of course I knew they were not wild ones, but it did at least settle the argument in favour of my men.

Before we moved on that morning the head man of the village came and asked me for compensation for damage done by the elephants to banana-trees during the night. He had actually got his bill down on paper, and brought with him a boy of seventeen, who could speak a few words of English and claimed that he had been educated. It was he who had put the head man up to this ruse to obtain money. I told White, who could speak Hindustani fluently, to deal with him. It did not take him long!

But from my point of view the incident was the first sign that we were reaching civilisation again. However, as we were not going south to link up with the Bishenpur track, but west, it turned out there was a very long stretch of uncivilised country still to cover. Nevertheless, we had by this time at least left the mountains. In place of precipices we struck jungle swamp in which the animals got bogged. In trying to cut across country above the junction of the Digli and its tributary we were forced to turn back and follow down one river-bed to the confluence and then up the other river. It involved eight miles in water, knee-deep, with semi-quicksand bottom. It was just as slow going for the elephants as for the humans. All the children and the majority of the women had to ride, but the younger women were quite game to carry on. A few dropped out, and we had to send elephants back to pick them up.

Following elephants along a creek with a patchy quicksand bottom is an experience which thoroughly tests one's endurance and one's temper. It amounts to floundering along and continually losing one's balance,

as one is always taking a step that meets with no resistance
—as though one had stepped into a hole. It is next to
impossible to carry anything, and the Gurkha girls soon
discovered it was equally difficult to wear anything. It
was not a time or place for false modesty and they were
quite beyond caring about such matters. So they just
handed up their garments, one after another, to the
oozies and floundered on, naked, unimpeded and
unashamed.

It was quite impossible to travel along the banks or
to keep near them, as the dense jungle not only came
down to the water's edge, but bamboos and canes grew
right across. These had to be cut to allow the elephants
to pass, and the sharp, twisted masses that resulted were
awkward obstructions for those following.

I estimated that we covered only ten miles between five
a.m. and five p.m. that day. Everyone was dead beat
when we arrived at the confluence. It was an amazing
sight to see the refugees sorting out their few wet rags of
clothes on an open patch where we had decided to
camp.

That last desperate day of floundering down the
river had brought us, I reckoned, to within one day's
march of the tea estate. But we agreed that to arrive
there with our entire party might not be popular, so I
decided to take the really sick along with me, on nine
elephants, and to leave the remainder of the party
camping as near the tea estate as we dared. I had the
astonishing experience of walking right out of the wall
of dense jungle into the open plain of the tea estate—
an ocean of green tea, as far as the eye could see. I had
come out exactly where I had planned on the map.
There were doves cooing. I felt a lump in my throat,
and could hardly believe my eyes. About a mile away
was a large bungalow, typical of so many planters'
bungalows in Assam. I went ahead to introduce myself
to the old planter and the lovely young wife whom we
had imagined.

It looked a homely bungalow. As I approached it I
could see a figure in a white shirt on the veranda, for

the bungalow was built on high ground, above the level of the surrounding tea bushes.

Before I reached it I was hailed by a man, speaking with a strong Scotch accent, " What is the hurry? What about a cup of tea? "

" No hurry, and nothing I should like better," I replied, and, swinging up his garden path, I walked on to a big open veranda with a breakfast table, with breakfast just laid.   The planter was James Sinclair.   He was a bachelor of forty-eight, and had no attractive young wife.   He had mistaken me for one of the officers of a Commando unit, which had just arrived in that neighbourhood.   Some of them were in the habit of dropping in to see him.

He asked me where I had come from and where I was going, so I gave him a brief account of my travelling circus.   He then said that he had heard a rumour that there was a party of Japanese somewhere on the move with a few hundred elephants, but that he had not believed it. Now it turned out to be true, but, thank the Lord, we weren't Japs!

I breakfasted off new-laid eggs and hot coffee, and during the meal he told me that he had been expecting to hear of some refugees who were supposed to be coming through that way.   Imphal had apparently signalled to Silchar about them.   He was more than surprised when I told him I had brought them with me.

White arrived presently with the very sick on nine elephants, and Sinclair gave us every assistance, by handing them over to his tea-garden doctor.

We were still twenty miles from Silchar, but I was able to telephone to the civil authorities about the refugee women and children.   It would be the greatest possible relief to hand them over, and have no further responsibility for them.

I was not able to communicate that day with the military authorities, and I was not particularly concerned to do so.   I was already six days overdue, and had kept three days' rations in hand.

The refugee women were handed over that evening,

I

so there was plenty of food left for my elephant-men. Two weeks later I was able to check up that all the sick among the refugees had recovered. I saw them in their camp, and they looked cheerful and happy. They were waiting to be sent farther on into India. They would have a fine story to tell their Gurkha menfolk when they met again after the war.

White and I stayed that night with Sinclair, and opened our last bottle of rum. Browne and Hann also had one at the camp. It had been agreed there was to be no rationing of their contents.

Next morning Sinclair invited all four of us to stay in his bungalow until I had got in touch with the Army and straightened everything out. The main elephant camp settled in about two miles from the tea-gardens.

That was the twenty-fourth of April. We stayed with Sinclair for a period of four months.

The Sub-Area Headquarters at Silchar were so astonished at our arrival that I thought I detected a note of disappointment! Supplies Branch had made fabulous calculations as to the amount of fodder they would have to provide for the elephants, and there was already a file of signals about the lost host of forty-five elephants, four officers and Burman personnel. The R.A.F. had apparently been trying to find us for twenty consecutive days, but we had vanished, only to pop up again, just after we had finally and happily been written off.

My demands on Supplies for elephant rations were nil, and my other requests easy and simple. So we immediately became popular.

I flew to Army Headquarters at Comilla, where news of our arrival had caused quite a stir.

By the time I got there our bodies and elephants were already up to auction to the Assam Forest Department.

One of my first enquiries was to discover what had happened to the wives and families of my elephant-men. But it was a month before I ran them down, through the refugee organisation of Assam, and discovered that they had been dumped at Parbuttipur, in Assam, on the

Brahmaputra River. Being Burmese, they attracted considerable interest. As soon as it was possible, I sent Browne and White, with two of the most influential elephant-men, to visit them, so that they could bring back first-hand news to the oozies about their families. I have never known any two men who got on with children better than Harold and Chindwin, and their reception at Parbuttipur Camp was described to me later by the officer in charge. They were mobbed by the delighted children, whose excitement was indescribable. All in the camp felt that my promise had been kept. The families had to remain separated through the monsoon months. But they made the best of it, set up their own hand-looms, and were actually trading in Shan woven silk bags and hand-woven cottons before they returned to their homes.

They accepted their share of the upheaval in a wonderful spirit, and this helped me to hold their men together for four years, although they were not enlisted and I had no disciplinary authority over them. The difficulties for high-ranking officers in time of war can be very great, but to be in charge of Elephant Companies, without even an Establishment, could at times be far worse. My elephants could not be taken to Delhi and officially branded as the property of the Indian Army. My oozies could not be sent in a body to Simla to be certified as Burmans of good repute to those who resided there, and they were many!

However, an Imprest Account, written chiefly in Burmese, did confuse the Army Accounts Department to such an extent that they were forced to take it on trust. The advantages of our irregular position came when the war was over, as it enabled us to be demobilised at once, without waiting for all sorts of papers to come through.

Chapter Seventeen

THE battle for Kohima and Imphal, which proved decisive, and led on to the reconquest of Burma, was then in its first most critical stages. But my horizon was limited to my own job. Having got rid of the refugees, my concern was my elephants. A prolonged rest, so that they could get into good condition, was essential for them. Otherwise nothing would ever be got out of them again. They would also have to be refitted and re-equipped.

Expert timber-dragging elephants like these were almost worth their weight in gold in the forests of Assam. The Army authorities hoped to put them to good use with the Assam Forest Department. Fortunately we were in the wrong valley. The Forest Department needed us in the Brahmaputra Valley, near the main Assam railway and trunk road. This involved a march of two hundred miles. The rains had broken, and I declared that it was impossible for us to undertake it before October.

I was very glad to be able to put off our working on timber extraction in India, for I knew that once we started it the elephants would not return to Burma during the war, and probably not for many years after it was over. If we could hold the Japanese attack during the monsoons, I felt certain that we should follow the enemy back into Burma when he cracked, and I knew that my elephants would be invaluable when that time came. I soon became involved in the usual type of Army paper war, of which I had little experience up till then. I rapidly learned the technique of obstructiveness in order to stave off the plan of sending us to work for the Assam Forest Department, which I determined to fight in every way I could.

Meanwhile, I took the opportunity to send each of

my three officers on long leave, for I knew that there would be little chance of any later.

The Imphal battle turned in our favour, and soon afterwards an opportunity occurred for me to get the question of the employment of the elephants settled as I wished.

I was called to visit Army Headquarters at Imphal, to supply information on a subject unconnected with elephants. But the interview made it clear that the elephants might soon be able to return to the Kabaw Valley. They were in the right place to do so directly the Bishenpur track was cleared. It was obvious, therefore, that the sooner any plans for employing them on timber extraction were dropped, the better. I therefore took the opportunity to ask for a definite ruling, and was given an interview by the Army Commander at Imphal, with results most satisfactory to me.

When I returned, the Burmans were delighted to hear my news of our future plans. Browne and White were to march the elephants back to the Kabaw Valley as soon as possible, and I planned to go back ahead of them, in order to pick up any stray elephants which our Army might have overrun or captured. The Japanese had been using large numbers of elephants in their offensive, and wholesale desertion by the oozies, complete with elephants, might be expected during their retreat.

I was, however, recalled to Headquarters with White, to be caged up in Intelligence Branch in Army Headquarters at Comilla with what would obviously be a ten-day job of work. I was rather amused by the manner of our return. We reached the large airfield near Silchar on a really dirty day of monsoon weather. The surrounding hills were enveloped in thick cloud, and while we were waiting Chindwin White said to me: "I don't know that I wouldn't prefer to walk back."

A few moments later a dirty yellow little Harvard Trainer came out of the rain-clouds and landed. Our names were called out, and we walked out to the aircraft, with our big rucksacks on our backs.

"Same bloody machine that nearly stampeded the jumbos," said White as we approached.

The pilot already had two R.A.F. passengers aboard, and called out to me: " I can't possibly manage you, sir, but we might squeeze in the little fellow, if he would take that hump off his back."

Chindwin was accordingly crammed in, and yelled to me: " There's a new bloody game on here. Everyone else is strapped in and has got a parachute. But don't you kid yourself, I'll hang on to the legs of one of these chaps if we do have to jump."

I joined him, an hour or two later, at Imphal, getting in on a Dakota in which there was plenty of room to spare. Chindwin went round telling everyone how I had got rid of him in a Harvard, and implied that I had been trying to get rid of him altogether.

It had been decided that, in spite of the monsoons, our Army would follow up the Japanese as fast as possible and keep them on the run. Unfortunately, White went down with a severe attack of malaria with complications. It was three months before he was well enough to come back. I was instructed to proceed to the Kabaw Valley to join the Commander of the 11th East African Division and, *en route*, to see the General Officer Commanding the 33rd Indian Corps. Hann had gone off to join a formation of Intelligence Branch in the field, and Browne was left to bring the elephants back alone. He was quite confident that he could, and he did so successfully, but he did not really recover from the exhausting strain of being the only officer in charge of them, for a whole year. He then went on leave to South Africa, with his job completed, four days after the Japanese surrender. No man ever deserved leave more.

I arrived in Imphal and Tamu. No words can describe the conditions of the latter place.

McVittie, the young Anglo-Burman to whom I had entrusted the women and children of my elephant-riders four months before, had got back before me, and was already building bridges with eleven elephants he had collected, whose oozies had deserted from the Japanese. The importance of the work these animals were doing can be judged from the fact that the necessary

gear and all requirements had been flown in and dropped
by air, as a top priority, and demands for priorities were
many at that moment. Other elephants were becoming
available, as the oozies and elephants were escaping from
their Japanese masters in their disorderly flight.

The lack of gear was the most serious problem which
held up our using these animals, and, as Browne's party
of elephants could not possibly reach us from the Surma
Valley under six weeks, I decided to make use of all the
equipment and hand-made harness which their oozies
had made in the rest camp, near the Baladan Tea Estate.
Fetching it took me three days in a lorry convoy.

The monsoons were by no means over in the Kabaw
Valley, but nothing was to stop the East African Division
going down it. Within three weeks I had collected and
equipped sixty recaptured elephants, and sent up what
reinforcements I could to McVittie. The rains were so
violent that log bridges built one day were often washed
away the next, only to be replaced the day after.
Japanese lorries were bogged all along the valley of mud.
The East Africans cut millions of saplings and threw them
across the road to keep it open. They gave out a stench
as they rotted which almost matched that of the bodies of
the Japanese, who had dropped out, all along the line,
and died of disease, starvation and exhaustion.

The streams were in such spate that it was next to impossible to keep log cribs in place for any length of time.
We therefore used elephants to haul discarded Japanese
lorries into the beds of the streams, and built our log
cribs on top of them. Had it not been for the exceptionally heavy late rains in September and early October,
1944, the Japanese retreating along the Tiddim road
would have run into the spearhead of the East African
Division, coming down the Kabaw Valley.

The sappers had now completely accepted elephants
as part of the necessary equipment. Oozies whom I had
not seen for seven months, and had since been made to
work for the Japanese, were now back again under me,
and were working with the East Africans. They were
given the same rations as the troops, and realised that

the Army had now really returned, and that there was no possibility of our withdrawing from the Kabaw Valley again. Air drops were as regular as clockwork, and elephants were used to carry the supplies dropped from the dropping zone to the distribution centre. These animals had been dive-bombed and machine-gunned from the air by the R.A.F., when they were being used by the Japanese as transport, on the tracks to Ukhrul and Jesami, in the Chin Hills surrounding Imphal. In one such bombing forty elephants had been killed, and elephants were being recaptured with gaping wounds which needed dressing. I therefore established a camp for sick elephants on the bank of the River Yu. To the best of my belief it was the first field veterinary hospital for elephants ever to be established. Some of the worst wounds on elephants' backs had been caused by acid spilt from wireless batteries, during transport. The Japanese had ignored the danger, and the oozies were not sufficiently familiar with acid to realise what the consequences would be. These cases were a warning to our own troops using elephants for transport, and enabled me to take precautions to prevent cases being caused by our own carelessness. In some beasts the flesh had been burned half an inch deep, and the elephants must have suffered slow torture while working in pack-harness. I treated them by dusting with M. & B. powder, and healing was remarkably quick. Many of our pilots have told me that they regarded attacking columns of elephant transport as a most loathsome job. The sincerity of these statements is beyond question, as I have also read reports from pilots, asking that elephants should not be a target for attack. Occasions arose, however, when there was no alternative but to stop the Japanese receiving supplies carried on elephants. This was particularly the case during the rapid advance of the Japanese to the Chin Hills and to Jesami and Ukhrul, preparatory to the offensive against Kohima. For had that succeeded they would have isolated China, and have overrun Assam and Bengal. The elephant transport trains were extremely difficult targets to find, as they marched by night, without lights, and were concealed in the jungle by day. The inspection of the sick and wounded elephants in my hospital camp was an extremely painful task—as painful for me as visiting field-dressing stations filled with wounded men would have been. The gun-horse has now been almost completely superseded by mechanical transport, and set free from the horrors of war. One can only hope that the unfortunate mule will also be superseded.

The Japanese had looted all the rice in the villages to the north and down the Chindwin; for their armies had been left without supplies after the failure of their plans to capture our dumps in the Imphal Plain. The villagers were therefore starving, and all my calf elephants under twenty were used to transport food supplies to these people. Demands came also for more elephants, to rebuild the road to the north to Myothit, and to the east to Sittaung. I was nearly at my wits' end in the valley, and so was Browne, who was travelling back with our original herd of forty-five. He arrived with them safely, after a journey of six weeks, but he was far from fit. He refused to leave me, however, and we struggled on, trying to meet all the demands that were being made on us.

The rains gradually came to an end and our troops were pouring into Burma. Roads were therefore needed over every track to the Chindwin, north, south, east and west.

Browne's arrival brought our strength up to one hundred and forty-seven elephants. Every fit animal was working full time. My head Burmans became my officers, and they managed remarkably well, considering what they had to put up with, in trying to please everyone.

I had no alternative but to attach parties of elephants to sapper companies, asking for one officer to be responsible for rationing the men and for general supervision. By this means I always had one man with whom I could deal direct. I owe these sapper officers a debt of gratitude. They got the best out of men and animals, by keeping calm under all circumstances, and by preserving their sense of humour.

One of these officers, named Alexander, who was a

young civil engineer in peace-time, became so completely wrapped up in the elephants and oozies working
under him that he learned all their names in a week,
and struggled hard to learn Burmese, bribing the oozies
with cigarettes to give him lessons in the evenings. All
was going well when a sudden disaster occurred. Oke-
thapyah (Pagoda Stone), one of his best animals, was
blown up by a Mark 5 land-mine near his camp. Alexander came rushing over a most fearsome track in a
jeep, arriving at two a.m., to tell me all about it. He said
its back legs had been blown off, but he had seen it move,
and was afraid it might be still alive! The Burmans
who came with him assured me in Burmese that the
animal was stone dead. I gave Alex a good tot of rum,
and told him I could not amputate an elephant's legs,
and we could only do our best to prevent such accidents
in future. He abandoned the subject, but asked me to
give him a lesson in Burmese—at two-thirty a.m.! I
went back with him, starting before dawn, taking an anti-
tank rifle, in case he had been right; but of course the
elephant was dead—a sad sight in the early morning
hours. The men had already discovered three more
Mark 5 land-mines, and led us to them.

I knew that they had been put down by a British
infantry battalion six months before, during the retreat,
and never mapped. Having been exposed all through
the monsoon rains, they were most uncertain things to
handle. However, Alex, being a sapper officer, considered it to be his duty to pick them up there and then,
and replace the safety-pins. He told me to take the
Burmans away behind trees while he was doing this.
Two of the men, however, flatly refused, saying that if
Thakin (Alex) wasn't afraid, they weren't, and anyhow
they wanted to see just how it was done. So we all stayed
and watched. While Alex removed the claw-clamp and
the lid, he asked me to explain the sheer wire and how the
pin had to be replaced. " Simple enough! " exclaimed
Tun Myin, one of the Burmans who was watching. And
next morning he brought in five more land-mines all with
their safety-pins replaced, just as Alex had done them.

When Alex was not at hand I always felt that, but for the grace of God, there goes Elephant Bill! It was not long before this business of land-mine recovery began to get on my nerves.

It was a standing joke with the oozies that all they were doing was only for the cold-season months, after which our Army would leave the valley once more. But I was able to arrange with the Army authorities to bring their wives and children back from Assam by lorry. This gave them new confidence that this time we had come back to stay.

By early December there were four roads fit for transport to the Chindwin River during the open season. The elephants built all the bridges on each of these roads: Tamu to Tonhe to the north, Tamu to Sittaung in the east, Tamu to Yuwa to the east, Tamu to Mawlaik to the south-east, Tamu to Kalewa to the south.

One or two small Bailey bridges had been brought up, but no bridging programme had been possible for these roads, as all bridging materials were wanted for the crossing of the Chindwin at Kalewa. No less than two hundred and seventy log bridges and log culvert crossings were put in by elephants over these routes, thus allowing all motor transport and tanks to move forward, before the main bridging programme was undertaken.

As the roads to the Chindwin were completed, Forestry Companies arrived, to obtain the timber required for building assault craft and small barges at Kalewa. Five hundred assault boats were built at Kalewa, from timber extracted by elephants and cut up at the sawmills. They also supplied the portable sawmill, with the timber required for decking the main bridges, for an all-weather road from Tamu to Kalewa.

During the war elephants had many jobs to do with timber, which they had never encountered in the routine of peace-time. One of these was to lift and pass logs up to a height of nine or ten feet—that is to say, from ground level to the bridge level. These logs weighed, on an average, a quarter of a ton each, and were often too heavy for the trunk to grip or hold. If the log were balanced on the outside of the trunk, on the tusks, there was always a danger that as the elephant raised its head to lift it the last foot or two the log would roll back, up its forehead, and endanger the life of the oozie, who was sitting on the elephant's neck at a lower level.

On one occasion I was watching, with one or two sapper officers, the last logs being handed up to a bridge under construction, and we witnessed a remarkable display of intelligence. The elephant was a particularly clever animal, and was beautifully handled by his oozie, but it was evening, and they were both tired. Several logs had slipped during their efforts to balance them, and it was quite obvious that the elephant was anxious about the safety of the oozie, who was placed in a dangerous position, just as the log was lifted to the highest point. There were still about three logs to be lifted. The largest of them was picked up by the elephant, and held in an endways position between the trunk and tusk, the signals for this being given to the animal by the oozie with his foot. The elephant then let it gradually slide, so that it lay across his trunk, at the point of balance, and the curving-up ends of his tusks acted as stops to prevent it rolling on to the ground, and then slowly lifted his head.

" God's truth! how marvellous! " said a Major, in a low voice.

" Hope to God it doesn't roll up his head," murmured the Brigadier.

I held my breath, and then said, in a calm voice, in Burmese: " Carefully now."

The animal at once dropped his head, and let the log crash to the ground. The oozie looked disgusted, and then, acting entirely without instruction, the elephant used his brains to devise a safe method of handling the log—that is to say, he thought of something which we four men ought to have thought of ourselves.

He moved to one side rapidly, and picked up a stout piece of wood, which had been shaped for use as a maul or club to drive pegs into the bridge. He rammed it in a vertical position, jammed between his tusk and his trunk. I at once saw what he had in mind. The oozie also had immediately understood, and put him hard at the log again. With almost vicious strength, and certainly with determination, the elephant picked up the log endways, lowered it, and balanced it as before and then raised his head. But this time the club-shaped bit of wood was there, to act as a vertical stop, so that the log could not roll back over his forehead on to his rider.

An oath came from the Major, a murmur of admiration from the Brigadier. I could feel my heart beating, as the animal moved towards the bridge platform, carrying the balanced log, and then, putting his fore-feet on to another log so as to gain a little extra height, lowered his head a little, at the same time curling the end of his trunk out of the way, so that it should not get pinched. The log rolled on to the platform, as gently and easily as if placed in position by an electric crane. It was one of the most intelligent actions I have seen an elephant perform. The remarks of the Major and the Brigadier as we returned to camp would have made that elephant purr with the complacent pleasure of a Persian kitten, if he had heard them, and he deserved them all.

Elephants were given strange jobs, and some strange sights were seen. As an experiment a landing-craft was built on the River Yu, in the hope of getting it down that waterway to the Chindwin. By the time it was completed, the water in the Yu was falling fast, which made the rapids more dangerous. The officer in charge, Connel, came to my camp one evening and asked if I could help get logs into place for his launching-slip, with elephants, and then help pull his craft over the shallows. Four tusker elephants were supplied for the job. They cleared the launching channel, and assisted in the launching, but when they started pulling his craft over the shallows there was a nasty noise, and they pulled her bottom out. However, he repaired her, and finally got her down to the Chindwin, where she was invaluable in helping a division to cross the river.

The DUKWS amused the Burmans a great deal. One of them broke down, and an elephant had to tow it to

the nearest repair workshops. The next things that
came along were locomotives loaded on low loaders.
They looked out of place, four hundred miles from the
nearest railway, travelling along a road through the
jungle. Two tuskers pulled one loader up an incline,
where wheelspin had been causing trouble. Elephants
were also used for clearing forest trees off new air runways.
Often they were working quietly alongside bulldozers.

There were a number of humorous requests for elephants : such as for cranking up stalled lorries with their
trunks, for spraying tar with their trunks, and ramming
in loose earth on air-strips with their feet.

Their last job, for the 33rd Indian Corps, was to put
a bridge over the Nayanzayah River for a squadron of
tanks, which was engaged in taking Kalemyo. It was
the only occasion on which I have seen elephants working
under gunfire.

The bridge had to be finished by evening, and elephants
worked from seven o'clock in the morning till seven
o'clock at night. Five animals stampeded, but were
recovered a few hours later. During the whole day
Dakotas were circling two to three hundred feet above and
air-dropping in a dropping-zone, not half a mile from
where the animals were working. Three Dakotas were
shot down by enemy fighters that day. By this time the
elephants had become so accustomed to aircraft overhead
that they took no notice whatever.

The elephants near the dropping-zone at Indaingyi
soon realised that salt was being dropped. Their peace-
time ration of fifteen pounds a month had come to an
end in 1942, and they were in need of salt. Therefore
as soon as they were released from work they went to the
dropping-zone in search of the broken bags of salt which
were lying about.

Indian troops, except the Gurkhas, were surprisingly
timid in dealing with elephants. So were the East
Africans. But the British troops would readily climb
on their backs for a ride, and it tickled their sense of
humour to do so. Their confidence, though born of
ignorance, was usually justified, but not always. A

sapper Major moved a stubborn tusker on musth off a main road, by offering it bits of bread, as though it were a zoo elephant. When he told me about it afterwards I could only say he was lucky in war. On the other hand, an Indian Army Service Corps driver, who had his truck held up by a tusker on the road, after screaming his horn and revving his engine without effect, shot it in the leg with his rifle. The bullet smashed the bone, and the animal had to be destroyed. Luckily, there were very few such incidents.

After the crossing of the Chindwin River at Kalewa, new forest areas kept falling into our hands, and I kept hearing of more elephants being found. The brigades which captured them did all they could to keep these animals as part of their own transport. This was not practical, as they had no officers who understood how to handle elephants or what their requirements were. As a result, I had many private wars to win before I could get the elephants back for proper organisation. On one occasion I exchanged six jeeps for ten elephants.

By the time the 4th Corps came down the Kabaw Valley every elephant in my hands which had been recovered from the enemy was fit and was equipped ready to start road construction on the line of advance south from Kalemyo to Gangaw, up the Myittha Valley, and over into the Yaw and Irrawaddy Rivers. By that time two experienced officers, Finch and Scanlon, had joined me. They at once took charge of one herd, and did a sterling job of work.

Browne at this stage had to give in at last, after a long struggle. He had a most fearful skin complaint, caused by his exposure for two years to the most filthy jungle living conditions.

I, too, was beginning to feel the strain of something wrong with me. I was suffering from an excruciating pain, high up in what some people call one's stomach. For two months I laughed with friends who tried to cheer me up by saying that the trouble was a few gin-corks I must have swallowed at odd times, by mistake, and that it would be a simple operation to have them extracted, once we were back in Rangoon. A Divisional Commander, however, who came to ask me to pop over the ridge to Mawlaik in an L.5, to give some information to a Brigadier who was about to cross the river there, spotted that it would be my last job for a time, and on my return from my flying visit sent one of his doctors to see me.

Red tape was put aside, and I was told that I should be flown from Htinzin strip in an L.5 to Army Headquarters at Imphal, where the Army Commander would see me. When I got to the strip, however, I found no waiting aeroplane, but only an urgent message from the new 4th Corps Commander saying that it was necessary for him to see me. Finch, my new officer, who was to deputise for me, was with me, so the jeep was turned to 4th Corps Headquarters. I had not then been told that the 4th Corps was to advance down the Gangaw Valley. Corps Headquarters staff was at lunch when I arrived, and the Corps Commander ordered me the one and only egg in their dug-out mess. For half an hour it seemed that that golden egg had cured me. It did at least give me enough energy to perform the task required of me before I left. This was to go forty miles up the Yu River Valley, and try to persuade six elephant camps to swim the Chindwin River, at noon the following day, as a blind for a force crossing higher up the Chindwin.

Finch went with me, and I have never known six more willing volunteers than the headmen of those camps. I spoke to the riders, and they, too, were full of enthusiasm, though they knew well enough what a difficult and dangerous task it was, at that time of the year.

They needed no one to go with them, and were ready to manage on their own, as I knew they would be. Finch and I then returned to Corps Headquarters, to assure the Corps Commander that it was all arranged, and would be carried out. He gave me a late cup of tea, and I was able to explain that Finch knew every yard of Gangaw Valley, and before nightfall the Commander realised that those six elephant camps would be far more use to him with his Corps, in the valley, than employed as a strategic deception, as he had originally intended. The order for their crossing the Chindwin was therefore cancelled at dawn the next day.

With a sad heart I left the Kabaw Valley, to drive to Imphal in the dark. I knew that road so well, but I had such a hell of a pain that the only relief seemed to be to lean against the driving-wheel of the jeep.

The Army Commander, who always gave one the feeling that he knew every man in his Army, saw me at once. I had no arrangements to make; I did not have to wait in any transit camp; I was told to go to a Hill Station hospital direct and to get back to my elephants as soon as possible.

For a brief period all the pundits thought they ought to remove my gall-bladder, but, by the grace of God, one of them who knew me spotted that it was a duodenal ulcer, and suggested that all I needed was three weeks in bed. This did the trick, and six weeks later I was driving back in my jeep from Shillong in Assam to Army Headquarters at Monywa in the Lower Chindwin.

The battle for Meiktala was then at its height. I shall never forget my return, and I shall never live down the story that I had been cut open in hospital so as to have a bunch of Gordon's Gin corks taken out of me.

On my return to the Kabaw Valley, and before pushing forward to Army Headquarters, which by that time had reached Monywa on the lower Chindwin, I at once saw Finch. There was much for me to learn of what had happened in the past six weeks, and I was prepared for the inevitable bad news, which is a part of war. Many of my friends, I knew, must have given their lives while I had been away. For the XIVth Army had forged ahead, and was already hammering on the gates of Mandalay.

Far in its rear, in the Kabaw Valley, Finch had been concentrating on feeding two sawmill units with seasoned teak and other hardwoods for boat-building. This was now of urgent importance, and Kalewa, on the Chindwin, had become an organised shipyard at which all sorts of river craft were being constructed. And no shipyard

anywhere had ever been better supplied with the finest
teak in the world cut to all necessary dimensions.

It seemed for those in charge of the elephants on that
job that they had taken the first step back to their normal
peace-time work. In one of the permanent camps of
elephants engaged in this work was Bandoola, who had
remained in perfect condition ever since he had led the
great climb over the mountains into Assam. Old Po
Toke was in charge of that camp, and Bandoola was
employed in handling the largest pieces of timber. The
camp was two miles away from the main military road,
and in it one could only just hear the grind of the incessant
stream of Army lorries.

Before I went forward to visit Army Headquarters,
I told Finch I would visit Po Toke's camp and inspect
elephants, for I thought that it would help to keep up
the morale of the oozies, who were already becoming
impatient for the war to be over, though the elephants
had, I think, become completely inured to it.

To my surprise, Bandoola was absent from the parade,
and I naturally asked Po Toke where he was.

He replied: " He has been missing for three days,
Thakin Gyi."

Whereupon Finch broke in with: " Nonsense! You
told me five days ago, when I was last here, that he had
not been caught."

I said no more, but, after inspecting the animals,
went on into Po Toke's camp, where his men were
quartered. I at once sensed that something was wrong,
and collected all the elephant-riders and tree-fellers,
and spoke to them as follows:

" You all know the difficulties we have with elephants
getting lost in peace-time, and how far worse it is in war.
Have you all been on an organised tracking party,
looking for Bandoola? "

No one answered me, so, looking at Po Toke, I asked
him: " Have you not organised one? "

Old Po Toke looked pale and worried and replied in a
low voice: " There is no trace of his tracks anywhere."

At the risk of incurring the wrath of all the Chief

Engineers in Burma, I barked out: " All dragging work
here is stopped until Bandoola is found, and there will be
no rations in camp either except plain rice; so get to work
at once."

Finch and I went back to camp with the feeling that
what we had heard was no normal story of a missing
elephant. I went on to Army Headquarters, and Finch
arranged to send me a signal when Bandoola was found.
But no signal came, and when I got back five days later,
I heard that Po Toke had been taken ill, and that the
whole camp seemed in a most depressed state, as there
was still no trace of Bandoola.

I went straight off, and blasted old Po Toke to hell.
The effect was electric. He burst into tears and, blub-
bering like a schoolboy, said to me: " Bandoola is dead
within four hundred yards of camp. Go and see him.
I am too ill to walk, Thakin Gyi."

Two of the oozies silently led me along a track leading
from the camp towards the hills, and before long I could
smell the frightful stench of a decomposing elephant.
The two oozies suddenly stood aside, and I walked on into
a cleared patch of short grass. There lay Bandoola,
the hero of my march. I could scarcely believe my eyes
when I saw him lying dead. But his enormous belly was
distended with decomposition—and then I noticed something else was wrong also. His right tusk was gone, and
there was only a butt of solid ivory, where it had been
sawn off at the lip. The left tusk, half imbedded in mud
and earth, on the lower side, had not been taken.

My feelings were a terrible mixture of grief and un-
controllable anger. I was determined to find out the
truth. Bandoola was a war casualty. He had been
shot. There was a bullet-hole in his forehead, and the
bullet must have gone straight through his brain; he
had obviously dropped dead where he was standing.
As far as I could see, there was no trace of the spot
having been visited for several days by any living soul.

I at once put a guard of five Karens, armed with Sten
guns, round his carcase, and there was no need to tell
them how to act if occasion should arise, or if any

intruders came back to get the other tusk during the night.
I told them I would be back next morning.

All I could get out of poor old Po Toke was the pitiful
statement that Bandoola's oozie had found him dead
one evening, ten days before, and on going with the
oozie to the spot next morning he had found that the
right tusk had been sawn off. In his panic and grief,
he had sworn all his men in camp to silence, and had
forbidden any of them to go anywhere near the carcase,
for fear of the Jungle Nats, which alone would have had
the power to kill his unconquerable elephant, Bandoola.
He pleaded that he had been unable to face breaking
such terrible news, as he knew that my grief and Finch's
would be as great as his own. It was useless calling him
a bloody fool and cursing him because his prevarication
made it far more difficult to discover the culprit. Such
arguments meant nothing to Po Toke. Bandoola was
dead, and his own interest in life was over. Nothing
mattered to him any more. It was late that night before
I turned in, and, to put it mildly, I was grieved, angry and
perplexed. By noon next day the left tusk had been
extracted cleanly from the skull by my Karens, and a
.303 bullet extracted from Bandoola's brain. The
slenderness of this, my only bit of evidence, can be
realised. Thousands of lorries passed nearby along the
Army's lines of communication every day. I had
enquiries made at every unit in the neighbourhood, but it
seemed most unlikely that any sepoy had been guilty,
as most of them belonged to non-combatant units. Every
check was reported to have been made on ammunition—
with the negative results that might have been expected.

There was, however, a Chin village only two miles
from the spot. I went there with an armed party, and
ordered the headman to produce all firearms within ten
minutes. He did so, bringing the owners with their
weapons. I disarmed six men, three of whom were
armed with old .303-calibre rifles, and put them under
close arrest while I made a house-to-house search of their
huts, hoping I might find the sawn-off tusk. But I
drew a complete blank.

The headman was extremely perturbed when I told him that all the firearms would be confiscated until he either produced the tusk or evidence as to which of his hunters had shot my tusker elephant. Again I drew blank.

I then gave orders to Finch to dismiss Po Toke and Bandoola's oozie, hoping this would produce some reaction by which I could discover the truth. Once more I drew blank.

Bandoola's death still remains an unsolved mystery. His left tusk is my most treasured souvenir of the war. I have often wondered whether old Po Toke had become so war-weary as to become slightly deranged in his intellect and whether he had shot Bandoola, rather than leave him to a successor when he resigned. The ways of jungle Burmans are strange, and it is just possible that he also has a souvenir of his beloved elephant. The secret, whatever it was, was buried with the body of that heroic tusker, who was exceptional in every way. Even his name was a most unusual one, being that of a Burmese general who fought heroically against us during the Burma War which resulted in the British annexation of Burma in 1886.

I insert here the official record of this remarkable elephant of which I was so proud.

BANDOOLA: No. SK. 895

1897	*November :* Born.
1903	Trained. Branded " C " both rumps.
1904–17	Travelling with Forest Assistants as pack animal.
1918–21	Ounging Moo River (*i.e.* salving logs from sandbanks in it).
1922	Transferred to Gangaw Forest.
1923–31	Timber camp of Maung Aung Gyaw.
1932	Injured in fight with wild tusker. Rested throughout the year. Fully recovered.
1933	Transferred to South Kindat Forest, Upper Chindwin River. Allotted to camp of Maung Po Toke. Extraction of heavy timber Mawku Reserve.
1934–41	Fit throughout. Prime Elephant of the forest.
1942	*January–April :* Employed on Kalewa-Kalemyo road, before the retreat of the Burma Army.
	May–October : Disbanded but kept in secret hiding from

the Japanese in side creek of Kabaw Valley by Maung Po Toke living in Witok.

November : Handed over again to Elephant Bill and Harold Browne at Tamu.

December : Enrolled as No. 1 animal, the nucleus, of No. 1 Elephant Company, XIVth Army. Employed dragging timber for bridges.

1943   *March–November :* Employed near Tamu collecting timber ready for the return of the Army.

November–March 1944*:* Bridge-building with the Army in Kabaw Valley.

1944   *April–May :* Leading elephant in the march out of Burma from Kanchaung to Baladan in Assam.

June–October : Resting in Surma Valley, Assam. Loose for one day in pineapple grove, estimated to have eaten nine hundred pineapples. Severe colic. Recovered.

November–December : Marched back to Burma.

1945   *January–March :* Attached to Forest Sawmill Units, R.E., teak-dragging for Army boat-building.

March 8*:* Found dead, shot by an unknown person near Witok.

During my absence in hospital and while all this was taking place, the work had gone on with accelerated speed. A log bridge built by elephants had been constructed over the Manipur River near its junction with the Myittha. Similar bridges had been constructed, as required, right through to Tiddim, and every tank going down passed over them without a hitch. No troops were maintained on the lines of communication behind this corps on this route, and no excavating machinery had to be used on the one hundred and twenty miles of this forest road.

I had a grand total of four hundred elephants working under my direction at this time, and I was making new contacts with oozies with their elephants who had deserted from the Japanese, and were hiding in the Mingin and Pakokku forests.

An American pilot, who had made a forced landing, had been given shelter and food and kept in hiding, for two months, in a camp of Karen elephant-men, who eventually brought him into our lines. The story was that when he was rescued by the Karens he gave them his money-belt, full of coins, as a reward. But, having nothing better to do during the two months he was in hiding, he taught the Karens how to play poker and won it all back. He gave it them a second time, and won it back again. But he went on with this once too often, for a Karen, called Po Doh, learned to play poker so well that he won all the money from the other oozies and the pilot's Colt .45 automatic from him too.

During their retreat the Japanese were pressing a party of Burmans, with a hundred elephants, forward into the dry zone beyond Saw, on the Irrawaddy River. The head Burman went to the Japanese officer in charge, and told him that even though the Japanese shot all the oozies and all the elephants they would go no farther. The Japanese officer referred the matter to his superior, but, without waiting to hear his decision, the whole party escaped with their elephants, and reached our lines after three forced marches.

This accession increased the number in our hands to seven hundred. Many of them had been so overworked by the Japanese during their retreat that they needed long rest and careful nursing.

Another fifty came into our hands on the Moo River after the fall of Shwebo. No more were recaptured in the dry zone, and it was not until the Prome, Pyinmana and Toungoo districts had been overrun by our troops that another three hundred fell into our hands.

The loyalty of these oozies to us was often strikingly shown. One Independent Brigade, crossing the divide between the Chindwin and the Moo Rivers, asked me if I could help in any way to provide transport for them down the Moo Valley.

It was quite impossible to get elephants over in time to assist the Brigade, which was desperately short of mule transport. So I suggested that a letter in Burmese, addressed to a contractor who had worked for me for seven years, should be dropped by one of our Spitfires. It was dropped on Naunggauk village, inhabited by men who had formerly worked for me. In the letter I asked that he should organise as many pack-elephants

as possible, from those which had deserted from the
Japanese, and as many bullock-carts as possible, for the
use of British troops who would be reaching them very
shortly.

When the Brigade arrived it was met by twenty-
three elephants and thirty-four bullock carts, all organised
as perfectly as though by one of our officers. The Brigade
made a landing-strip for light aircraft, and shortly afterwards I landed there in an L.5, to meet the men who had
acted so loyally. I took a large sum of money to distribute
among them as a reward. But I found they were terrified
of accepting it, owing to the lawlessness and dacoity
prevalent in the district. So I made arrangements to
arm them as well, and the money was soon in circulation.

After the 33rd and the 4th Corps had all gone down
into the dry zone, and the hot season was almost at an
end, elephants were kept working on only one main
line of communication—that down the Kabaw Valley
from Tamu to Kalewa. A new all-weather Bithess road
was to be constructed there before the monsoon broke.
A hundred and fifty elephants were employed in clearing
all the culverts, in preparation for its construction. The
Bithess road was an extremely expensive experiment, but
it was the only possible method by which an all-weather
road could have been constructed down that valley in the
time available. It was, in its essence, a carpet of water-
proof hessian material made in strips two feet six inches
wide, treated with bitumen or tar. The strips over-
lapped eight inches and sealed the road surface. Camber
was obtained by laying the two outside strips first, and
building up with overlaps to the centre.

After it had been completely organised, the rate of
progress in laying the road was one mile a day. The
early storms of the 1945 monsoon had broken before it was
completed, but the road carried seven hundred tons a day
during the critical months.

By July 1945, the road had "cracked." Over some
sections stretches of a mile were awash, and a quagmire
resulted. After this the only hope of keeping the road
in use was to build log causeway diversions. Five miles

of such causeways were constructed by elephants during the 1945 monsoons. This meant laying two thousand five hundred logs per mile, or a total of twelve thousand five hundred logs, which had to be felled and cross-cut, and then dragged and put in position by elephants. All this work was done by No. 1 Elephant Company, under the most appalling monsoon conditions. At every flood the culverts were soon jammed with jungle debris, and the elephants were kept busy, continually clearing them. But they kept the road open. Over it, all the petrol for the Army was carried.

As the labour which had formerly been employed in taking rafts of teak logs down the Chindwin became available, it was organised for taking rafts of petrol drums from Kalewa down to Monywa and Myingyan. The work had been well planned. A month before Kalewa had been captured, and the Chindwin bridged, Burmans were set to work on the Upper Chindwin, above Mawlaik, in cutting cane and bamboos to build rafts. These were then floated down to Kalewa, when the time came. A million bamboos were delivered to Kalewa by the jungle Burmans for this work.

A small group of officers operated in the forward areas of the Kabaw Valley. Thomas and Keeley did most valuable work in this. They could, and should, have been reinforced by large numbers of others, who were sitting in Simla, waiting for the fall of Rangoon, which they seemed to imagine was the only gateway to Burma.

The fall of Rangoon, however, was in sight. There would undoubtedly be a great demand for timber. No one knew what supplies of it would be found there. Before the war there were about three hundred thousand teak logs, within easy call, at depots supplying the Rangoon mills. It turned out there were less than three thousand easily accessible logs within ten miles of the city when it was occupied. The elephants would be kept busy for some time in getting the teak logs left in the creeks since 1942 forward to meet the demand for timber. They would be wanted immediately they could be released from Army work.

Chapter Eighteen

CONSIDERABLE information had been gathered from the Burmans and former employees of the timber firms on the use the Japanese had made of elephants during their occupation of Burma.

During their advance of 1942 the Japanese used elephants to transport mortars and ammunition over the Caukeraik Pass from Siam into Burma. It is probable that this had been planned in advance, and the operation was successful. It seems very unlikely, however, that the Japanese had intended to make other military use of elephants in Burma before their invasion. For we know that they had made preparations for an organisation to work the forests under military control. A Japanese company, called the Nipponese Burmese Timber Union, was formed soon after the fall of Burma. The company did round up a considerable number of elephants and their oozies, who remained inseparable from their animals. They appointed as many of the Anglo-Burman assistants of the timber firms as they could find, as officers. But these Anglo-Burmans were never trusted by the Japanese. Such suspicions did not make for efficiency, even if the men had been trying to work. No British firm would have ever paid a dividend, unless it had done the same work in less than a third of the time that the Nipponese Burmese Company took over it. As a matter of fact, though they made an effort to show that they intended to develop the forests, they did very little extraction of timber from the forests, and relied almost entirely on what had already been hauled to the waterways or rafted to the depots. This may partly have been due to the fact that the Japanese military had a prior claim on elephants, and would send for working parties of a hundred elephants whenever occasion arose for their use. No Anglo-Burman was ever appointed to command these columns of elephants for military purposes, and the Japanese had to rely on the small number of Burmese-speaking officers in their army to coerce the oozies. There were many causes of difficulty and trouble. The rations of the Japanese soldier were inferior to what the oozie was accustomed to, and this was undoubtedly a principal cause of discontent.

The Japanese also insisted on elephants being tied up after a day's work, and being hand-fed by the oozies. This meant more work for the men, who had to cut fodder, and less food for the elephants, which always do best when they can pick their own food. After feeding their animals, the oozies were themselves kept penned in camp under guard. I found that most of the oozies who had worked under the Japanese hated them so much that they preferred not to discuss them. They were eager to forget as soon as they could. " They lived like dogs; they ate like dogs; and they died like dogs," one of the oozies said to me, in summing up the invaders.

The elephants and their oozies were of the greatest military use to the Japanese. The big Japanese offensive to break into India via Imphal, Ukhrul, Kohima and Jesami from the Upper Chindwin, depended largely on elephant transport. This accounted for their rapid movement over jungle paths in very difficult country.

On 13 March, 1944, the Japanese crossed the Chindwin by night, with a column of three hundred and fifty elephants, which they marched direct to the Chin Hills. A Japanese N.C.O. was in charge of every thirty animals. The elephants were used over precipitous and impassable country, linking up with motor transport and bullock-carts when they reached roads once more. Their transport system was improvised *ad hoc* from all available means and, though it did not look smart, it functioned and moved fast.

The Japanese did not ill-treat elephants in the sense of being cruel to the animals, as their management was left entirely to the oozies. But they pushed them hard, and never gave them opportunities to get the full amount of fodder they needed. I have already referred to the careless indifference which led to injuries from acid spilt on elephants' backs.

The Japanese had, however, a passion for ivory, and practically every tusker elephant which had been in Japanese hands had his tusks sawn off, as near to the nerve as possible. This work could not have been done by the Japanese themselves, as it demanded expert knowledge. It was no doubt done by Burmans of the toughest type, who wished to curry favour with Japanese officers, who were mad about ivory. No serious damage was done to the health of the elephants by this. I did not see a single case in which the nerve had been exposed. But, nevertheless, it was criminal, as it greatly reduced the value of a tusker for timber work, since the tusks left were not long enough for him to get under a log in order to move it. The Japanese, however, were more concerned with using elephants for transport than they were with timber extraction. Perhaps they thought the elephants looked less dangerous without their tusks. Early in 1943 I was present at the examination of a full pack, dropped by a Japanese soldier, when avoiding a patrol of ours on the east bank of the Chindwin. The pack weighed approximately seventy-five pounds, and contained two tips of tusks weighing six pounds in all. The soldier obviously valued his souvenir, to add it to such a heavy load. I don't think, however, that the Japanese got all the ivory obtained in this way, as the Burman also has a passion for it.

" Four thousand elephants used for hauling timber have disappeared in Burma." This statement appeared in the *Daily Mail*, and was quoted in *Punch* with the query: " Have you looked everywhere? " Well, the answer is that we had not, and nobody ever will. The statement appeared before we had completely cleared the Japanese out, and a few more may have come to light. I can, however, claim to have discovered the whereabouts of one of the missing four thousand. He is the Regimental Mascot of a famous Indian regiment, which captured him, and would not surrender him to me. On their return from the Burma Campaign he was marched across India to the Regimental Depot. Unfortunately, there is on his behind a capital C branded on with white phosphorous paint when he was seven years old. This proclaims his real ownership—the Bombay Burma Trading Corporation—and all the dhobies in the Punjab can never erase it. The Quartermaster is advised to get busy with the regimental tailor and fit him with cloth of gold trappings to cover it up. When the regiment reached Assam a language difficulty arose. The Burman oozie wished to return home, and it was decided that an Indian mahout must be found among the ranks of the battalion. Not one could be found, so it became a Brigade request, and eventually a sepoy, who claimed to have been employed in a Rajah's elephant stable, was appointed.

The handing over of the Regimental Mascot by the Burmese oozie to the Indian mahout was planned to be a ceremony of importance. Many officers were present, including three Battalion Commanders and the Brigadier. There was considerable speculation among those on the parade-ground as to how the elephant would react to orders spoken in Hindustani, for the animal's understanding of Burmese words of command had become a byword in the regiment.

The new Indian mahout arrived on the parade-ground in bottle-green battle-dress, wearing boots, belt and side-arms. The Burmese oozie sat on the elephant's head, dressed as usual in his lungyi skirt and a Japanese cotton vest. The Indian wore a look of immense self-importance, the Burman one of complete indifference. Not a word was exchanged between the pair as the oozie ordered the elephant to sit down on all fours. As the Burman slipped down off the elephant's head, the Indian mounted, and the animal stood up. The Burman walked off the parade-ground, and then came the great test, as the Indian was left to prove himself. Drawing his bayonet from its scabbard with a flourish, he first held it at the sword present arms. Then he gave the elephant a probe with it behind the right ear, and, to the astonishment of everyone, exclaimed in English: " Now, Mr Bloody, come on ! "—and off they marched.

In all, one thousand six hundred and fifty-two other elephants were recaptured from the Japanese between November 1942 and the date of unconditional surrender. They went back to their working lives. Before I left Burma I visited and said good-bye to four hundred and seventeen of them, working in the Kabaw Valley in Upper Burma, where they were still being employed in pulling out the tail of the XIVth Army. They were all that was left of Elephant Companies Nos. 1 and 2. The rest had gone back to their pre-war work of timber extraction, and were soon happily scattered through the teak forests of Burma where they belong. Some were war-weary, some were battle-scarred, but they were in good hands, and would be nursed back to good health and good condition. Of the lost host of three thousand nine hundred and ninety-nine (according to the *Daily Mail*), many hundreds lost their lives owing to the folly and ruthlessness of man. There can be no roll call of the survivors. But there were numbers of wounded who, though they may have had a hard fight for existence to gather their food, would recover after they had treated their wounds in the traditional elephant fashion, by sealing them with mud two or three times a day. When they recovered they would set forth to leave the valleys which had become hells in the jungle during the war, for peaceful areas. But many must have escaped unhurt.

Those that had stampeded and those that survived their wounds must greatly outnumber those that lost their lives, and I know well enough where they are now. For the herds of wild elephants show no resentment when domesticated animals join them. They have none of that herd instinct directed against the stranger that one finds in cattle, in small boys and among many grown-up men. This tolerance is just one of the things about elephants which makes one realise they are big in more ways than one. No doubt some attempts will be made by the jungle Burmans to recapture branded animals from the wild herds. The only successful way to do this is for two very daring oozies to ride a really trustworthy animal into the wild herd as it is grazing in open kaing grass and to edge it alongside the animal they are trying to recapture. One of the oozies will then begin to talk to it, very quietly, and if it listens without alarm, he will slip across from the animal he is riding on to its back. A short stampede is almost certain to follow, but a good oozie will soon gain control as the wild herd disappears. But those that will be recaptured in this way are few indeed, and with Burma in its present condition I like to think of the hundreds that will remain leading their happy wild life, undisturbed by the restless demands of man.

Elephants have recently been nationalised in Burma, which means that they will lose their best friends in captivity, the European Assistants, many of whom would never have gone on with their work in the jungle but for their interest in the most lovable and sagacious of all beasts.

THE END